MAINSTREAM AND MARGINS

MAINSTREAM AND MARGINS

JEWS, BLACKS, AND OTHER AMERICANS

PETER I. ROSE

Transaction Books
New Brunswick (U.S.A.) and London (U.K.)

Library of Congress Catalog Number: 83-4693
ISBN: 0-87855-473-4 (cloth)
Printed in the United States of America

Library of Congress Cataloging in Publication Data

Rose, Peter Isaac, 1933-
  Mainstream and margins.

  Includes index.
  1. United States—Race relations—Addresses, essays, lectures.
2. United States—Ethnic relations—Addresses, essays, lectures.
I. Title.
E184.A1R716   1983   305.8'00973   83-4693
ISBN 0-87855-473-4

For Charles D. Lieber and Charles H. Page

Acknowledgments

The author gratefully acknowledges the following publishers and publications for granting permission to reprint copyrighted material:

"The Ghetto and Beyond: Reflections on Jewish Life in America" (originally published as "Reflections on Jewish Life in America"), *Humanistic Judaism* 2 (1966): 3-11.

"Tensions and Trends: American Jews in the 1980s" (excerpted from *Group Status in America*). New York: Institute of Human Relations, American Jewish Committee, 1981.

"Country Cousins: Small-Town Jews and Their Neighbors" (originally published as "Smalltown Jews and Their Neighbours"), *Jewish Journal of Sociology* 3 (England, 1961): 174-91.

"City Lights: The Children of Small-Town Jews," in *Strangers in Their Midst*. Merrick, New York: Richwood Press, 1977.

"The Black Experience: Issues and Images," *Social Science Quarterly* 50 (September 1969): 286-97.

"Race and Education in New York: The Challenge Moves North" (coauthored with Stanley Rothman), *Race* 6 (1964): 108-16.

"Social Physics: The Resurgence of Ethnicity" (originally published as "The Resurgence of Ethnicity") *They and We: Racial and Ethnic Relations in the United States,* 3rd ed. New York: Random House, 1981. © Random House, Inc.

"Blacks and Jews: The Strained Alliance," *The Annals of the Academy of Political and Social Sciences* 454 (March 1980): 55-69, © 1981, all rights reserved.

"On the Subject of Race: Thinking, Writing, and Teaching about Racial and Ethnic Relations" (originally published as "The Development of Race Studies"), in *Race among Nations* ed. George Shepherd and Tilden Lemelle. Lexington, Mass.: D.C. Heath, 1970.

"Problems in Conveying the Meaning of Ethnicity: The Insider-Outsider Debate" (originally published as " 'Nobody Knows the Trouble I've Seen' "). Northampton, Mass.: Smith College, 1978. © Peter I. Rose and the Trustees of Smith College.

"It's Almost 1984: Sociological Perspectives on American Society" (coauthored with Myron and Penina Glazer and originally published as "A Sociological Debate about American Society"), in *Sociology: Inquiring into Society,* 2nd ed. New York: St. Martin's Press, 1982.

Preface

Mainstream and Margins is a collection of essays on race and ethnicity written over the past twenty-five years. It is a reflection of my own thoughts and expressions as they developed and changed. Selecting which pieces to include and then preparing them for publication was a strange but rewarding experience. It forced me to think about things I had nearly forgotten, especially the circumstances—and people—that had sparked my interest in the subject of these essays. Among those who had influenced me most were my parents, Aaron and Lillian Rose; my mentors, Douglas Haring and Nathan Goldman at Syracuse and Robin Williams, Edward Suchman, and Allan Holmberg at Cornell; and, in a curious way as I explain in the introductory essay, the sculptor Malvina Hoffman and the poet Robert Frost.

August 1982

Contents

Roots and Branches: An Introduction

It is difficult to say when my involvement in sociology began or how I happened to be drawn to the field. Thinking back to my early life, I remember at least three possible factors. First and perhaps foremost, my parents were social workers involved in the community center-settlement house movement. Through them I had very early exposure to a variety of people, rich and poor, Black and White, native born and immigrant—and several refugees from Hitler's war who came to live with us between 1935 and 1944.

The second "factor" was both art and artifact. It was a poster from an exhibition of Malvina Hoffman's sculpture "The Races of Man." On the poster were photographs of many of her figures scattered about a map of the world indicating their place of origin. Fascinated by the differences between the physiognomy of the Sioux and the Ubangi, the Mediterranean and the Malay, I decided that some day I would like to learn about the racial differences portrayed by Malvina Hoffman—and also about the human resemblances of those who sat in our living room.

At the age of fourteen or fifteen, I read a poem by Robert Frost which contained the line: "My object in living is to unite my avocation with vocation as my two eyes make one in sight." I liked the sentiment expressed and the phrase became a sort of personal motto. But in those days I had other interests besides that of becoming a social scientist. At the top of the list was a love for skiing and the outdoors. In my late teens I thought I would try to achieve Frost's double goal by becoming a professional skier. The trouble was that I was not good enough.

My fall back position was more realistic. I would study and teach about people. As an undergraduate at Syracuse University a good deal of time was spent shuttling back and forth between the Zoology Department where I took courses in natural history, evolution, and physical anthropology, and the Maxwell School of Citizenship where I studied cultural anthropology, sociology, and contemporary issues, influenced especially by Douglas Haring, author of *Order and Possibility in Social Life,* and Nathan Goldman, a clinical psychologist with a Ph.D. in sociology from Chicago. Haring introduced me to the rich

1

literature of anthropology; Goldman to the works of Robert Park, Robert Redfield, and David Riesman among many others.

Nearing graduation, and having abandoned all hopes of becoming another Hannes Schneider (the then premier ski instructor in the country), I was still in a quandary about which direction to go within the general realm of social science and its application. I finally opted to do graduate work in the Department of Sociology and Anthropology at Cornell, hopefully under the guidance of Alexander Leighton, the psychiatrist-anthropologist, whose early work, *The Governing of Men,* a study of the relocation of Japanese Americans in the 1940s, I had read in a Maxwell course.

Leighton was away for most of my Cornell years. Instead, I studied with a number of sociologists and anthropologists, including Robin Williams, Edward Suchman, and Allan Holmberg, who taught me to appreciate the connections between theory (mainly Parsonian), research (decidedly Lazarsfeldian), and practice (uniquely Holmbergian). That combination was to have a decided impact on some of my subsequent work, even as I came to question many aspects of the institutional approach, survey research, and interventionist anthropology.

While members of my "cohort" read Marx and Veblen, Simmel and Mills, most of us began our careers functionalist in thought (especially interested in the study of value consensus), applied in research orientation (hoping to expose those places where the order seemed to break down), and reformist in action (determined to bring conduct in line with creed). Not surprisingly, we hailed the "Brown" decision of the Supreme Court in 1954 as a triumph of our position.

Starting Out

When I was finishing graduate work, I accepted a position at a college in Baltimore, a border city undergoing the early pains of desegregation. The years in Baltimore were both productive and educational. At Goucher College I was part of a two-person team, expected to teach everything from introductory sociology to anthropological theory. It was quite an initiation. I also served as a consultant and researcher at the Council of Social Agency's Research Department, becoming involved in two studies of "Unreached Youth": a general study of White delinquents (a colleague was doing a parallel study of Black delinquents), and a series of interviews for those engaged in the epidemic of swastika smearing that occurred in 1959. To my chagrin, in several instances my subjects in the second study turned out to be some of the same young men I had interviewed in the first.

In 1960 I moved to Smith College in Northampton Massachusetts. It was not until I left the metropolitan area and the near-South that I began to write about Black and White relations, the subject that had occupied so much of my thought and activity for so many years.

The early 1960s were, for many young social scientists, a time of reawakening. With our students, we were beginning to learn and see more of "the other America" and to recognize the depth of the chasm that divided the society. We read Paul Goodman and laughed at his lampooning of sociologists while finding his analysis profoundly socio-logical in its own right—and disturbing. Americans did seem to be growing up absurd, and many "consensus-oriented" sociologists seemed to have failed to recognize fundamental differences between those who had made it and were trying to get out of the closed rooms and the others who peered in and sought entry. I was especially impressed by the growing paradox within what we still called "the Negro community." On the one hand, many of its members were precisely the outsiders who wanted in. ("What do you want?" we asked in one questionnaire and interview after another. They an-swered, "What you have.") On the other hand, Blacks could not forever remain supplicants waiting to be admitted to the Big White Room.

I became convinced that they would have to go it alone or, at the least, feel they were determining their own destinies. Ironically, my first real break with liberal integrationists was when I went back to Baltimore and gave a lecture on the need for Whites to step aside, for Blacks to move into middle- as well as upper-level (and not just titular) leadership positions, and for all to recognize the necessity for what, in a rather Durkheimian presentation, I called "the coalescence of com-munity." I even said that some separatism on the part of Blacks might be required to allow them time to regroup, organize, and then confront the system with a unified front so people on all sides could deal with one another from a posture more akin to political parity. That, I argued, could lead to real negotiations and more meaningful integra-tion. But the message got lost and I (who in 1962 was advocating some sort of Black Power although I did not call it that) was viewed as a supporter of apartheid. (Ten years later *not* to advocate separatism or at least indicate an understanding of the desire for it meant being labeled a typical racist.)

During the early years at Smith I became increasingly involved in the affairs of the profession, mainly, though not exclusively, in the Society for the Study of Social Problems, the Society for Applied Anthropology, the Eastern Sociological Society, and the American Sociological Association (ASA). Most of the involvement was with committees on intergroup relations and minorities, but in time I worked on other activities. As I got to know sociologists throughout the country, I also found myself increasingly concerned about the narrow paths on which many seemed set. They were becoming more and more concerned with professionalism, I with the problem of reconciling what was to me a humanistic discipline with the scientism that others stressed. (This was not long after the time when the American Sociological Society changed its name to the American Sociological Association.)

I also gained some notoriety for constantly speaking up at annual meetings about civil rights and the war in Vietnam, and urging fellow members to take collective stands in opposition to policies which seemed to be violations of democratic principles and matters especially relevant to those professionally concerned with human relations. My remarks (and those of others with similar views) were not always greeted with equanimity. Many stood up to challenge us, saying that meetings of learned societies might be arenas for discussion of some of these matters, but taking public positions, especially in an official way, was most inappropriate. Others did not even think they should be discussed at all.

As we moved further into the 1960s, others, far more radical than I, voiced stronger sentiments in those ubiquitous Hilton ballrooms, often couching their critiques in revolutionary rhetoric. Splinter groups and caucuses formed to effectively mobilize for action inside the organization and in the world beyond. The targets were many besides Johnson, Nixon, and members of Congress. Among them were social scientists who consulted for government agencies and, it was said, helped solidify the "Welfare-Warfare State"; social researchers who "manipulated" people, especially those described as "culturally deprived"; and social theorists who wrote uncritically of this society where ethnocentrism was fostered and prejudice instilled, where one learned about achievement by being taught to accept the principles of meritocracy in a manner that urged them to blame themselves and not the system for their failure to achieve. Much of what they said made sense, but what was troubling was that few of them—and equally few of the liberals—had a viable plan to reorganize society to make it both free and fair.

I remained active in the civil rights and antiwar movements inside the sociological associations, on campus, and to some extent in the streets. But I frequently found myself in the awkward position of agreeing with what many around me were saying while strongly objecting to some of the techniques used, most especially a growing left-wing McCarthyism which sought to stifle any who might disagree with the blanket condemnation of "Amerikkka." By the end of the decade there were fissures in society and fragmentation within the ranks of those who studied it. There were not just good guys and bad guys, but various types of protesters, all proclaiming universal truths to very partisan cohorts. (Many engaged in what Michael Lerner once aptly called "respectable bigotry": they loved the Blacks and the poor but somehow found the working class, in their "ticky-tacky houses," ideal scapegoats.) Society was reeling. So were the Eastern and American sociological associations.

At the height of the upheaval, old friends found themselves ideological enemies, old socialists were attacked as fascists, integrationists were called racists, liberals were labeled reactionaries, and YPSLs were finks. Tensions outside the campuses (and the Hiltons) flowed through the gates and into the classrooms where a new band of young sociologists, instructors and students, often served in the vanguard of the frontal attack on the system. Still, the general message did get across and at least some segments of society (and the ASA) responded to charges of elitism, racism, and sexism. By the mid-1970s it seemed everyone was regrouping, including the sociologists. During a stint on the ASA Council in 1974–77, I observed some significant changes in official policy, self-examination (see for example reports on the status of minorities and women), and the composition of that ruling body itself. One result (that some critics saw as cooptation) was a growing sense of respect for differing viewpoints, a return to civil discourse even in consideration of potentially explosive issues.

As I tried to address myself to some of the issues that were so pressing in those days, I felt a growing sense of inadequacy in terms of my education and that of many sociologists. I felt we were limited in our understanding of history and poorly informed about literature that was not *the* literature (of the field). I began to do more comparative work with both European and American historians, and began to read more widely, most particularly in those many ethnocentric ethnographies, the first novels of immigrants and other minority writers. I also began to find a new outlet in writing essays through which I could combine *my* varying interests and concerns, à la Robert Frost, including pieces on "The Black Experience," "The Ghetto and Beyond," and sometime later "Nobody Knows the Trouble I've Seen."

Moving On

Something else happened to me back in the 1960s that had a profound effect on my later work and interests. I spent the year 1964-65 in England (at the University of Leicester). For the first time, I was not only exposed to another kind of sociology, but to life in a somewhat different society. There I learned, for example, that in some places everyone talks about social class, not just sociologists. I also discovered that my interest in intercultural relations extended far beyond our borders. I found it very stimulating (and depressing) to observe race relations there and to write "Outsiders in Britain," one of the first of the sort of essays just mentioned.

That year abroad whetted my appetite for more foreign experience. Three years later I was back in Europe and have been abroad every year since, usually for at least two months. My work as a consultant, lecturer, and researcher has included teaching stints in Japan, Australia, and Sweden, and shorter visits to lecture and conduct research in many countries of Europe, Asia, and Africa.

Becoming peripatetic, new interests in comparative higher education and intercultural exchanges were added to my particular "fields of specialization." A two-year study of the Senior Fulbright Program in East Asia and the Pacific gave me an opportunity not only to evaluate a program which I had known as a former Fulbrighter, but required the conducting of interviews with over a hundred top-level academicians in eleven rather different countries in the area.

In many of the places visited I was asked to talk about American society in general and racial and ethnic relations in particular. This led to increasing contact with students in foreign universities and to a growing involvement with what many call "Americanistics." Back at Smith I became involved in and began to direct a rather unique Diploma Program in American Studies for foreign graduate students.

In recent years many disparate interests and personal commitments—international and intergroup relations, problems of marginality and loss, of forced migration and the search for asylum—have been pulled together in a study of the rescue, relief, and resettlement of refugees. This has meant looking at the limited sociological literature on the subject and trying to develop a sociology of exile. It has meant field work, including first-hand observation of some activities of international organizations here, in Europe, and in Southeast Asia, interviews with U.S. government personnel, representatives of voluntary agencies, refugee workers in camps and centers, and refugees themselves.

One of the most satisfying aspects of the "refugee project" has been the opportunity to interest students in the problem through the development of new courses and research activities in which they can combine sociological investigation with humanistic concerns. A number have opted for careers in international social service with such organizations as the office of the UN High Commissioner for Refugees, the Hebrew Immigrant Aid Society, the American Joint Distribution Committee, Save the Children, the U.S. Catholic Conference, Church World Service, the Intergovernmental Committee for Migration, and the International Rescue Committee. Several have gone on to graduate school hoping to write dissertations on some aspect of refugee policy.

One of the most troubling aspects of the project has been that while many students (and others) have become interested in the plight of refugees, there has been an increasing backlash against the pressure to admit more and more displaced persons to this country. Part of the reaction is related to a resurging nativistic sentiment; part to the continuing failure of our society to resolve what long ago Myrdal called the American dilemma, the legacy of deep-rooted racism; and part may reflect the ambiguity of a policy which, despite recent changes in immigration laws, still favors certain asylum seekers over others.

Like many of my generation, I am not only concerned with the direction our society has been taking and what has recently been described as the rising "meanness mania," but with the direction many of those in our discipline have chosen. There was a time when C. Wright Mills lambasted his colleagues for doing either "Abstract Empiricism" or "Grand Theory." This dichotomy still exists, especially in those circles where, almost in counterreaction to the politicization of the field in the 1960s (and the deep involvement of sociologists in political action), there has been a retrenchment, a turn back to "scientism." With others I have grown to realize that sophisticated quantitative methods are important. But they are not the be-all and surely not the end-all. "Not all things that count can be counted." The proclivity, once again, to try to assure our students and each other that we are true scientists, reveals a continuing uncertainty (some would say a paranoia) about who we are and what we are about.

At bottom, we are humanists, and our field is a double bridge: between C.P. Snow's "two cultures" and between the social asepsis of the laboratory and library and the ordered chaos of the world beyond. Allowing ourselves to range more widely, to be more speculative, to include in our "data base" much more of that soft material that is not so easily measured, to become less concerned with statistical significance and more so with social importance, does not mean abandoning the sociological perspective. It means enhancing it. That orientation still offers to provide the framework within which to understand what is being explored, observed, summarized, and analyzed—the larger picture of the systems in which people live, work, play, and suffer.

Elaborating on this point a few years ago—in one of the essays included here, I suggested:

> After all, blacks like whites, Jews like Gentiles, Chicanos like Anglos, Irishmen Protestant and Catholic, institutionalize their behavior patterns, set criteria for the conferring or denying of status, indicate the tolerance limits of accepted and expected behavior, and maintain social systems of great intricacy even when they, themselves, have difficulty articulating their character. To explain these things is and should remain the primary role of the sociologist.

I believe that what I said in the conclusion of that paper still obtains:

> I now feel very strongly that much of our work is like that of the Japanese judge in *Rashomon,* the one who asks various witnesses and participants to describe a particular event as seen through their own eyes. Like the judge, neither teachers of sociology nor our students can be allowed to get off the hook. We must analyze the disparate pieces of evidence and then try to figure out how they fit together. If we use the suggested approach . . . then, perhaps, we will be better able to know the troubles others have seen and be better able to understand them.

About the Book

What follows is a collection of previously published essays, including several of those mentioned above, all focused on some aspects of racial and ethnic relations in the United States and the problems faced by those in three overlapping social categories: European immigrants, especially Jews; non-White minorities, mainly but not exclusively Blacks; and the sociologists who write about both. They differ somewhat in style (some, especially the earlier ones, are more traditionally sociological and "academic" than others); in form (dictated in part by the place in which they were originally published); and in approach (there are those based on hard data, and those that are speculative, reflecting my own position on a few of the issues of the day).

While united by a common theme and yet different in the ways just mentioned, there is something that should strike the reader as it struck me in going through a batch of reprints filed in chronological order. In many ways these are period pieces. I deliberated long and hard about which of my essays I would include in this collection and how I would present them. Early on I decided to eliminate several long reviews of such works as Nathan Glazer and Daniel P. Moynihan's *Beyond the Melting Pot,* Milton M. Gordon's *Assimilation in American Life,* Ulf Hannerz's *Soulside,* Andrew M. Greeley's *Why Can't They Be Like*

Us?, Michael Novak's *The Rise of the Unmeltable Ethnics,* and Stanford M. Lyman's *The Black American in Sociological Thought*—all of which had made significant impacts on the thoughts of many about mainstream and marginal Americans and their mutual relationships. Rather, in some places, critiques of these studies—and many others—were woven into the slightly revised papers that were to form the core of this book.

A second decision was related to organization. Originally the plan was to present the material in strictly chronological order. In the end the idea was rejected for two reasons: first, because there might appear to be an implicit continuity when, in fact, several articles, chapters, and books had been published "in between" the essays selected for this volume; second, because there was another, more logical way to deal with the problem, by topic or, as it were, subtopic. The book is thus divided into three parts, beginning with a set of papers on American Jews, followed by one on Black/White relations, and ending with my analyses and thoughts about what has come to be called "ethnic studies" as well as some other matters.

My early research and continuing interest in Jews as a quintessential marginal minority—and the invitation to write a lead piece for a new journal, *Humanistic Judaism*—led to the first essay included here. "The Ghetto and Beyond: Reflections on Jewish Life in America," begins with a comment about the differences between the old ghettos and the new, and includes some comparisons of Jews' earlier experiences on the Lower East Side of New York and the more recent experiences of Blacks in Harlem. In the main, it is a social history and sociological assessment, ending with the situation in 1967 when, coming out of an era of philo-Semitism, Jews were becoming increasingly sensitive to attacks from the Right, Left, and "below."

That their fears were partially justified is discussed in the second essay in the section. In "Tensions and Trends: American Jews in the 1980s," part of a report prepared for a special task force of the American Jewish Committee, I attempt to reassesss the previous decade and examine the current status of Jews relative to that of other Americans. Among the issues addressed are group identity and group rights. While the original paper contained considerable material on Black-Jewish relations, that has been deleted from chapter 2. It is dealt with in detail in the last essay in the second part of the book.

From the mid-1950s to the present I have been particularly interested in the study of "marginality" and the "exemption mechanism," two important sociological concepts. The former refers to being both a part of and apart from a dominant society (hyphenated Americans being a good case in point); the latter to being accepted by those in that dominant society despite one's membership in another, often marginal, group. ("Oh, he's not like other Jews, he's a regular guy.") These interests led me to write a master's thesis and eventually to conduct doctoral research on both subjects. They were combined in my study, originally published under the title *Strangers in Their Midst: Small-Town Jews and Their Neighbors* (1977). That book was the culmination of many years of work and three studies, the first two conducted in the late 1950s and first reported in an article in the *Jewish Journal of Sociology* in 1961. The early research concerned the life histories and perceptions of Jews in some seventy-five rural hamlets in upstate New York, Vermont, and along the New York-Pennsylvania border; and the views non-Jews had of these "strangers" in twenty communities in the same area. Years later, a follow-up study of many of the Jews originally interviewed and many of their now grown children revealed the predictions about a tiny minority that would become even smaller to be proven true.

In 1957, as is explained in the third essay, "Country Cousins," the small-town Jews had seemed to feel that, as one put it, they "had the best of both. . . . Judaism, with all its traditions, its stress on culture, on learning, on freedom . . . and the fact that [they] live in a small town, with nice people and good clean air. . . . [They] wouldn't trade either for the world." Owing to the critical role of exemption, they found acceptance even when their gentile neighbors continued to harbor traditional stereotypes about Jews in general. And they thought their assimilated children were quite secure in their little villages.

"City Lights" tells something of what was learned nearly twenty years after the first studies were conducted. The children had rejected the provincialism of the small towns and had sought a parochialism of their own. Drawn by the opportunities they felt abounded in the metropolis and by the desire for Jewish contacts, almost to a person they eschewed the rural town for the urban scene.

Long involved in the study of intergroup relations and as an active participant in some aspects of the civil rights movement, I published several academic pieces on the subject in the early 1960s, including a short essay, "Radical Pacifism and the Negro Revolt." However, it was not until the beginning of the school crisis in 1968 in New York City that I began writing for a wider audience. The first of a series of pieces was a collaborative effort, written with my colleague Stanley Rothman, a political scientist who grew up in the part of Brooklyn where much of the drama was to be played out. Our article "Race and Education," the first in Part Two, was the result.

Shortly thereafter I wrote a much longer essay, "The Black Experience: Issues and Images," in which I presented one observer's opinions about the causes and consequences of the shifting climate (mentioned *en passant* in "Race and Education"), most especially the joining of previously separated streams—one of which I once labeled "ethnocentric blackwardness," the other "soulless militancy"—which were to merge in the Black Power movement and its corollary Black Consciousness. The militants' tactics, the emphasis on political revolution and cultural recrudescence, were to have an influence beyond their original purposes. They became the models for the mobilization of many other minorities—racial and ethnic, and also women, the handicapped, and the aging (Gray Panthers).

Once completed, "The Black Experience," first published in the *Social Science Quarterly,* was expanded and divided into two parts, each to form an introductory essay for a two-volume set of readings called *Americans from Africa* (1970), dealing with eight controversies then extant. Volume 1, *Slavery and Its Aftermath,* included papers on "Africa and the New Americans," "The Legacy of Slavery," similarities and differences in Southern and Northern experiences, and "Community, Class, and Family Life." Volume 2, *Old Memories, New Moods,* asked "Who was Nat Turner?" and how significant were his and others' revolts, discussed the quest for "Freedom Now," sought answers to the question "Whither Black Power?", and ended with a consideration of Afro-American identity and the acceptance of being Black. The last section was called "Negroes Nevermore."

While completing the manuscript for *Americans from Africa* two phenomena were forcing changes not only in society but in the ways social scientists approached the subject and in the content of curricula in "minorities" courses. The first was the Black Power movement itself; the second, the reactive (or perhaps in some ways imitative) resurgence of ethnicity in various quarters of the White community.

In 1964, *They and We: Racial and Ethnic Relations in the United States* was published. It was very representative of the current thinking about intergroup relations and stressed the nature of prejudice, patterns of discrimination, and the reactions of minorities. It did not have much to say about how those who were to be called "White ethnics" reacted to the pressures of non-White minorities. Ten years later, in preparing a revised edition of that already dated text, I included several new chapters. One of these, "The Resurgence of Ethnicity," sought to capture the spirit and offer some sense of what had happened in the intervening decade, especially to those who felt they were being forced to pay for the sins of other people's fathers. Their indignation was expressed in a variety of ways, such as strong opposition to forced busing and affirmative action and other results of the civil rights movement. The seventh essay in this volume, which I call "Social Physics," is an abridged version of that chapter written for the second edition of *They and We* and later revised and updated for the third edition (1982).

The final essay in Part Two brings the reader (and me) back full circle, connecting issues raised in the previous chapter to those discussed in the introduction to the first one. "Blacks and Jews" was originally written for a special issue of *The Annals of the American Academy of Political and Social Science*. In its pages I attempted to show the bittersweet and symbiotic relationship between two principal American minorities. Their relationship was summarized in the paper's working title, "Strangers, Neighbors, Friends, and Foes." The essay seeks to indicate that all four terms aptly describe some aspects of the "strained alliance."

Of all the previously published pieces that appear in this volume, none have prompted more mail and discussion than "Blacks and Jews." By and large the comments have been most gratifying, particularly from individuals, both Black and Jewish, some of them members of various civil rights or defense organizations, who felt that I had gotten beneath the rhetoric or, as my friend anthropologist Gerald Berreman would put it, "behind the mask."

Penetrating beneath the surface or getting behind the mask is an important concern of many social scientists. It has long been a concern of mine. It has been central to my life as a teacher as I have wrestled with the character and quality of dominant/minority experiences. In the last part of this book this issue is a recurrent theme (most explicit in the second essay). The first chapter of that last set is one of the few scholarly papers published here. It, too, has a story.

Having completed work on a small book, *The Subject Is Race* (1968), dealing with traditional ideologies and the teaching of race relations, I was asked to prepare a chapter for a volume, *Race among the Nations* (1970). The invitation provided the opportunity to dig more deeply into the evolution of studies in the field and the thoughts of many American social scientists about them. A part of that summary and a commentary on a number of major works by writers such as Pierre van den Berghe and Richard A. Schermerhorn that were to have a considerable impact on teaching, writing, and thinking about dominant/minority relations are presented here under the title "On the Subject of Race."

Having taught courses about intergroup relations for twenty years, I continued to be puzzled by and worried about the difficult question of the best way to convey the meaning of ethnicity. Like others, including Norbert Elias, Robert K. Merton, and William J. Wilson, who had written about the "insider-outsider debate," I was interested in exploring the differences between the judgments of insider-members and outsider-observers. Once having examined the bases for each party's claim to truth, I wanted to see if there might be a way to close the gap to work through the epistemological and pedagogical—and in the case of this subject, political—problem. "Problems in Conveying the Meaning of Ethnicity" was the result. First presented as a lecture and later published, it provoked some controversy and encouraged me to try to go on with the arguments. For several years I thought of doing so but was drawn away by two old interests: one was intergroup conflict, mainly between Blacks and Jews; the other, the plight of refugees, a topic in which I had been interested for many years but had written little about until the mid-1970s.

The last chapter is a sort of experiment in trying to indicate to students the ways different sociologists see the same thing and how they interpret such matters as social stratification, immigration, racial conflict, changing mores, and a host of other social issues. Originally written as an epilogue to a textbook, *Sociology: Inquiring into Society* (1982), my coauthors Mickey and Penina Glazer and I were determined to get away from the standard format of presenting one position after another, then summarizing each. Instead I thought an imaginary talk show on national television might provide the forum for a hypothetical debate. That debate is "moderated" by fictitious Tom Kelly.

Perhaps the most pleasing response to the publication of that epilogue, a section of the book our original publishers were a bit dubious about including, was that students not only found it interesting and stimulating but often took it so seriously that I was frequently asked to provide full citations of such made-up treatises by our imaginary sociologists as *Freedom and Control: The American Contradiction; Meritocracy and Democracy: A Functionalist Analysis; Peasants to Parvenus; The Plural Society;* and *Consensus and Dissensus: The American People at Bicentennial.*

In the previous pages I have followed my editor's suggestion and tried to provide a sense of myself and some brief introductions to those previously published essays included in this book, indicating how they came to be written. Hopefully, knowing something about how one's life and work can offer reciprocating satisfactions will underscore the significance of that line of Robert Frost's that had such an impact on a very impressionable youngster.

Its sentiment still affects me at 50 as I think about the future and chart a series of mid-course corrections that will take me to new ports of call (and new callings, perhaps) while continuing to provide the opportunity to combine "my avocation with my vocation as my two eyes make one in sight."

Part I
The Marginality of a Model Minority

1
The Ghetto and Beyond: Reflections on Jewish Life in America

(1968)

The Jewish quarter is generally supposed to be a place of poverty, dirt, ignorance and immorality—the seat of the sweatshop, the tenement house, where "red lights" sparkle at night, where the people are queer and repulsive. Well-to-do persons visit the ghetto merely from motives of curiosity or philanthropy; writers treat it sociologically, as a place in crying need of improvement.[1]

This summary of popular images of New York's Lower East Side, written almost seventy years ago, sounds strikingly similar to what one might read of Harlem, Hough, or central Newark today. But the echo has a hollow ring. Regardless of what outsiders say, today's ghetto is not the same. It has a different character.

The Old Ghetto

When the Lower East Side teemed with Jewish immigrants trying to eke out a meager living in the overcrowded buildings of a worn out slum, they too were often poor, hungry, bewildered, and bedraggled. But they knew what "soul brother" meant long before that expression was to enter the American vernacular. Their word was *landsmann* and, in many ways, the fellowship it stood for made the old poverty tolerable. The *modus vivendi* of the poor Jew's existence was dominated by mutual assistance and a sense of community. It was also pervaded with a belief, an underlying faith, that "America is different."

And for them America *was* different. In his "Afterword" to a reissue of Michael Gold's *Jews Without Money*, Michael Harrington summed it up succinctly:

> The "old" poverty was the experience of an adventurous poor who sought, like the characters in *Jews without Money*, a mythical America

17

where the streets were paved with gold. They became disillusioned, to be sure, yet they shared the solidarity of a language, a religion, a national memory. If there were countless human tragedies and terrible cycles of unemployment and want, there was still an expanding economy and the possibility of battling one's way out of the ghetto, either individually or as part of a community, as in the labor movement.[2]

The demonstrable successes of those who had arrived but a few years (and sometimes mere months) before, kept the faith alive. Despite the repeated mutterings of *a klug tzu Columbus* (a curse on Columbus), one could make it here—and many did. The Jews' ghetto, unlike the Blacks', was a gateway. It served to help them get in rather than to keep them locked out.

The Jews of the lower East Side, the "Jews without money," were not the first to settle in America. Merchant traders from Recife, Brazil arrived in Manhattan in 1654. By the time of the revolution there were nearly 3,000 Jews in America and established congregations were to be found in Newport, Savannah, Philadelphia, Richmond, and New York. Their numbers were to increase a hundredfold by 1870 as economic conditions and political unrest prompted the emigration of Jews from Germany. When they arrived some stayed in the East. Others went South or West. German-Jewish immigrants followed the wagon trains selling their soft goods and hardware to the pioneers and eventually settling among them. Backpacks were replaced by wagons, replaced in turn by little shops, some of which became great emporiums with names like Levy's, Goldwater's, Nieman-Marcus, I. Magnin, and Miller Stockman. By 1870 a quarter of a million Jews were residing— and often prospering—in this country.

Although not always welcomed with total equanimity, most found acceptance as they settled in cities, towns, and hamlets across the land. Anti-Jewish barriers were rarely erected against the social or physical mobility of these American Hebrews (as they were sometimes called). The ghetto as a place of ascription or solace was hardly in evidence on this side of the Atlantic in the antebellum period. It emerged as East European immigrants began to arrive on the eastern shore in increasing numbers during the late 1870s. Within ten years the number of Jews increased to 500,000 and within twenty years it exceeded a million. By 1924 when the Golden Door was shut for good, more than 3.5 million Jews had come to the United States.

These poor "greenhorns," with their sallow faces and strange clothes, their few belongings and their many children, their curious dialects and mysterious religious rites, were to change the character of Jewish life in America—and America's characterization of the Jew.

From their ranks (and not from the earlier German group) came the poets and painters, the polemicists and provocateurs. This is not to deny that stereotypes already existed. They did. Shakespeare was widely read and the image of Shylock was not unknown (nor were Jewish peddlars spared the comparison). As many social novelists of the gilded age pointed out, wealthy German Jews were often seen as its quintessential parvenus.[3] Still, prior to the "new immigration," Jews as a group had made but a slight dent on the consciousness of the average American and had even less of an impact on American culture (save perhaps for Levi Strauss's dungarees). All this was to change dramatically with the arrival and settlement of the "Russian" immigrants on the American scene.

The immigrants themselves (from Warsaw and Lublin, from Vilna and Kovno, from Bialystok, from Kiev, from a hundred little villages in the Pale of Settlement, Austria-Hungary, and Rumania) came to find in the United States what seemed eternally elusive in Europe—the privilege of being a part of society rather than mere parasites on the body politic. America was seen as offering something more as well. Not only could one belong; one could also be oneself. Once here, the immigrants began to recreate an urban equivalent of the *shtetl* they had left behind. It came to be called a ghetto, not by those who lived, worked, and played out life's dramas there, but by the outsiders who peered into these "exotic" and "oriental" enclaves.

The American ghetto was from its inception a combined product of communal assistance and societal denial. Realities quickly intruded on the optimistic visions of the open society and Jews found that, while they could join the society, the price of membership was high. Mounting fear over the "wretched refuse" of Europe had led to a growing antiforeign semtiment throughout the country. And none decried the influx more quickly than those who had so recently been immigrants themselves. Such tensions exacerbated a tendency that already existed among most groups of newcomers and certainly among Jews. This was the tendency to seek one another out and develop institutions (or remodel existing ones) to aid their kith and kin. Perhaps the most striking characteristic of the Jews was the extent to which they felt united by membership in a single, if greatly extended, family.

Jews and Others

To be asked whether one is a "member of the tribe" was (and remains) more than a facetious question. It is a request for identification, for placement in a meaningful social category. As Erich Kahler has pointed out, such a feeling of kinship with fellow Jews may have little to do with personal relations. One may be much closer to Gentile friends than to Jews. One may even be the sort of Jew who is uneasy in the presence of those displaying "Jewish peculiarities" (which in its extreme form may take on the character of intense self-hatred).[4]

For the Sephardic and German Jews who had come to America prior to the great migrations for example, Jewish identity was a relevant part of personal existence and few denied their lineage or heritage. Still, they tried to minimize their "differences" from the social world into which they sought admission. They wanted to be seen by their gentile peers as bankers, not Jewish bankers, as lawyers, not Jewish lawyers. And they tried to model their lives accordingly. Being a Jew was important; being *Jewish* was often quite distasteful.

With the entry of millions of East European Jews (many reflecting those "Jewish peculiarities"), emotions were stirred and conflicts arose. The German Jews, both elite and parvenu, came to be grouped willy nilly with their "cousins" from Russia, often to their profound dismay. They who had organized Reform temples with choirs, organs, and Sunday services, who belonged to the best clubs and traveled in the highest circles, who had eschewed all traces of the "ghetto mentality" (or thought they had), were chagrined at what the migration might, and indeed did, portend. Some sought to dissociate themselves from their less reputable "relatives," but because the uncouth newcomers *were* relatives, they could never be completely abandoned.

One way of reconciling desired social distance with social responsibility deeply (though often painfully) felt was to employ these new people in their own shops and factories or help them find employment in those of Christian friends. Another way was to aid in the organization of societies such as the ubiquitous free loan associations to assist poor Jews. There are many explanations for the motivation of German-Jewish philanthropists (including the obvious notion of charity beginning at home), but one too frequently overlooked is the desire to alter the stereotype of the ghetto dweller by helping the newer immigrants help themselves.

Growing antiforeign, and especially anti-Semitic, sentiment throughout the country touched all American Jews—old-timers and newcomers alike. By the turn of the century many strange and sometimes strained alliances had developed between the German Jews and the "Russians," between the bosses (many worked in the Jewish-dominated needle trade) and the workers. The deepening cleavages between Jews and gentiles intensified the feeling of Jewish interdependence, whether one lived on Central Park West or in Brownsville. If exclusion inhibited the ease with which Jews could overcome the caste lines of privilege, it served to coalesce an ethnic community which could then mobilize its varied resources for mutual assistance.

More Jews, of course, were apt to be found in Brownsville than on Central Park West:

> We were the end of the line. We were the children of the immigrants who had camped at city's back door, in New York's rawest, remotest, cheapest ghetto, enclosed on one side by the Canarsie flats and on the other by the hallowed middle-class districts that showed the way to New York. "New York" was what we put last on our address, but first in thinking of the others around us. *They* were New York, the Gentiles . . . we were Brownsville—*Brunzvil,* as the old folks said.[5]

Other immigrants also felt the sense of separateness. Jews were not entirely unique. But Jews were bound and determined not to let any barrier divert their quest for a respected place in American society. For one thing, Jewish immigrants, unlike, say, their contemporary sojourners from Italy, had almost all taken one-way tickets to America. One in five of the Italians went back home after they had made their nest egg (or after they had repeatedly failed to do so). The Jews had no homes to which to return.

In yet another way their difference from other European immigrants was significant. Unlike the Italians (or the Irish or Poles) they were not former members of the lower levels of peasant societies. If they had come from societies that still showed the marks of a feudal social structure, *they* had never been in peonage. They had lived metaphorically as "eternal strangers" in the Eastern countries where for centuries they had been relegated to marginal occupations and where in more recent times they had been left to practice their own traditions, periodically disrupted by acts of terror wrought by the czar's officials or their loyal subjects.

The "Russian" Jews, unlike almost every other ethnic group to come to this country, brought skills and values more in keeping with the society into which they hoped to move than with those from which they had come. Their skills were often entrepreneurial and their values aspiringly bourgeois (though few would admit it). Although many were religious (if they kept the faith, they were Orthodox—at least in the beginning), they felt no allegiance to a dogma imposed by a dominating church and enforced by a bureaucratic hierarchy. Each *shul* was a world of its own; each congregation was a circle of close friends and relatives. What united the disparate groups was a tradition that encouraged searching inquiry and constant questioning. As the Protestant ethic had once been secularized into a social one for the early settlers, the Talmudic tradition in the early 1900s became transformed from a part of the central core of spiritual life into a *modus operandi* in the streets and workshops of urban America.

Finally, the well-known belief in the sanctity of the family, respect for law and justice, and the faith that education could lead to both aesthetic and material benefits, all strengthened Jewish ambition to catch up with and eventually overtake the Joneses of America. Although few American Jews played out their lives as if Horatio Alger, Jr. had written the scenario, their successes came to represent the clearest case of the American dream becoming a reality. It seldom happened overnight, but conquering the obstacles of language and culture and social discrimination, many East European Jewish families moved from rags to riches in three generations.

Generations

Best seen as members of cohorts in different stages of acculturation rather than of strictly chronological periods, the generations of Jews varied markedly. What is usually referred to as the first generation pertains to that phase dominated by the immigrants and those old enough to have been directly affected by life in an East European culture. While the immigrants faced the upheaval of uprooting, traveled in steerage across a forbidding ocean, experienced the culture shock of arriving in a strange land and the debilitating effects of life and work under the most adverse conditions, they proved amazingly resilient. Because they tried to reconstruct so much of the world they had left behind, the problem of culture conflict may have been less acute for them than for their immediate descendants. They seldom wandered far—geographically or psychologically—from their "quarter."

The children of the first generation lived their early lives scurrying between two worlds. For most, the centripetal attraction of the wider society often transmitted by public school teachers was too compelling to resist. They were to learn, often through bitter experinece, that the accent, dress, and manners learned in their neighborhoods precluded easy access into the American mainstream. Some, disillusioned by both antiforeign and anti-Jewish attitudes, withdrew to their territory. Others became actively engaged in radical activities that stressed universal brotherhood and rejected parochialism in all guises—save its own. Most continued to press for admission or at least tried to adjust their lifestyle to fit more readily into that toward which they aspired. Old ways were modified (the new, American "denomination" *Conservative* Judaism was a case in point) and others were cast aside. For those of the second generation, Jewish/Gentile stories and jokes abounded—many self-denigrating; but the lore of the *shtetl* and the sayings of the rabbis were left behind. As the old-timers died, the Yiddish theaters lost their patrons and Yiddish newspapers their readers.

What remained was the sense of communitiy and the desire to maintain familial ties. As individuals became more successful they moved farther away from the old ghetto area. But as they went out from the lower East Side of New York, the South Side of Chicago, or central Baltimore and moved uptown, or as in Boston, to the west (or eastward in such places as Syracuse and Rochester), they settled in what came to be labeled "Jewish neighborhoods." This pattern of sticking together continued right out into the suburbs where homogeneous ethnic enclaves became countrified versions of the American ghetto—now adorned with million-dollar synagogues.

Often members of the second generation were the first of their families to enjoy the benefits of what their hard-working parents had longed for: a living wage. Some became very wealthy. Newly rich, they could lavish on themselves and their children what had for so long been denied. Homes, automobiles, and manners of dress were often ostentatiously garish. With these manifestly nouveau riche characteristics came a growing awareness that money could be used as well as spent. Increasingly, these parvenus (a twentieth-century version of their German-Jewish predecessors) began to use their money to give their children superior educations in elite universities. In time, these children would often find themselves embarrassed by the crude, uncultured ways of their elders. More often, the second generation had to struggle, and for every Jewish boy who went to Harvard, a hundred went to City College and *then* on to better things.

The children who grew up in old-law tenements or in the gilded ghettos built by the immigrants or their sons and daughters formed the third generation. This generation has now reached maturity and is raising and struggling to understand an even more ungrateful fourth. The grandchildren of the immigrants, and their children too, live in a very different world. Almost everything has changed. Despite the phenomenal rate of acculturation, the rate of assimilation, as measured by intermarriage and even by interfaith socializing, has remained exceedingly low.[6] Or, to use Milton Gordon's terms, there has been a good deal of cultural adaptation but little structural assimilation.[7] Jews may no longer be very Jewish, but they are still Jews. And most not only want to remain so but wish their children to remain so too.

Socialist grandparents lived in slums and yearned (and often campaigned) for better working conditions, better wages, and better times for their children. By and large, they were to get them. The second generation saw their fortunes rise, fall, and rise again as the economy expanded, depressed precipitously, and was rejuvenated through New Deal innovations and especially the wartime boom. (Said one: "I started life as a Communist, then I became a Social Democrat, then a New Deal Democrat, then just a plain Democrat. Now I'm a full professor.") Jewish grandchildren enjoyed the fruits of parental success and the opportunities offered in a society noticeably free from anti-Jewish barriers. The last point is extremely relevant.

During the first half of the century attitudes toward Jews varied markedly. In the early days Jewish workers had to contend with a good deal of prejudice and discrimination, exacerbated by involvement in radical causes and by an old but unfounded belief that Jews threatened unfair competition in the marketplace. Anti-Semitism rose and fell during the immediate post–World War I years only to rise again during the Depression. In the late 1930s and the early 1940s active German-American Bundists and members of the Christian Front sought to exclude Jews from various spheres of life, and many unaffiliated Americans sympathized with their views. Most did not, and discrimination against Jews in the United States even during the Depression tended to be of the social variety: quota systems on college and professional school enrollment, restrictions on buying into certain neighborhoods or working in certain industries. Perhaps the most pervasive view in those days was that Jews were all right as long as they did not get "too pushy." American officials displayed little sympathy for the plight of European Jews during the early days of the Nazi regime in Germany. Reluctance to offer sanctuary to the millions who were displaced and who eventually died in the gas chambers extended to the highest reaches of society.

Today it is argued that the desperate plight of European Jewry was simply not understood at home. The argument has more than a kernel of truth; few Jews and far fewer Gentiles knew the true story of Nazi atrocities. But the horrors revealed as the camps were opened sent a shockwave through the country and, perhaps in a spirit of expiation, led to a changed view of the American Jew. Revelations about the depth of German calumny brought forth concern for the fate of those who survived. When the United Nations granted statehood to Israel,

America vied with the Soviet Union to be the first to ratify, and Americans in general felt the need to offer a homeland for Jewish displaced persons. The caricature of the Jew ingrained in the mind of Americans was soon to become seriously modified by the notion of the heroic fighter. Israel's victory over the Arabs in 1948 (and in 1956 and 1967) evoked admiration even from those who were not otherwise kindly disposed toward Jews. (One recent commentator has suggested wryly that figures such as Moshe Dayan represented the penultimate portrait of the "the Jew as *goy.*")

Everyman a Jew

For the majority of Jewish young people, things looked bright in the late 1940s and the future even brighter. In many ways, they had made it *into* American society and, in this sense, they "had it made," or at least thought they did. Few anticipated the day when Christian Americans or some middle-class Americans would begin to want to "think Jewish"—or at least think "thinking Jewish" was "in."

Some have argued that televison provided the first wedge in opening the door to a Jewish era. Perhaps. Ethnic humor, especially Jewish humor, made its first nationwide appearance as old-time vaudevillians from the borscht circuit found the new media receptive to the public recounting of their very personal *tsoris*. Soon many Americans were larding their language with choice Yiddish phrases and the homely philosophy of Jewish mothers.

The turnabout probably came out of something more significant than the birth of the televison age. It was part of a mood of frustration, anxiety, and for many, bitterness, of a generation raised on depression, war, and unconditioned surrender, on Pax Americana and the world-is-our-oyster imagery—the silent generation, which included many young American Jews in college fraternities, medical schools, law offices, in apolitical lethargy by cold war realities, Korea, and McCarthyism. The aura of detached optimism was darkened by a realization that the end of the war did not signal the beginning of a new era of world peace maintained by American largesse and good intentions, but a time of upheaval and change—first abroad and eventually at home.

Among the first to "tell it like it was" were Jewish "sick" comedians who, while speaking from inside the box, or more often from the nightclub stage, vented not only their personal frustrations, but the general irritations of hundreds of thousands of Americans. To these iconoclasts nothing was too sacred to examine or decry. The "sick-niks" were attacked as ghouls, as desecrators of the pantheon of

America's most revered heroes, as ingrates for lampooning living legends such as President Eisenhower, J. Edgar Hoover, and Mom. Whatever their views, they were listened to and imitated. A whole new genre of "ethnocidic" humor was born, humor that was associated with Jews even when they had nothing to do with it (as in the case of Tom Lehrer). "Listen to this record . . . Listen," they were saying in Boston and Boise and Des Moines. "Those Jews sure got a lot of nerve." And they listened and laughed (often at themselves though they may not have known it).

Most Jews, now fairly prosperous and middle class, were embarrassed by the "sickniks" with whom they were fearful of being identified. What they feared was that once again they would be singled out as being different. (Of course, they still *were* different. Even as they listened to the same programs and records as other Americans, they took special pride in *really understanding* the subtleties projected and the sources from which the allusions sprang.)

But the fears might have been allayed, for America—at least literate America—was about to enter its most philo-Semitic phase. The poignant stories of growing up in the ghetto told by stand-up comics from the Catskills had warmed the hearts of many Gentiles, who were themselves not so far removed from Shantytown, Little Italy, or even Winesburg. The chutzpah of the iconoclasts pricked the social conscience of their children, or at least made them laugh. But what had even greater appeal was the new American novel with the Jew as protagonist.

Jews were no longer being portrayed simply as suffering philosophers out of touch with the real world, as conspirators in some radical campaign to overturn the social order, as tintypic shyster lawyers, grasping merchants, or unloved physicians. In place of the old caricatures were people who happened to be Jewish. For perhaps the first time in American literary history, the Jew became everyman and, through a curious transposition, everyman became the Jew. Characters in the widely read fiction of Salinger, Bellow, Malamud, and Roth—the "Frannys" and "Herzogs" meant something to most literate Americans, not to Jews alone.

Too White, Too Red?

The latest generation then, began growing up in a new kind of milieu, at least for American Jews: troubled on the outside but, for them, quite tranquil within. The grandchildren of Jews from Eastern Europe knew little of first-hand anti-Semitism and even less of deprivation. They entered a world in which Jews were not only tolerated but also accepted.

Melvin Tumin implies that some, perhaps many, Jews (at least those over thirty) have become too complacent, enjoying their acceptance and success and internalizing the spirit of a sort of "cult of gratitude." They have become too far removed from radical grandparents who manned the battlements for the rights of workingmen or from anarchist uncles who mounted the soapboxes to harangue their audiences for freedoms great and small. They hardly remember. And many shrink from thoughts of being considered too outlandish in their political views, if they think about such matters very deeply at all. For good or ill, most American Jews are part of the big wide—and White—Establishment. Some of their children (although far from all) have discovered with chagrin the soft, rather passive nature of their parents' liberalism. Many have come to resent the bourgeois views of parents who seek to prevent them from "going where the action is," or who fail to understand why they want to go at all.

This is not to say that the Jewish parents of college-age children are unconcerned with the fate of others. They have, for example, long been supporters of the civil rights movement. Many have contributed and petitioned. Some have marched. A few have died. But many of their children are claiming that when it comes to such matters as civil rights for Blacks one feels the Jew "doth protest too much." What may not be understood is the difference between naiveté and gentility.

The vast majority of America's Jews is committed to seeing Blacks accepted as a free people and full citizens. Most go farther and support the idea of offering compensatory services to overcome the inequities of the past. But like many other middle-class Americans, there are those—especially the ones so recently out of the ghettos themselves—who are fearful of what they see as the disruption of their communities and the disturbance of their children's education and growth by a rapid influx of lower-class Blacks into neighborhoods or school districts. For all the involvement in "the movement," there remains in some Jewish circles a paternalistic aura of noblesse oblige toward the Black cause. ("They should be grateful for what is being done for them.") Much of this is said only in the confines of the home or neighborhood because of what might be called "Jewish gentility" ("How can you say that Harry? People won't understand"), but it exists just the same.

For many Jews, confrontation is still a way off, and those who say that liberalism increases the farther one gets from the problem may well be right. Some Jews remain, or their property remains, back in the old "quarter." They are the special targets of verbal and, increasingly, physical abuse by Blacks who live there and on whom they depend for a living. They live in fear of these neighbors as their Old Country parents and grandparents had once feared Russia's landless peasants. Milton Himmelfarb sees this estrangement as an irreconcilable conflict in which, once again, poor Jews face even poorer *muzhiks*. (This is not to discount the fact that there are Jewish "merchants" and "slum-lords" in the ghettos who do exploit the Black residents. But most Jews living there are not rich, nor are they oppressors. They would dearly love to get out, leaving to others—perhaps the city itself—the thankless task of trying to salvage something from the ruins of their old neighborhoods.

Recently, Jews in Harlem, Brooklyn, and the suburbs have become targets of anti-Semitic attacks by certain Black Power groups who claim they are not really interested in the cause of Black people but only in their own security. As the tempo of demands increases, an even greater rift between Jewish liberals and Black militants may be expected. Still, the remnants of the established civil rights movement look to Jews for continued support and participation. As the nation awaits the next phase of the struggle, its Jewish citizens wonder which view shall prevail. It is no idle matter for, like most White liberals, the Jews (at least those middle-aged and older) will wait warily and react rather than take the initiative on civil rights in the future.

The children are not as skeptical, but they also seem deeply troubled and confused. In the early 1960s many militant young Jews walked hand-in-hand with their "Black brothers." Half of the "visiting" White people in Mississippi during the fateful summer of 1964 were reported reliably to have been Jewish. Now these Jewish youngsters are not sure where to turn. They are no longer wanted by many of their old friends, who tell them to go back to Westchester and work with prejudiced Whites. Some have done so (not without difficulty, for it is often hard to go home again). Some have opted out altogether and become hippies. And some have found a new outlet for radical passions on the campuses and in the peace movement.

The war in Southeast Asia has also affected the parents of these draft-age youths. On this issue, the majority of Jews find themselves with their liberal friends: not pacifists, but opponents of the government's war policy. While not all doves are Jewish, most Jews are dovish. Despite the fact that advertisements opposing the war in Vietnam in the *New York Times* and other newspapers contained a very high percentage of Jewish-sounding names, few anti-antiwar spokesmen singled out Jews as being a disloyal group. Jewish defense agencies and many Jews feared a backlash, especially from conservative groups that viewed any protest against the war as an affront to America's fighting men and who tended to view dissent as tantamount to treason. Aside from right-wing pamphlets, it was only after the first week of June 1967 that the issue was raised at all.

The barely concealed elation of American Jews (including most Vietnam doves) over Israeli military successes caused some to question why they have been unwilling to support America's fight against Communist aggression in Vietnam while they eagerly endorsed Israel's war. Following the Israeli victories, neo-Nazi polemicists wrote Streicher-like tracts on the "genocidal policies of Israel" and of "American-Jewish complicity" in these "atrocities." Others began to raise troubling questions about whose side the Jews were on. The questioners were robbed of the one strong point that usually accompanies such diatribes: alleged collusion between Zionists and Communists. The Soviet line (in certain ways much like the American Right) gave little ammunition to *that* sort of propaganda campaign. It may well be that the television coverage of the Security Council debates served to reduce the potential tension that might have been created by the seemingly inconsistent position of American Jews. Not a few Jews were aware of this. They were also relieved that the desert war had been swift and decisive, for they feared the questions that would have been raised had the Israelis found themselves at the mercy of the Arabs with the United States reluctant to intervene—as well might have been the case.

American Jews delighted at Israeli victory in the Six-Day War have evinced much less enthusiasm for their own country's protracted conflict in Southeast Asia and its stalemated war against poverty at home. Other groups in American life share this frustration. In the search for scapegoats that may soon ensue, Jews may find themselves most vulnerable to attack from Right, Left, and below. By seeking reform and compromise on most issues instead of radical change, they may increasingly come to appear too white for the Black militants, too red for the White conservatives, and too yellow for their own children. Jews are not unaware of such possibilities. They know that latent anti-Semitism can be revived in America as it has been in the past. But they do not seem worried. They feel they can ride out the coming storms. Like their forebears who came to settle on the lower East Side, most Jews still believe in America and its people.

As for their dissident children, they feel (rightly or wrongly) that they have heard it all before. New Left protest, at least when voiced by Jewish youth, sounds strikingly familiar. Irving Howe sums up the sentiment in one succinct sentence (writing about dissent in the thirties): "You might be shouting at the top of your lungs against reformism or Stalin's betrayal, but for the middle-aged garment worker strolling along Southern Boulevard you were just a bright and cocky Jewish boy, a talkative little *pisher*."[8] The same is being said today—though the cause, the occupation of the listener, and the boulevard are different. Today's young Jewish activists will grow up too. When they do, they will probably find themselves radical in thought, reformists in action, bourgeois in manner—and Jewish. Just like the rest.

Notes

1. Hutchins Hapgood, "Foreword," in *The Spirit of the Ghetto: Studies of the Jewish Quarter of New York* (New York: Funk & Wagnalls, 1902).
2. Michael Harrington, "Afterword," in Michael Gold, *Jews without Money* (New York: Avon, 1965): 232. See also Moses Rischin, *The Promised City: New York's Jews, 1870-1914* (Cambridge: Harvard University Press, 1962).
3. See John Higham, "Social Discrimination against Jews in America," *American Jewish Historical Society* 47 (September 1957):9.
4. Erich Kahler, *The Jews among the Nations* (New York: Ungar, 1967): 5-6.
5. Alfred Kazin, *A Walker in the City* (New York: Grove, 1951): 12.
6. Marshall Sklare, "Survivalism or Assimilation: Changing Patterns in American Jewish Life," Proceedings of the Jewish Orientation and Training Seminar for Social Workers (New York, mimeo., 1958).
7. See Milton M. Gordon, *Assimilation in American Life* (New York: Oxford University Press), 1964.
8. Irving Howe, *Steady Work* (New York: Harcourt, Brace, & World, 1966): 353.

2
Tensions and Trends: American Jews in the 1980s

(1981)

Whatever the agencies of government say, Jews are still a minority in America. In a population that has recently topped 225 million, they are but a very small slice of the demographic pie, less than 3 percent. But Jews are an important minority; for many they are a model group. If success is to be measured by educational, occupational, and political mobility, Jews are to be ranked at the very top of the scale, for they have done extremely well in America.

Success is not security, however. Spanish Jews in the fifteenth century, Russian Jews in the nineteenth, and German Jews in the twentieth were also successful minorities but, it turned out, terribly vulnerable ones. Without drawing comparisons or suggesting that American Jews face the possibility of a similar fate, even among these well-established, well-placed Americans there is a gnawing sense of apprehension that something may go awry, that hard-won achievement and acceptance may be called into question, thwarted, or reversed. Certain recent trends have caused concern that the ever-smouldering embers of anti-Semitism may be fanned by those jealous of Jewish accomplishments, or those in need of scapegoats for personal misfortunes, or those who feel betrayed by what they see as a Jewish retreat regarding certain social causes, or by those who side with the enemies of Israel (and use such slogans as "Zionism is Racism" to advance their cause).

Tensions have mounted in recent years and spirits that soared in the early 1960s when, with other liberals, Jews felt we were truly at the edge of a New Frontier, have flagged considerably. The disquiet is not specific to Jews, but they seem to have been most affected by the events of the late 1960s and the reaction to their involvement by White conservatives who, as I predicted in 1967, did come to see them as

"too red," and Black militants who came to see them as "too white."
Few anticipated an even sharper turnabout caused not so much by
domestic activities but by international concerns—the oil crisis
touched off by the Yom Kippur War of 1973. Since that time, many
Jews have felt that even old friends and allies in the Christian community and in government circles have been backing away, shrouding
their own anxiety about energy matters in a veil of rhetoric about
"evenhandedness." (They are especially troubled by a reluctance of
others with whom they stood to stand with them—and by those who
talk of their unswerving commitment to Israeli security while selling
AWACs to the Saudis.)

In the face of these and other signs of "distancing," Jews have been
reminded again and again that, whether officially recognized as minorities or not, their group status remains as much a critical part of their
public persona as it is a critical part of their individual and collective
psyche. To friend and foe alike, here as elsewhere, a Jew is a Jew. He
may be many other things but this designation, like that which members of other ethnic categories carry with them, is of central significance in almost every sphere of life.

While it is doubtful that many American Jews envy what their Israeli
cousins have—a harsher life in a bureaucratic society where real
danger lurks at every border, they often covet one aspect of existence
in that far-off state: not the Jewish environment which, to many, is less
Jewish in many aspects than that found in an American suburb; not
even the proximity to sacred places and biblical roots. It is the fact of
being a master in one's own house, of being, for once, in the majority.
Saying this does not mean that American Jews are about to make
massive *aliyah*. This is home for approximately six million (including
many recent refugees from the Soviet Union and Iran and several
hundred thousand *yordim* who have "come down" from Israel to seek
their fortunes here). [1] Still, there is uneasiness caused in part at least by
a continued sense of marginality (a combined product of associational
inbuilding and defensive insulation) that exists alongside their entry
into the mainstream of almost every part of American life. Of late this
has meant not only toiling in the work rooms, but access to the board
rooms and executive suites; not just behind-the-scenes politicking, but
elective and appointive representation at the highest levels of local,
state, and federal government; not just affiliation with the academy, but
a significant presence in the senior professoriate and the top administration, as college deans and university presidents, too. But even for
those at the top there is a psychic tension that many feel even when
they have difficulty articulating its character. It is (still) summed up in

the common refrain, the repeated phrase, the not-so-rhetorical question: "Is it good for the Jews?" The question is prompted by the realization that, while highly successful individually, there is always that matter of vulnerability in the aggregate.

The age-old epigram—"is it good for the Jews?"—has long served as a silent preface to many a personal reflection on social issues and public policies. It was surely *the* underlying issue for those of us who joined together to examine "Group Status in America" and other issues taken up by an American Jewish Committee special Task Force on the 1980s, one of a number of efforts to review recent trends and address current concerns (and which prompted me, once again, to offer a commentary on Jewish life in America). The question itself is not an idle query, for what others say and do has always been of concern to Jews in the Diaspora, including those who live in the United States.

Current Concerns

Despite the fact that any number of opinion surveys have indicated steadily lowering rates of racial and religious prejudice in the United States between 1950 and 1980,[2] of late there seems to have been a sharp reversal of the trend. The evidence is to be found in rising tensions, in the growing ranks of hate organizations such as the various neo-Nazi groups and the Ku Klux Klan, and in public display of anti-Semitic and anti-Black activity. Some see it as a temporary aberration; others as a more profound—and ominous—rise in the "meanness mania."

It is too soon to know the longevity of the current course, but its onset has been attributed to several things: a conservative political climate, anger over welfare policies, concern about inflation and recession, apprehension about the U.S. role in the world, and the general decline of civility and reasoned discourse. Whatever the cause, meanness has been manifest in a variety of ways. There has been an alarming increase in the number of violent crimes and general vandalism, and in discriminatory actions directed against certain groups. Even while Gallup polls find that Jews are a minor issue in the general public mind (in October 1980, for example, only 8 percent of Americans asked thought Jews had too much influence), there is increasing evidence that the rate of anti-Semitism is rising.[3] Reporting on this trend, Nathan Perlmutter of the Anti-Defamation League of B'nai B'rith said it "suggests that there is a high quotient of anti-Semitism and anti-Jewish hostility which still exists just beneath the surface of American life."[4]

Specialists in intergroup relations meeting in New York in January

1981 suggested that evidence of anti-Semitism is found in various spheres of life: the increasing willingness, among working- and middle-class Prostestant and Catholic Americans, to tell anti-Jewish jokes; increasing expressions of symbolic hatred—swastika smearing, grave-yard desecrations, graffiti painting—and more direct acts of intimida-tion and violence; and continuing evidence of Black disaffection from their old Jewish allies. The reasons for these manifestations are mani-fold, but four sometimes overlapping factors must be considered: traditional anti-Jewish feeling deeply imbedded in the fabric of Chris-tian societies, which periodically surfaces; reactions to frustrating circumstances and the search for scapegoats to blame for such matters as economic setbacks and government intervention; "timely" forms of vandalism and imitative behavior on the part of young people; and what Gordon Allport once called "earned reputation." The last is the view that those who are targets are at least partially to blame for their plight. Thus some Black leaders are aware of the opposition of various organized Jewish groups and agencies to certain aspects of the affirma-tive action programs. In their eyes it is a clear example of Jewish betrayal, even a kind of complicity in growing opposition to Black advancement. This, of course, is not true, but as W. I. Thomas said long ago: "If men define situations as real, they are real in their consequences."

Writing at the same time as W. I. Thomas, John Dewey also believed in the importance of self-fulfilling prophecies. One of his most famous expressions was the idea that "in America the hyphen connects instead of separates." He was referring to the symbolic link between the Old World and the New with which every immigrant had to deal, a link connecting ethnically specific attitudes and behavior patterns and a set of values, principles, and lifestyles that are American to the core.

Several sociologists have suggested that in the United States the ethnic group is a new social form. It contains elements of the old—often linguistic, occasionally sartorial, always gastronomic, but even in the ghetto, barrio, or suburban enclave, its members become different from their cousins "back home." The American ethnic group is a product of both ends of the hyphen.

It has long served the double purpose of providing solace and strength. Solace is offered through the security of knowing that there are others who share one's fate and to whom one can turn for protection from the ravages of poverty and the glare of rivals and enemies. Strength comes through collective action, the banding to-gether with fellow "ethnics" to gain protection, access to opportunity, and social advancement. "Bloc power" is an old political device well known to urban historians and members of almost every American "nationality" and racial group.

Ethnicity is not merely a response to negative forces. Being connected to others like oneself enhances self-esteem and provides a feeling of camaraderie, a pride in peoplehood, and a sense of having roots in a fixed location and sociocultural space. As Kurt Lewin pointed out long ago: "It is not the belonging to many groups that is the cause of difficulty, but an *uncertainty* of belongingness."[5]

Ethnic identity—for Jews, for Blacks, for others—is a complex phenomenon. Some say that in these days of uncertainty and widespread uneasiness about the future, it is only natural that people should seek out kith and kin in a return to the *Gemeinschaft* (even to a *Gemeinschaft* writ large, like an ethnic group). Others feel that ethnicity, while useful in the past, has served its purpose. Opponents warn that today such a reversal of an "enclave mentality" may be counterproductive, "largely an ideological revival wrought by alienated and disenchanted intellectuals and activists in a dangerous alliance with conservative political demagogues."[6]

Irving Levine suggests that while critics may be correct in warning of the hazards of ethnocentrism and group chauvinism, they are misreading the American reality by so easily discounting the power of ethnicity to remain an important contemporary force. They too easily dismiss social, psychological, and political needs for ethnic identity, and underestimate the positive force of ethnic social cohesion.[7] Levine's point is well taken, but it continues to come under attack by those who say that the resurgent emphasis on cultural ties is not a search for a lost community or for an anchorage in an increasingly anomic society but a defensive and tribalistic reaction to the events of the 1960s and 1970s, when the collective rights of those officially labeled "minorities" threatened to block the paths of others who had also known discrimination based on group membership. For some, it is argued, the reaction was less a search for roots than a demand for equal time, prompted ironically as a quid pro quo response to Black Power and similar categorical demands such as those manifest in ethnic studies programs and affirmative action activities.

Jews, those "outsiders within" and "allies in the struggle," have been caught up in the debates themselves. Perhaps better than most, they know that ethnicity and group membership are highly functional in terms of personal adjustment and ego development and as a protective device. Like many others with special concerns, Jews have always sought to protect and assert their group's interests. But even in doing so they have often expressed ambivalence about extending that notion to claim categorical prerogatives or what has come to be known as "group rights."

Group Rights and Group Interests

In an advance paper circulated to all members of the AJC Task Force on Group Status, the following statement was included:

> In the 1970s, a powerful movement developed to allocate social and economic goods along group rather than individual lines. In court cases, such as *DeFunis, Weber, Bakke,* and *Fullilove,* and in administrative decisions, racial and ethnic classifications became increasingly prominent in making key decisions. This trend generated great controversy and is sure to constitute one of the major social issues of the 1980s. One major development has been the proliferation of groups claiming special status based on race, ethnicity, age, gender, sexual orientation, and degree of handicap.

It was immediately apparent to all assembled at the first meeting of the group that the affirmative action debate was one of the most controversial the task force would take up. Why the concern? Few issues have been more troubling to Jews than this one. They are caught in a double bind. Aware that, without dramatic alterations in structural arrangements, traditional patterns of discrimination may well continue, they are nonetheless worried about the fairness of "favoritism," which is how many view affirmative action.

While such a view is widely held, it misses an essential point. Affirmative action is not a device to render favoritism but a label for a series of approaches to equalize opportunity. It includes ways of casting wider nets for applicants, means of ensuring that not only conventional criteria are used for screening purposes, and guarantees that prior handicaps are taken into account. As the American Jewish Committee suggested in its brief in the Bakke case: candidate A, who has demonstrated through achievements the capability of surmounting the hurdles of severe economic or cultural deprivation due to racial discrimination, may have the potential to become a better physician than candidate B, whose test scores are higher but who has been reared without experiencing discrimination and in the lap of luxury. "What we did urge," reported Samuel Rabinove, director of AJC's Discrimination Division, "is that medical schools evaluate each applicant individually as a total person, not just how the applicant did in school, but how he or she did in life."[8]

Being especially sensitive to the issue, and aware that special circumstances sometimes call for special intervention, many Jews claim that such a position is tenable. But even so, some supporters worry about being propelled down a slippery slope, where more and more "points" are allotted for ascriptive characteristics and fewer and fewer for achieved ones. There are others who, having known denial and its consequences, see themselves as authorities on ways of overcoming barriers by dint of hard work and personal initiative. This is not to say they revel in their ability to deal with adversity; but many who remember when times were very different for them are not averse to pointing out that "nobody ever gave *us* that kind of advantage," or to asking—"Why can't they be like us?"

Wherever they stand, most Jews seem to hold the view that what is most needed is the assurance of equal opportunity under well-enforced law. Nothing more, nothing less. What bothers many is the new approach which carries the whole thing a giant step further, suggesting, in the extreme, that the only way to overcome discrimination is to discriminate in reverse—denying Pinkas to assist Paul. This pits the concept of justice *against* the idea of equity rather than combining the two. One critic, Lisa Newton, writes that

> If justice is defined as equal treatment under law for all citizens . . . injustice is the violation of that equality, discriminating for or against a group of citizens, favoring them with special immunities and privileges or depriving them of those guaranteed to the others. When the southern employer refuses to hire blacks in white-collar jobs, when Wall Street will hire women only as secretaries with new titles, when Mississippi high schools routinely flunk all black boys above ninth grade, we have examples of injustice. . . . But, of course, when the employees and the schools *favor* women and blacks, the same injustice is done.[9]

Newton and many others call this reverse discrimination, for it undermines the rule of law, destroying justice itself, at least in its political sense. She suggests that the problems raised by such reverse discrimination are insoluble "not only in practice but in principle." Two sets of questions arise: Who are the victims? Only Blacks? Only women? Who should qualify, when many have grounds for special pleading? And, once such difficult queries are answered—How much privilege is enough? When will the price be paid, the balance restored?

For many of the "preferred minorities" these arguments have a hollow ring. They are not concerned about the philosophical debates any more than they are in hearing the stories of how Jews overcame discriminatory practices and made their way into the mainstream. Recognizing, if not publicly admitting, that one of the most serious problems many racial, ethnic, sexual, and other minorities face is lack of self-respect, it is important to remember that the affirmative action movement originated as a by-product of the consciousness-raising activities of the 1960s and early 1970s which sought to turn negative self-images into positive ones.

The move was expressive but also instrumental, a calculated turn-about that left friends, mentors, and benefactors hanging. Heightened intergroup antagonism is an almost inevitable correlate of such revolutionary and recrudescent mobilizations, a relationship well-known among behavioral scientists. Freud, writing about such phenomena, pointed out that "in the undisguised antipathies and aversions which people feel toward strangers with whom they have to do we may recognize the expression of self-love—of narcissism."[10] An important function of self-love is to build ego defenses. Similarly, an important function of ethnocentrism is the enhancement of group cohesion. Such ethnocentrism, as manifest in Black consciousness (and later the Women's Rights Movement, Gay Awareness, Gray Power, and the rest), sought to consolidate pride by asserting power. And a way to assert that power was to make another inversion of principle: group rights to offset group wrongs. With the compliance (some would say the complicity) of the courts and administrative agencies, the rhetoric was reified. It was "officially" assumed that if one belonged to a particular group, one was ipso facto a victim and in need of special assistance.

Not all minority group members agree that categorical treatment is the answer. A significant faction has argued that demanding to be judged primarily by group membership instead of on an individual basis is counterproductive. It serves to corroborate the views of outsiders that certain types of people are incapable of competing on an equal basis and reverses the cause it seeks to serve "by officially stressing inferiority." However, most do not share these views. They believe that racism, sexism, and general prejudice against the old and the handicapped are so deeply woven into the fabric of society that merely ensuring equal opportunity is not sufficient.

Few mention other factors, such as regional and class biases, that are also responsible for keeping people from entering the mainstream regardless of race, creed, color, and other legally recognized stigmata. There is only grudging acknowledgment of the fact that, in many areas today, there are clear differences between advantaged and disadvantaged members of each of the "preferred" minorities, or that it is the former who tend to benefit more than those whom most programs were designed to assist.

While exercising a commitment to redress grievances of the past, it seems equally appropriate to indicate concern about abuses of the affirmative action principle, which often reward those least deserving of assistance and harm those most vulnerable (like teachers, municipal employees, factory workers, and others) who are dropped in quota-based investigations, and are bypassed, down-graded, or replaced by less qualified petitioners. Perhaps the problem is that discrimination itself has become a shibboleth, a code word that is at once too broad and too narrow. It may be too broad because it assumes that all who belong to a "preferred" category are sufferers, and too narrow because it excludes many sufferers who are not "preferred."

One way out of the current philosophical, political, and semantic trap might be to attempt to change the ground rules, to begin addressing the problems of those who are disadvantaged, irrespective of color, national origin, or gender. Such a shift in emphasis would not exclude members of minority communities who are barred from access or suffer from inadequate preparation; on the contrary, they would be more apt to benefit than they do today. Putting the emphasis on the poor, for example, would help men, women, Blacks, and Whites. While most poor in this country are White, most Blacks are poor. They, and women, many more of whom are treated unequally than men, would still receive a greater share of assistance. Stressing aid to the disadvantaged would also open up opportunities to "nonpreferred" poor and working-class men and women who have felt especially ill-served by the emphasis on minority group rights.

Coalitions of Conscience and Interest

From the early part of the twentieth century, American historians have noted that Jews have been in the forefront of many movements to seek human dignity and unfettered opportunity for all. They were active in the labor movement, in the founding of the NAACP, in a wide variety of liberal causes, and in many radical activities which sought to challenge the power of entrenched elites and insecure parvenus. They were also prominent behind the scenes of many a political coalition, playing the roles of benefactors and brokers, movers and shakers.

For many years their participation in liberal coalitions was a marriage of principle and interest, a most convenient arrangement. Jews formed strong alliances with Blacks, with labor and human rights groups, and despite their diversity successfully pursued common causes, especially during Franklin Delano Roosevelt's presidency. Reform was the primary mechanism, fairness the principal goal. In many ways the Jews and their allies succeeded in substantially altering traditional practices regarding the treatment of ethnic minorities, the poor, the handicapped, the very young, and the very old. The coalition outlived FDR and became the main vehicle for promoting New Deal solutions to social problems. For two decades it served both as the conscience of liberal-minded activists and as a potent force for political action.

In the early 1960s many societal changes began to affect the once-firm bonds between various factions in the liberal coalition. Some said that the glue that held the fragile structure together was so old it had become brittle, that it was no longer strong enough to hold the pieces together in the face of the severe strains. But it was not the dried-out cement that made the old coalition come unstuck. It was the shifting agendas of the constituent members, the growing orientation toward separatism among the very groups that had for so long felt the need for interdependence. This shift led to sharpened debates within the less-than-unified parties.

Elsewhere[11] I have discussed the ways Jews reacted to the events of the 1960s and 1970s: to struggles for community control, the ascendancy of Black Power, the formation of new coalitions by their old allies (as when some Blacks became more identified with Third World and anti-Zionist movements than with their traditional partners). Not discussed were differences of opinion within the Jewish community about what was happening and what the events themselves might portend. There were those who claimed to appreciate the Blacks' position, asking their fellow Jews to understand how difficult it was to be always dependent on others. The time had to come, they said, when even friends are rejected as patronizing. "You can't expect them to thank us—or to love us." Some did try to understand. Many others, however, were annoyed by the seeming shortness of memory; they felt abandoned. Some felt betrayed and broke ranks with the traditional liberals altogether. And there were those, many of whom had never felt fully comfortable with the course the civil rights movement had taken, who said "we told you so."

While members of particular ethnic groups often express unanimity on certain critical survival issues, they rarely sing with one voice and there are disagreements about many things. Jews are no exception. There have always been divisions within the American Jewish community: historical divisions based on what part of Europe people came from, when they came, and why; religious divisions far greater than the Orthodox, Conservative, and Reform differences known even to non-Jews; ideological and political divisions ("But what *kind* of a Zionist are you?"); socioeconomic divisions between uptown Jews and those left behind; and cultural divisions, as between the "Jewish" Jews and the "JASPS." Many of these divisions persist, although the issues within the categories have shifted over time. Which part of the Pale one came from, for example, is of little significance today, but religious differences and concerns are as important as they were twenty years ago, and there are sharp debates over such issues as the protection of Orthodox traditions, the support and funding of parochial schools, the preservation of communal institutions. Ideological lines have also been reetched and sometimes redrawn; witness the splits between the old Left and the new, between the old liberals and the neoconservatives.

Public stereotypes notwithstanding, not all Jews are rich or upper middle class. Many are lower middle class—clerks, civil servants, schoolteachers, and many are workers—taxi drivers, waiters, semi-skilled laborers. Some remain truly poor. Social stratification still exists in the Jewish community, and not all Jews view economic and social policies with the same eyes or vote for the same candidates. (Key Orthodox Jewish neighborhoods in New York City reportedly voted 3-1 for Ronald Reagan in November 1980.) There are still divisions between the provincials (who are often city folk themselves, members of tightly circumscribed urban villages) and the cosmopolites.

In light of such differences of status and perspective what has been distinctive in the past was not how fragmented Jews were, but how often they set aside their many disagreements to deal with issues relevant to their common values and collective interests. Many now argue that their involvement in the old liberal coalition—sometimes grudging, sometimes enthusiastic—had to do with the things that united Jews. But of late even that unity has become strained, and there are deepening cleavages between various segments of the American Jewish community.

Not only is there a continuing intellectual dialogue in Jewish and non-Jewish journals of opinion about the efficacy of various approaches to domestic and foreign policy, there are also strident voices in the street, many of which were rarely heard outside the old neighborhoods. For example, increasingly militant Orthodox Jews have assumed the mantle of "Jewish activism," becoming outspoken lobbyists for their causes, putting the old liberals on the defensive, and worrying the neoconservatives as well.

Disillusioned with some of their erstwhile partners and uneasy about traditional solutions to new problems, many Jews are still wary of joining with old adversaries, especially since such arrangements inevitably involve certain compromises. "How," many ask, "can we work hand-in-hand with people whose religious principles and beliefs are so far from our own? How can we join with the Moral Majority when, among other things, we want to keep prayer out of the schools? How can we support Roman Catholics—or seek their support—when we disagree on the issue of abortion?" The last question offers the clue to why, for others, thinking the unthinkable is possible: "Or seek their support." Some Jews, streetwise and astute in survival tactics, feel they may have to resort to new sorts of coalitions. It is argued, often defensively, that alliances with groups Jews do not ordinarily perceive as allies could serve to pull people (who are also in need of partners) closer to the center and help isolate them from the extremes. It should be remembered that the Moral Majority is not a majority. Not yet.

But does not compromising in one area mean selling out across the board? Some say no, it is merely good pragmatic politics. Others say it is the first step toward the abandonment of a self-imposed sacred trust. Within the Jewish community there is little agreement. At one end are those disillusioned liberal Democrats who would have voted for anyone but Goldwater in 1964 and for anyone but Carter in 1980—and did. At the other are those like Rabbi Alexander Schindler, president of the Union of American Hebrew Congregations, who worries aloud about the "chilling power of the radical Right" and states that it is "no coincidence that the rise of right-wing Christian fundamentalism has been accompanied by the most serious outbreak of anti-Semitism in America since the outbreak of World War II."

While Schindler and those in his camp know that the Jewish community cannot seek total ideological agreement on every issue, they are extremely wary of forming alliances of short-lived convenience, even with those who are supportive on the most emotional of all issues, the survival of Israel. Those still affiliated with the liberal Left feel it is far more advantageous to cast their lot with old allies, including the liberal Protestants in the National Council of Churches—who on nine of ten issues are on the same side as the Jewish defense agencies—and try to patch up the quarrel with Blacks, than to turn away from either in pique over playing Faust to Falwell.

Their critics retort pointing again to the fact that the participants in that old alliance now all march to different drummers. Jews, they say, must stop reversing the order of Hillel's famous queries and again proclaim, first, "If I'm not for myself, who will be for me?" Coalitions of convenience are the only strategy of the 1980s for vulnerable groups like Jews who will have a better opportunity to survive and prosper if they stop forgetting to ask: "But is it good for *us?*"

Is there a middle way? Must Jews choose between quixotic attempts to revive the past and decisions to deal with those they fear most? Do liberal-minded Jews have to stand on their principles in a lonely left field or turn a sharp right? There is such a place as the progressive Center. Progressive because it does not suggest that yesteryear was the best of all times and that old solutions will solve all problems; a Center because it recognizes that, for Jews at least, extremism of Left and Right are both potent dangers. Any new coalition must put clear priorities on its objectives, and high on the list will be several items which neither neoconservatives nor old liberals can gainsay: a commitment to free expression and the right to "life, liberty, and the pursuit of happiness"; a demand for equity in the court of justice; unrestricted competition in the marketplace and the academy; and assistance to those who are clearly disadvantaged, regardless of race, creed, color, or gender.

New Americans

In the decade ahead all Americans will be affected by the social and economic changes brought on by forces often beyond their immediate control. Also affected will be a number of people who, despite our problems, see this country as far better (or safer) than their native lands, and who will try to become Americans too. For most Jews the old phrase, "America is different," has a very special meaning. American Jewish history and folklore are filled with stories of struggle, setback, survival, and success. Now new waves of immigrants are coming to the United States hoping to build new lives in a new land. (Ten percent of the total number of Jews in the United States today are recent immigrants, most of them from the Soviet Union or Israel.)

There are marked differences between the character of the society into which my grandparents sought admittance and modern America. But the argument that the old *goldene medina* was far more open, with an expanding opportunity structure, than today's closed system in which unskilled laborers are superfluous, is only a partial truth. While unemployment rates are high, more people are at work than ever in our history, and many low-level jobs go unfilled for lack of people willing to take them. Many beyond the gates are eager and willing to do the menial work, to try their hand at "making it" in America, much in the manner of the earlier immigrants, by combining their efforts and helping members of family and "nationality" groups. (These attitudes are additional ammunition in the arsenal of arguments of those who believe in maintaining, if not fostering, ethnicity as against those who would try to wipe out all vestiges of hyphenated identity or marginal cultural activities.)

The new immigration, which began with only 250,000 a year in the

1920s—after a record of up to 1 million a year between 1900 and 1914—
has grown tremendously in recent decades: 250,000 each year in the
1960s and early 1970s. Then, beginning in 1975, a still more rapid
increase took place. More than 800,000 immigrants were officially
admitted to the United States in 1980, including about 230,000 refugees, most of whom were Indochinese "boat people" or Soviet Jews.
In addition, many hundreds of thousands of "illegals," mostly from
Mexico and other Latin American countries, also crossed the border.
The great influx is evidence that America is still seen as the land of
asylum and opportunity. It also means that once again newcomers will
change the face of the country. This time the complexion is changing as
well; the largest percentage of recent arrivals are non-White and non-
European. These newcomers often vary from one another as markedly
in their values, aspirations, and outlooks as they do in appearance.

Predictably old nativist sentiments have begun to resurface, opposing the influx of "alien elements." This time, other views have been
added, those of people who might be called the neonativists. They
argue that, until society takes care of its own, it should not allow others
to enter. Some of these neonativists are White ethnics, others are
members of American minority groups: Blacks, Puerto Ricans, Native
Americans, and Chicanos. These groups express the view that a double
standard is being applied in the selective immigration policies and
resettlement practices which favor immigrants from certain areas like
Indochina or Communist-bloc countries while tending to ignore those
from others such as Salvador, Uganda, or Afghanistan. They also argue
that it is they who will have to pay the highest price for refugee relief,
through the diversion of funds they need to more dramatic and politically appealing causes, as well as through direct competition in the job
market, since the undocumented aliens will sell their labor most
cheaply, undercutting growing pressures for fair wages. Both points
sound strikingly similar to what was said by Know-Nothings in the
mid–nineteenth century about the Irish, what the Irish said about
Italians and Southern and Eastern Europeans, and what some of those
White ethnics—and some Jews—have been saying about favoring
Blacks and other "preferred minorities" more recently.

Two of the most critical areas of controversy surrounding immigration are Americanization and bilingualism. *Americanization* is an old
code word used by many who firmly believed that assimilation into
Anglo-American ways was the only way outsiders could ever be
accepted. Critics have long argued that Americanization was responsible for turning ethnic pride into self-hatred and for leaving many
immigrants in the unenviable position of being cast adrift on an alien

sea. Supporters, by contrast, echoing the ideas of such early assimila-tionists as George Washington and John Adams, voice the opinion that only when foreigners cast off their alien skins and forget the customs of the past, can they really be absorbed. They admit the immigrants would have to give up a great deal, making tremendous sacrifices; but, they argue, "think of what they would be getting."

Bilingualism is a more modern concept. Jewish, Italian, Greek, and Polish immigrants who came here in the late 1800s and early 1900s took it for granted that they and their children would be taught in English and not in their native tongue. But the large migration of Spanish-speaking Puerto Rican Americans to the New York area, prompted by the economic boom of the post–World War II period and the availabil-ity of cheap and fast air service, changed the culture and character of the city—and brought about vigorous resistance to assimilation. Some sociologists have speculated that clinging to their Hispanic heritage was a way for Puerto Ricans to separate themselves from the Black Americans with whom they were often grouped. Others say that easy access to Puerto Rico made acculturation less necessary or desirable.

The latter argument also came to be used to explain the resistance of many Mexicans to Americanization. The closeness of the motherland meant that one could *be* in one world (American), while in a sense *living* in another (Mexican). Whatever the reason, the result is that many Mexican Americans, like many Puerto Ricans, feel they should be allowed to retain their ways and language. Some argue that their children should have instruction in Spanish and that their language should also be used as a vehicle for moving down the road to learning to use English in everyday life. (In 1974, in the case of *Lau v. Nichols,* the Supreme Court ruled that Chinese-speaking students in San Fran-cisco were being discriminated against by being taught in a language they did not understand.)

Because Hispanics make up the largest linguistic minority in the United States, many bilingualism debates revolve around the teaching of Spanish and the provisions for bicultural as well as bilingual pro-grams for them. However, they are not alone. Other groups have pressed for similar opportunities. Nor is bilingualism the only policy debate with respect to new Americans. Others include questions about how assistance is offered and given, especially in the placement of refugees. Should Soviet Jews, Khmer Buddhists, or Cubans be encour-aged to cluster, to form and maintain enclaves where they can find security through familiarity, or should they be scattered to encourage their early absorption into the mainstream?

If past history is any indication, it would seem most logical to allow people to develop ethnic communites, thereby easing the transition from often totally different cultural milieux. While some immigrants, especially those with higher education and familiarity with the language and customs, have successfully assimilated into dominant communities, the evidence suggests that for most, the acculturation process is painful and often prolonged. The support of others in (and often from) the same boat can be very helpful in preparing them to live in the heterogeneous society.

Finally, the most difficult question of all: Who should be admitted? At a recent conference on The Acculturation of New Immigrants, one participant, an economist, asked the assembled corps of policymakers—representatives of major volunteer agencies that work with immigrants and refugees, members of several ethnic organizations, and some foundation personnel and academicians—how many would favor unlimited immigration to the United States. Not one said he would. But the experts could not, or would not, say whom they would admit and whom they would exclude.

Some members of minority groups who were there later commented that most Americans would probably be willing to welcome as many Indochinese as wanted to come, as well as other anti-Communists from Europe, including Soviet Jews and other Whites, but would balk at large-scale requests from Africans; or argued off the record that it was not racial prejudice but cultural bias, a preference for people with an Anglo-Saxon value system or its functional equivalent.

Symptomatic of the debate, which is far more heated outside the grounds of elegant conference centers, is the view expressed by some that data showing how similar Vietnamese and Soviet Jews were—in terms of achievement motivation and the success of their children—compared to Mexican Americans in the same city, demonstrated why the first two groups should be preferred over the third. Others argued that this only highlighted a narrow perception of what it means to be a good American. Should America favor only highly motivated applicants whose cultures are dominated by a work ethic similar to that touted by many Americans? Ironically, many who themselves had not come out of that tradition, who in fact once resembled the Mexicans in the above sample more than those with whom they now aligned themselves, would answer that question affirmatively.

It is essential to keep several points in mind. First, that the gains of the Refugee Act of 1980 must be preserved, including the broadened definition of "refugee" and the possibility of admitting large numbers of refugees in emergencies. Second, that family reunification and the saving of refugees—principles which have formed the basis of the preference system since 1965—are now under attack from those who want immigration geared primarily to labor trends. While it is necessary to be mindful of economic problems, these should not be allowed to take precedence over humanitarian concerns for those seeking asylum and new lives in America.

Finally, it is suggested that for reasons of both coalitional interests and concern for its effect on American society, Jews must think seriously about the problem of illegal and undocumented aliens. A dual approach—generous amnesty for those already here but far better enforcement capabilities in the Immigration and Naturalization Service (and the Border Patrol)—seems appropriate. But even as debate over the plight of illegal aliens continues, it is necessary to support the protection of civil rights of those already here and provide them and their families with educational opportunities, health care, and fair judicial procedures.

Into the Eighties

American Jews can and should take pride in their successes. But in doing so, two caveats must be borne in mind. First, having made it does not mean that ipso facto, they "have it made." There are those, even today, who do not see Jews as models for emulation but as scapegoats on whom they can project their failures, as usurpers of what they see as their God-given places, or as exploiters who, they claim, made their way at others' expense. Jews may be successful and prominent, but they are not entirely secure, even in America. While they have attained considerable prominence in American society, Jews are and always will be a minority here. This has long made them particularly sensitive to the importance of defending their group's interests. At a time when storm clouds threaten on the horizon, efforts must be redoubled to ensure that Jewish rights are protected.

In asserting those rights for themselves, American Jews cannot forget their responsibility to others. Despite the conflicts and disagreements of recent years, they cannot abandon their historic commitment to the profoundly Jewish goals of justice and mercy. Racial discrimination, religious intolerance, and sexist policies still exist in parts of this country. Jews cannot rest until all men and women are free. This means they must be willing to reforge alliances of good will and speak out clearly and act forcefully against the persisting scourges of racism and all forms of bigotry.

Notes

1. "Jewish Population in the United States, 1979," *American Jewish Year Book* 80 (1980): 159. The figure given for 1979 is 5,860,900.
2. See Harold Quinley and Charles Y. Glock, *Anti-Semitism in America* (New York: Free Press, 1979). See also a report on a Louis Harris poll in *Newsweek* (26 February 1979): 48.
3. Peter Khiss, "Survey Finds Sharp Rise in Anti-Semitic Incidents," *New York Times* (30 December 1980): 49.
4. As reported by Anthony Lewis, "The Deeper Problem," *New York Times* (4 January 1981): op-ed.
5. Kurt Lewin, *Resolving Social Conflicts* (New York: Harper, 1948): 179.
6. Irving M. Levine, "Bolstering the Family through Informal Support Groups: A Group Identity Approach" (New York: Institute on Pluralism and Group Identity, American Jewish Committee, 1978, mimeo.): 6.
7. Ibid.
8. Personal correspondence (23 December 1980).
9. Lisa Newton, "Reverse Discrimination as Unjustified," in *Reverse Discrimination,* ed. Barry Gross (Buffalo: Prometheus, 1977): 373–78.
10. Sigmund Freud, *Group Psychology and the Analysis of the Ego* (New York: Boni & Liveright, 1950): 55. Arabs.
11. See chapter 8 of this volume.

3
Country Cousins:
Small-Town Jews and Their Neighbors

(1961)

For many years social scientists and historians have been trying to piece together a composite portrait of American Judaism. Owing to their predominant pattern of city residence, research has been focused on urban-dwelling Jews; and the Jews of the United States have been characterized as a metropolitan people. There is, however, a scattered minority of American Jews living in little hamlets and rural villages who do not fully fit this urban image. Such people do not reside in old-style ghettos, in ethnic neighborhoods, or in modern homogeneous suburbs. Unlike their urban coreligionists, they are not members of ongoing Jewish communities. They are strangers in alien territory.

Critical examination of Jewish life in the small community would seem to be alogical extension of research in the study of American Judaism and the nature of Jewish-Gentile relations. Yet while the literature offers a wealth of information about urban Jews in America, there is a dearth of published material about their "country cousins." What little there is is limited to sketchy life histories, journalistic descriptions, and anecdotal recollections of the experiences of individuals who have lived in, visited, or passed through little villages appearing in such publications as *Midstream, Commentary,* and *Congress Weekly.*[1]

In an attempt to add to the general literature on Jewish life on the American scene, to assess Jewish-Gentile relations in this neglected setting, and to reexamine the ubiquitous concept of "marginal man," an extensive study of the small-town Jews of New York State was conducted in 1958.[2] Because the small-town Jew is so often cast in the role of being an ambassador of "his people" to the Gentiles, a parallel study was simultaneously carried out with non-Jewish small-towners also living in upstate New York.

49

Data were gathered to seek answers to several questions. To what extent do group traditions persist in cases of relative isolation? Does identification wane when unsupported by fellow members of one's own group? How intensive are relationships between the stranger and the world in which he has chosen to live? What kinds of adjustments does he have to make? To what extent does interpersonal contact with an isolated minority member influence stereotypic conceptions and misconceptions held by the majority group members about him?

The Research Design

Investigation was confined to one particular area of the country: "rural" New York State. "Rural communities" and "small-town Jews" were operationally defined as follows: "Rural communities are those communities with fewer than 10,000 permanent residents, in non-metropolitan counties of New York State, excluding all towns in the Catskill mountain region, in Westchester County, and on Long Island. Small-town Jews are persons identifying themselves as being Jewish living in 'rural communities' having 10 or fewer Jewish families." The first of the two studies was an attempt to document and analyze the background, beliefs, and behavior of small-town Jews and study and record their attitudes relating to the communities where they reside. I was particularly anxious to explore the areas of religiosity, community satisfaction, and patterns of social interaction.

Respondents were located through initial contact with twenty individuals I knew; each lived in a small town in one of twenty different counties. These persons provided the names of all the Jews they knew who fit the criteria established for designating "small-town Jews." They, in turn, supplied additional names. This technique, called "snowballing," provided 180 names in two weeks.

Of the 180 names twenty were randomly selected; and these individuals and their families, together with the original key informants, were personally interviewed in the Spring of 1958. The 160 in the remaining group were mailed detailed questionnaires which asked a number of questions about origins, family life, satisfaction with small-town living, religious beliefs and practices, organizational affiliations, and attitudes about their relative isolation. In every instance—whether in the interview setting or in responding to the survey—respondents were told that research was being conducted on Jews living in small towns and that *their* help was needed to tell *their* story accurately. In no cases did those to be personally interviewed refuse to cooperate; and in the case of the mail survey, 80 percent responded.[3]

The second study was designed to gather information on the impressions and attitudes of small-town community leaders about themselves and their images and attitudes about minority groups. Data were collected on the relationship between generalized prejudices and attitudes toward Jews, Blacks, and "foreigners"; the extent to which isolated Jewish persons might influence stereotypes; and the nature of interpersonal contact and socialization between Gentiles and Jews in rural communities.

The names of community leaders were obtained by writing to the mayor or clerk of each village selected and asking that a form designating twenty-five statuses of leadership—in business, the professions, in government and politics, in education and social service, and in agriculture—be filled out with the appropriate names and returned. Twenty towns were included in this second survey. All had fewer than 5,000 residents. Ten towns had from one to three Jewish families; the remaining group had none. In all, 315 questionnaires which complemented those sent to Jewish participants were mailed. With two follow-up appeals a total of 60 percent were returned.[4]

Jewish Life in the Rural Community

Dealers and Doctors

The Jews of New York's rural areas are almost all outsiders and not natives. Most are urban emigrants who settled in small towns after having spent the early part of their lives in American or European cities. Only 4 percent were born in the communities where they now live. Of the remaining majority, half were born in one of the large American metropolitan centers and 12 percent in middle-sized cities in the United States. Thirty percent in middle-sized cities in the United States. Thirty percent were born in Europe, many of them refugees from Nazi-dominated Germany and Austria.

How did these urban Jews happen to settle in such hamlets? Two-thirds said they had come for business reasons. These respondents were mostly second-generation East European immigrants. Many had begun their careers as traveling salesmen and peddlers who settled down and started a little general store in one of the towns along the circuit. There they remained and there they prospered.

In addition to those "dealers," the other major group were refugee physicians who had fled to America only to find it difficult to establish practices in urban areas. A large number of such doctors were placed in small towns by refugee agencies or professional groups. Besides these two major groups, there were several lawyers, teachers, insurance brokers, cattle dealers, and farmers in the sample.

When asked to place themselves in the upper, upper middle, lower middle, or working class, 74 percent marked "upper middle." Only three respondents felt they were "working class": two teachers and one tenant farmer. It was from the ranks of the professional people that the greatest percentage of upper-class self-ratings came. The high self-evaluation of socioeconomic status is reflected in the relatively high incomes of the small-town Jews. In response to the question: "Roughly, what was the total income for your family last year?" 30 percent said their income exceeded $20,000, 37 percent gave $10,000—$20,000, 30 percent $5,000—$10,000, and only 3 percent indicated that they made less than $5,000 a year.

Owing to the large proportion of professional Jews in the sample (36 percent), it was not surprising to find a high level of education. Seventy percent of those questioned held at least a Bachelor of Arts degree or its European equivalent. The small-town Jews indicated that only 11 percent of their parents had college diplomas, and 56 percent said that their parents had gone to the eighth grade or less. As for their own children, nine out of ten parents in the sample indicated that one or more of their children would (or did) obtain at least a college degree.

When asked about their political affiliation, 27 percent said they considered themselves Republicans "in most political matters"; 29 percent were Democrats, and the rest marked "independent." However, a number of "Republicans" wrote in the margin of the questionnaire saying that they were "registered Republicans whose loyalty lies in the Democratic camp." Finally, respondents were asked the following question: "Basically, do you consider yourself more a rural person or more an urban person?" Two-thirds of the group said "urban."

Once a Jew. . .

Eighty-six percent of the small-town Jews placed themselves in some "Jewish" category: Orthodox, Conservative, or Reform. All expressed some feeling of religious and/or cultural identity with Judaism. Those who said they did not fit into any of the three categories were not apostates, as their response to this particular query might suggest. They tended to qualify their answers with statements like: "I'm a liberal Jew," "My family are ethical Jews," or "We're Jews, that's all." Three-fourths said they belonged to some religious congregation. At the same time almost all said they rarely or never attended religious services because the synagogue to which they belonged was too far away (estimates ranged from 15 to 100 miles).

While they were too isolated to establish some form of Jewish communal existence, many kept traditional observances at home. For example, over half celebrated the Passover holidays, 25 percent never served bacon or ham, and 15 percent maintained strictly kosher homes importing meat from distant cities. The attempt to maintain the traditions of the faith was found in both the immigrant and refugee groups. The latter, however, was less likely to display Jewish and Israeli artifacts in the home.

The deep-seated sense of Jewish identification is evident in the following random excerpts from several interviews:

> I came to this community from New York. There I was raised in a real ghetto. All my friends and associates were Jews. I went to *heder,* to *shul,* etc., like everybody else. This was our way of life. Although I wanted to get out of the city and away from the ghetto, I never wanted to forget I was a Jew. This is my fate and I try to live up to it in every way.

Another respondent phrased it this way:

> Although I was born in the city I have lived in a small community practially all of my life. Here there are few Jewish families, but when you get right down to it I'm sure I prefer being with people of my own religion. I guess being a Jew is in my blood and in my soul.

And a third:

> Most people like us are city-folk living in rural areas. While our homes are here, our roots are somewhere else. . . . We bring the past with us when we go into upstate communities like this. Part of this past is our religion. We see ourselves as Jews and so does the community.

Most small-town Jews maintain some affective connection with their religion even when they leave the geographic boundaries of the urban Jewish community. A housewife summed up the expressions of many when she said:

> We're not what one might call observant Jews. Yet there are certain traditions we like to keep. We have a *mezuzah* in the doorway and a *menorah* on the mantle. We celebrate some of the holidays like the High Holy Days and Passover. We light the *Shabbas* candles and things like that. And, I must say I like a good piece of *gefilte* fish when I can get it. Yet we eat pork, work on Saturday . . . why sometimes I even go to Midnight Mass with my friends.

"Irrespective of whether you follow religious practices or attend synagogue, do you consider yourself a religious person?" Each person answered this question by placing himself somewhere along a continuum of "very religious" to "not religious at all." Five percent considered themselves "very religious," while 62 percent felt they were "moderately" so. Thirty-six percent said "somewhat religious" and 7 percent said they were "not religious at all."

A strikingly high correlation appears when one compares the degree to which people consider themselves religious with the extent to which they practice religious observances, and with the nature of affiliation— Orthodox, Conservative, or Reform. Taking these three items together a religiosity scale was constructed.[5] This allowed me to simplify analysis by using this single measure of "traditional" religiosity. Respondents were broken into three groups: high, medium, and low religiosity.

In communities having several Jewish families the presence of coreligionists tends to reinforce religious identity and support religious practices. Table 3.1 illustrates the fact that in towns with more Jews, religiosity is higher among Jewish respondents.

Table 3.1   Religiosity and Number of Jews

	Number of Jewish Families in Town			
	1	2	3–5	6–10
Religiosity				
Low	66%	62%	59%	42%
Medium	27	32	26	26
High	7	6	15	32
	100%	100%	100%	100%
	(31)	(21)	(44)	(24)

In addition to this demographic factor it was found that religiosity is correlated with several background factors. Those highest in socioeconomic status (by self-rating and income) are lowest in religiosity. In relation to occupation, those in the medical arts (mainly of the refugee group) are most apt to be low in this expression of religiosity while those in agriculture tend to be the highest. This was borne out in the interviews. I spoke to the daughter of an immigrant from Russia, a man who became a cattle dealer in a small upstate community where he raised his family. She related:

> Our religion was very important to us. We sang Hebrew songs and spoke Yiddish in the house. I couldn't speak English until I first went to school. . . . To my father the family was the core of Jewish life and so we learned

about Jews and our religion through discussions at home, through books, through stories. We were always very Jewish.

And a Jewish farmer had this to say:

> It's funny, but though we're really out of touch with Jew's we're the ones who try to keep up the traditions. . . . We think of ourselves as more Othodox than anything. You know, the Gentile farmers around us are pretty religious too. If you can't go to church, then you have to bring religion into the home.

It was found that small-town Jews who are low in religiosity are more apt to see themselves as more urban than rural, even though these very people live, most often, in the tiniest hamlets. And those low in religiosity tend to feel Gentile members of the community consider them different from rather than typical of most Jews, while those highly religious stress the reverse; they feel non-Jews think they are typical of Jewish people.

Although respondents were asked the difficult question of telling how they felt others saw them, it seems that they answered mainly in terms of their own self-images. Among those who said they felt they were viewed as different, the following kinds of reasons were given: "don't conform to stereotypes," "better assimilated," "differ in physical features," "gentler and less crude," "quieter." Most of the adjectives were related to personal demeanor. This group felt that Gentiles considered them as unique Jews and suggested that they were more likely to be seen as exceptions to commonly held beliefs.

Those who felt they were seen as typical tended to give quite opposite reasons related to positive stereotypic images. "I'm wealthy and well educated," "I still maintain the traditions and practices of Judaism," have a Jewish name."

Ambassadors to the Gentiles

Being strangers in a Gentile world, many respondents appear to be more conscious of being Jewish than their urban cousins who live in the centers of ethnic communities. In one form or other every respondent indicated that there were times when he was called upon to represent the Jews. Here, as several stated, they are "ambassadors to the *goyim*." Most often this occurs when interfaith functions are held in the community. There the local priest and minister are accompanied by the Jewish merchant to "give balance to the program."

Frequently the Jew serves as a "representative of his people" in less formal settings. He is called upon to give "the Jewish point of view" or to explain why Jews do one thing and not another. When the townsfolk turn to the Jews for information, the respondents related that they often felt a deep sense of responsibility and inadequacy. For example, one man told me:

> You know, we're curiosities around town. The people always heard about Jews but never met one. Then we appeared. Real live Jews. After some hesitancy they began to ask us all kinds of questions. . . . Often I wished I could answer all of them.

A housewife said:

> My children have been asked to explain about Chanukah, to tell the story of Moses, to explain what the Mogen David is. They wanted to know and my kids were the likely ones to ask.

And a merchant:

> "I can't understand it. As kids we learned that the Jews killed Christ. Tell me [respondent's name]," he says to me, "is it true?" As a Jew, and the only one this guy ever knew personally, I'm supposed to have all the answers.

Small-town Jews were asked: "Are you most conscious of being Jewish when you are with other Jewish people or when you are among non-Jews?" Those who were most conscious of being Jewish when with non-Jews were those most isolated, that is, those in smaller communities having few, if any, other Jewish residents. "Religious or not," said one real isolate, "we're curiosities around here."

Friends among Neighbors

In small towns Jews find that there are few limitations on formal and informal social participation and interaction. All but 17 percent indicated that they were members of some mixed organization. Over 45 percent said they belonged to professional, business, and social groups. In addition, one-third were members of fraternal orders like the Masons or Elks. When asked which organization (national or local) gave them the most satisfaction, almost every respondent listed some local (thereby non-Jewish) group. A druggist said:

> I think I've been a member of every damn organization in this town. From member of the volunteer fireman to president of the school board. Discrimination? Not in any organizations, that's for sure.

And the owner of a small chain of department stores:

> This is my community. These are my people in many more ways than Jews are. After all, our neighbors are friendly, all the organizations accept us, so we make friends here. This is home. When I join an organization they know they're taking in a Jew but it doesn't make any difference . . . I've been President of Rotary, on the Chamber of Commerce, a member of the Masonic Lodge, and Secretary of the Rod and Gun Club.

This reflects the attitudes of most people interviewed.

What about discrimination? Eighty-seven percent said they could not think of any community organizations they would not wish to join because of anti-Semitic feeling. In addition, 81 percent said they knew of no discrimination of any kind being practiced in their communities. While most said they had not experienced anti-Semitism, many thought that latent anti-Semitism existed among some community members. Fortunately I was able to compare these expressions with those of non-Jews. In the second study it was found that what Jews feel as the true pulse of community sentiment is not always the reality of Gentile attitudes.

In predicting what would be found along the lines of socializing between Jews and non-Jews I hypothesized that close proximity to Gentile neighbors and lack of opportunity to have day-to-day contact with members of a Jewish community would lead to a degree of intimate interfaith socializing unparalleled in larger communities. The majority of persons interviewed substantiated this prediction.

> Everyone has close friends. In the city Jewish people tend to cling together. But in the rural village, when you are a minority of one, you associate completely with Gentiles. While it's rare in the city for Jews and Gentiles to be invited to one another's home for informal visiting, this is an everyday occurrence in the little community.

In small towns Jews are more than participants in formal community functions. In most instances they are an integral part of the social life of their towns. For adults this includes such activities as parties, trips, dances, bridge clubs, and just plain "dropping in." For the children this often means playing together, going to parties, and frequent instances of dating. In over 50 percent of all cases small-town Jews designated a Gentile person as their closest friend. Yet 30 percent said they felt more comfortable with Jews than with non-Jews, especially in social situations. Those highest on religiosity identifying most strongly with traditional Judaism were most apt to feel this way.

The Next Generation

That the strength of identification with Judaism plays a major role in determining patterns of and feelings about informal socializing with Gentiles becomes even clearer when we examine the attitudes of Jewish parents toward their children. Since 90 percent of respondents were parents, I was able to get reactions to a number of questions; reactions which indicated a firm conviction that Jewish identity should not only be maintained but intensified. While a high degree of informal interaction is practiced, small-town Jews, like their urban coreligionists, are anxious for their children to keep the faith and marry Jews. As a result they send them to Jewish summer camps and, when they are through with high school, encourage them to attend large, metropolitan universities. And although they themselves are satisfied with rural living, few expect their children to return to the small town after graduation. Here is the opinion of a retired businessman:

> We've lived here ever since the children—I have three—were born. They grew up among Gentile people. I don't think they ever met another Jew until they were fifteen or sixteen. In no case were they ever discriminated against. My son was captain of the basketball team and played ball for the local Altar Boys Baseball Club. My daughters always went around with local kids and dated boys from school. I can't say I was happy about this, but I didn't try to stop them. Yet, despite a number of crushes on certain fellows, they never got real serious about any of them. . . . When they graduated from high school they all went to college in the city. There they met Jewish people. . . . I'm really happy that my children all married Jews. It's easier that way.

Small-town Jews are similar to city-dwelling Jews to the extent that they want their children to remain Jews. They are firmly opposed to interfaith marriage. To them this represents either the confrontation of too many social problems or alienation from Judaism; both are considered highly undesirable. Assimilation into the Christian community is not their goal.

The Best of Both

Stonequist, Park, and others have characterized the Jew as the classic "marginal man,"[6] the eternal stranger[7] unable to reconcile the traditions of his people with the counterforces of the majority world; "one whom fate has condemned to live in two societies and in two, not merely different, but antagonistic cultures."[8] One might expect to find ample support for such a definition among small-town Jews living away from the mainstream of Jewish life. Yet rather than being on the periphery of two cultures, ex–urban Jews seem to have internalized the best of each. They are more a part of their communities than they are apart from them. They are far more assimilated to the Gentile milieu than their urban cousins. But they remain Jews.

While they strongly identify with fellow Jews—a reference group they can "feel" rather than "touch"—and in many ways express a feeling of kinship with their people, they have adapted to the folkways of the small town in a variety of ways. They enjoy the advantages of sharing two "cups of life" and, in a word, are bicultural. This duality (rather than marginality) causes the majority of respondents to agree with one who stated:

> You see, we feel we have the best of both . . . Judaism with all its tradition, its stress on culture, on learning, on freedom. . . . And the fact that we live in a small town with nice people and good, clean air. . . . We wouldn't trade either for the world.

Those who can reconcile the past with the present find that they can share a little of each of their different cultures. Those who find satisfaction in the small community generally seem to agree with one woman who said:

> It's funny. I never thought a city girl like me would like small-town living. But I've changed. I honestly enjoy the lack of sophistication at Home Bureau meetings, the knock-down-drag-out fights at school meetings, the gossip that never escapes anyone. I love the scenery, the simplicity, and the lack of formality here. Sometimes I miss the city. A good play, a concert, a corned beef sandwich! But we get away each year and spend a few days in New York. After about three days I've had enough. I'm ready for home.

And with a lawyer originally from New York City:

> I guess having been raised in the city makes you appreciate a community such as this even more than if you were born here. It's just nice not to have to be on the go all the time. . . . There was a time when I would have laughed if somebody suggested that I might wind up in the sticks. But here I am and loving every minute of it. People accept you for what you are, not who you are.

Naturally those who gave such enthusiastic testimonials for small-town living were among the most satisfied with their lives in the rural community. Yet only 14 percent of all respondents expressed true dissatisfaction. Two main reasons were most frequently given for disliking the small town. First, there was general dissatisfaction with rural living. "This town is too provincial for me." "Progress is nil. I just wish we could get out." "I'd take the impersonality of the city any day over the gossipy closeness of this burg." The second kind of dissatisfaction related to isolation from other Jews. "Frankly I would be much happier if we could be with Jews more often." "My wife is not happy here. She'd much rather be some place where she can pick up the phone and talk to the girls. We miss Jewish contacts." "If I had it to do over again, I surely wouldn't move out to the sticks. I'd rather be where there are more Jewish people." Why do they not move out? The answer was provided by a merchant:

> We always plan to leave here for a larger community. My business keeps me here, as it furnishes me with a good income. If I could leave I would. The small town is too backward for me.

It must be remembered that the dissatisfied residents are deviant cases. Most respondents expressed some degree of satisfaction with their communities. They were either "very satisfied" (50 percent) or "somewhat satisfied" (36 percent). Satisfaction seems to depend on whether town people are cordial and accepting of strangers. In most cases isolated Jews are, as several interviewees put it, "curiosities and strangers." Generally the burden is on the Jews themselves; at least they think so. If they accept the ways of the rural village in which they reside, that is, if they join the local lodge, contribute to the funds, buy food and some clothing in town, take an interest in community affairs, they're "in." According to a storekeeper:

> The secret of a Jew living in a small town—happily—is to assimilate as soon as possible—but always to remember he's a Jew.

And a doctor said:

> In small rural towns one is accepted for what he is. Religion plays a minor role in your being accepted. If one is honest and equitable in his dealings with others, you are placed in the forefront of things.

Minority Adjustment

The brief description of the findings of our study of Jewish life in the small town are but excerpts from the original report. Yet it is hoped they shed some illumination on the life of the isolated member of one minority group and indicate the role of the ethnic ambassador. From this first study several generalizations are suggested. (1) Those who leave the confines of the ghetto or ethnic community are frequently anxious to seek economic and social betterment, to find acceptance in the new setting without loss of ethnic identity. (2) Once the minority member enters the new "alien" situation, he finds himself in the position of representing his "people" to the community at large. As a stranger his ethnic identity becomes particularly salient to the community and to himself. More often than not, consciousness of minority membership increases when one becomes an isolate. (3) The minority member who lives in the milieu of the majority has infinitely greater opportunity to adapt to the folkways of the dominant group than does one who lives in the middle of the ethnic community.

Opinions of Community Leaders

For that part of the research which was designed to tap the attitudes of the majority group I chose to get reactions of community leaders. Such individuals were selected because it was felt that they would have the greatest opportunity to have contact with the widest number of persons in their towns. In addition, being in positions of formal leadership in such small villages (average population 2,500) meant that these same persons would most likely play informal leadership roles as well; they would be the pace-setters for community opinion. It also seemed logical to assume that a higher percentage of community leaders would have closer contact with Jews than rank-and-file citizens. Many of the same kind of questions used in the first section of the study were asked of respondents in the second. In addition, a number of items referred directly or indirectly to attitudes about Jews and other minority group members.

Piecing together the varied comments of several different Gentile opinion leaders, all of whom lived in one village in central New York State, we have a rough image of "native" small-towners, their attitudes toward the community, general prejudice, and the effects of contact with minority representatives.

> I have lived in this town all my life. . . . I feel that in the small, rural community people are friendly to one another. A common greeting is "Hello Joe" . . . truly a warm feeling, one of belonging. . . . I love it here.

> Well, I'm an American, since before the War of 1812. I guess I feel this makes me a little better. I'm not prejudiced. I just prefer to be with my own kind and I'm sure they'd [Jews, Blacks, and foreigners] prefer to mix together too.

There are only two Jewish families here and they are highly regarded—
one man is a businessman. The other is a very fine attorney. No
comparison with New York City Jews. They're different.

I run a store and come into contact with salesmen of different races. I
have three Jewish salesmen, all three are good men. There is none of this
pushing and trying to sell stuff you don't need like in the city.

The Natives

While the small-town Jews were generally outsiders who had mi-
grated to the rural comunity, most Gentile respondents had been born
and raised in their towns or in similar small villages. Only one-fifth of
the total group had been born in cities and a mere 2 percent had been
born abroad. Like the Jews, some who had come from the outside had
done so for business reasons. But unlike the Jews, most "newcomers"
had settled down in small towns because of marriage to a community
member, cheaper housing, or for health reasons.

These people were mainly of old "Yankee" stock with 38 percent
claiming that their families—their fathers' fathers' family—had come
to America before 1800. Members of this group tended to call themselves "American," "Scotch-Irish," or "Holland-Dutch" in their self-
descriptions. Those whose families had immigrated during the nineteenth century were more apt to be of German or Irish descent. The
most recent group were most often of Italian origin.

The occupations of these respondents were widely varied, ranging
from farmers to bankers, from ministers to mill-hands. Like the Jewish
small-towners, most placed themselves in the upper middle class.
Their average annual family income was half that of the Jewish
respondents—$7,500. Half of the Gentile participants were self-em-
ployed as compared with 80 percent of the Jewish group.

Thirty-nine percent of the Gentiles said they had a college education
or had gone beyond college; 64 percent had at least a high school
education. Like the Jews they too had high aspirations for their
children. Seventy-six percent of these persons were Protestant (the
remainder Catholic); two-thirds were Republicans; and two out of
every three saw themselves as more rural than urban.

When asked about satisfaction with their communities the most
typical response was: "This is home." By and large, respondents were
highly satisfied with their communities (68 percent) and an additional
one-fourth expressed moderate satisfaction. For this group community
satisfaction depended on such variables as length of residence, ties to
one's home town, and the progressiveness of the community. When
asked for comments a highly satisfied respondent wrote:

This is a small, rural, closely knit community where newcomers have to make every effort to become insiders. The effort, however, I feel is well worth it. We are not too far from a large city (but far enough to be away from the clatter), our school is excellent, and religious relations in this community are excellent. While this town is pretty conservative, I find a great deal of satisfaction in the slow, easy-going pace. I've lived here since I was a boy and wouldn't leave for anything.

For contrast here is the comment of a dissatisfied resident of the same community:

Passivity, complacency and a sheer lack or neglect of economic intellect in this community has been responsible for the apparent degeneration of atmosphere and attitude in all things related to even a reasonable degree of progress. This, of course, offers nothing of value to the high school generation. It offers nothing to newcomers. All in all, a community which was once great is slowly but most certainly annihilating itself.

Ethnocentrism and "The Good Old Days"

In some instances dissatisfaction with one's town was unrelated to whether the community is a good place to live and work or not; rather it seemed to depend on the image of what the town itself should be (or what it might have been) and what it had become. Although lack of change or progress appeared as the most significant factor for dissatisfaction with community life, there were some residents who said they had *become* dissatisfied precisely because changes *had* occurred. Not the least of these changes was the influx of outsiders to a number of small towns. In almost every village included in the sample there were two or three respondents who longed for the old days, who resented the intrusion of newcomers, who could not accept change as progress:

I am sure foreign people make a mistake in keeping customs of their own land alive and featured in this country. If this country meets their expectations, they should forget the folklore of Europe, St. Patrick's Day parades, German days, and get behind American things. If they can't do this they should be returned to the land they love. This country is supposed to be the world's melting pot. If they won't melt, they should not belong.

We have a lot of foreigners here. . . . They're all right, keep in their own place, go to their own church. But I must say it isn't really the same any more. This town has a great heritage, it was settled before the revolutions . . . I don't mean to imply that I am prejudiced or that I dislike foreigners. We all have our place in this great country of ours. I just think it a shame that outsiders like those who live here, have to keep their old ways. It makes it harder for them to be accepted.

Such persons were among a small group of respondents (21 percent) who agreed with the following statement: "This country would be better off if there were not so many foreigners here." They were also in agreement with: "Religions which preach unwholesome ideas should be suppressed," and were 56 percent of the sample group; and with the statement: "Americans must be on guard against the power of the Catholic church," with which one-quarter of all respondents also agreed. Such attitudes indicate ethnocentric thinking. A Scale of Ethnocentrism [9] based on responses to the first two questions cited above and one which stated "Some people say that most people can be trusted. Others say you can't be too careful in your dealings with people. How do you feel about it?" was used to assess general prejudice.

A high degree of ethnocentrism was in most cases, highly correlated with low-paying jobs, low educational attainment, small-town origins, occupations involving working with "things" rather than "people," and "old family" status. If one was ethnocentric, one tended to be more "success-oriented" and less apt to want to be "independent." The highly ethnocentric individual was more likely to indicate a need to belong and express a strong desire to be accepted by others. Those who saw themselves as upper class and those who felt they belonged to the working class were higher in their distaste for outsiders than "middle-class" individuals. Little difference was found between Catholics and Protestants or along political lines.

Does the opportunity to interact with minority members affect the general prejudice expressed by the small-town Gentile? Without a panel study over time it is virtually impossible to answer this query. However, the data do indicate that contact is related to the amount of generalized ethnocentrism one feels, but *only* when this contact is close enough to permit social interaction to occur. As shown in Table 3.2, those who have close association with Jews and Blacks have a much lower degree of ethnocentrism than those who rarely communicate with members of these two groups or have no contact in the community at all.

Attitudes toward Jews and the "Exemption Mechanism"

Prejudice against Jews was more prevalent in the attitudes of Gentiles (at least among community leaders) than Jews imagined. Many community leaders subscribed to traditional sterotypes about Jews. For instance, 83 percent agreed with the statement that "Jews tend to be more money-minded than most people"; 80 percent agreed that "Jews tend to be shrewder businessmen than most people"; and 77 percent

Table 3.2   Ethnocentrism and the Nature of Contact with Jews and Blacks Living in the Community

	Jews			Blacks		
	No Contact	Impersonal Contact	Personal Contact	No Contact	Impersonal Contact	Personal Contact
Degree of Ethnocentrism:						
High	32%	33%	10%	30%	50%	13%
Medium	34	32	36	36	14	31
Low	34	35	54	34	36	56
	100%	100%	100%	100%	100%	100%
	(88)	(46)	(39)	(124)	(14)	(39)

agreed that "Jews tend to be more aggressive than most people." These figures are *not* significantly altered when the nature of contact— "none," "impersonal," "personal"—is used as a control. Most respondents felt that Jews in general possessed these "characteristics traits." Whether or not a Jew lives in town is not crucial for changes in stereotyping. Merely buying in a "Jewish store" or visiting a Jewish physician may only perpetuate generalized images of Jews.

Many of the small-town Jews in New York State *did* fulfill several of the classic stereotypes, especially for those who never got to know them individually. As a group, they were frequently in business. They were more liberal politically. They tended to posses an urban demeanor and were thus natural objects of the traditional suspicions of "city slickers." And their children, being strongly motivated (or pushed) by parents, tended to do especially well in school. Here there is ample support for the "kernel of truth" hypothesis.

Yet expressions of attitudes and actual behavior were sometimes contradictory. Close examination of the data disclosed that when interaction took place at an *equal status* level, community leaders, even those with negative images of Jews as a group, tended to accept individual Jews as exceptions to the rule. They saw them as "different."

In general, respondents who had personal and intimate contact with local Jews viewed their close acquaintances as less clannish, quieter, less flashy, and less radical than they imagined Jews to be. Here are three excerpts of statements appearing on the last page of the mailed questionnaire:

> My experience as to Jewish residents of this community is probably not typical. A high-class, wealthy, cultured, refugee Jewish family came

here in 1940 and we have been very close friends ever since then, both professionally and socially. They seem to me very different from most Jews.

Frankly, I'm not too fond of Jews. I've heard too much about how they stick together, how they can chisel you, how they try to get ahead. Yet, here in——there is a Jewish family who are not at all like this. They are fine, intelligent, honest citizens and very close friends of ours.

When the——came to this community everyone was suspicious. We knew what Jews were like and we didn't like what we knew. After a while we found that they were pretty nice folks. We looked at them as a different kind of Jew. They didn't seem the Brooklyn type. Thinking about it now I have the feeling that our children build their image of what a Jew is supposed to be from the contact they have with the children of this Jewish family. Sometimes we have warped ideas about what we think is true.

Repeated *personal* and *informal* contact in the home and around town can serve as a significant factor leading toward the ultimate reduction of prejudice against Jews. Exemption may well be an important intermediate step in breaking down predispositions toward minority groups. One further statement serves to illustrate this proposition:

When a Jewish family first moved in we wanted them to prove themselves to us. It must have been hard on them but they came through like troopers. They became an important part of the community. They showed us a different kind of Jew. No Shylock. Knowing them for twenty years now when I think of Jews I think of them. I used to think about some mean, hook-nosed character.

Dominant Group Perspective

The following generalizations are tentatively offered based on the study of the community leaders of twenty small towns in New York State. (1) In the small community the minority group member is constantly in direct contact with the majority group. As he gets to know their ways, they cannot help but get to know him. He stands on the threshold of influencing deep-seated images. He can reinforce such images or aid in recasting them through those with whom he interacts. (2) The isolated minority member rarely constitutes a threat to the established order and community members are often willing to accept the individual outsider despite articulated expressions of prejudice. (3) Repeated and intensive contact and personal association often tend to change the mental picture of the isolate from "different from" to "typical of" the group he represents. Exemption is viewed as an instrumental step in the ultimate reduction of prejudice.

Success, Satisfaction,
and the Question of Survival

Mordecai M. Kaplan, writing in 1948 on the future of American Jews, stated that Jews were in a woefully abnormal and startingly unprecedented situation, on the threshold of disintegration. He warned that something must be done to alter the course they seemed to be taking.[10] A year later Trude Rosemarin reaffirmed Kaplan's view and asserted that a dissolution of Judaism was occurring in America.[11] According to one commentator:

> These individuals [like Kaplan and Rosemarin] agree that there has been a widespread assimilation of Jewish culture to every phase of the general culture, with the result that American Jewry as a group is showing distinct signs of disintegration and the individual members of that group are suffering psychologically from the effects of this loss of orientation. . . . The consensus among students of this matter appears to be then that the question of Jewish survival or Jewish extinction is to be found in the nature of Jewish communal life.[12]

Jews in a Gentile World

The arguments of those who prophesize the decline and fall of American Judaism are mainly expressed in terms of culture conflict between that of the Jewish community of yore and the modern society in which Jews find themselves today. Here is a rebirth of the "marginal man" argument, which sees Jews as prototypical cultural schizophrenics who cannot reconcile communal, religious in-group existence with the forces of a secular society.

Yet even in the immediate postwar years there were others, like Will Herberg[13], Nathan Glazer[14], and Marshall Sklare[15], who did not feel that the conflict was the inevitable result of participation in aspects of two seemingly divergent ways of life: "Multiple roles are not necessarily contradictory, in fact they may be complementary; that multiplicity of roles may be contradictory leaves out the whole complementary aspect. It leaves out the aspect of reinforcing values."[16]

No better example of multiple cultural membership is to be found than in the small rural community where the Jewish resident is often cut off from both urban life and day-to-day contact with his own coreligionists. If one were to support the pessimistic lamentations of some writers, certain predictions would be in order: a disintegration of Jewish identification, alienation from Jewish culture, and perhaps even total assimilation into the Gentile world of the small town.

The research conducted in the late 1950s tends to disprove all these assumptions. The small-town Jews of New York State strongly identify with Judaism, feel part of and not apart from Jewish culture, and adapt rather than assimilate into the Gentile world of their neighbors. Small-town Jews appear to be as aware of their Jewishness as city Jews—perhaps more so. They find themselves acting as representatives of "their people" to the general community and as such tend to be highly conscious of this particular role, which they tend to accept as part of everyday existence. They and their children find themselves in the position of describing Judaism to friends, explaining the rituals, telling about holidays, and often being the only Jewish members of interfaith ceremonies along with local ministers and priests. There is little evidence of a dissolution of Jewish identity based on physical removal from the Jewish community.

Changes have occurred in the ritualistic expressions of Judaism and in the degree to which small-town Jews observe the traditions of their forebears and parents. These changes are not unique. Even the ethnically based suburbs of today bear little resemblance to the urban ghettos of an earlier period. Like the surburban Jews of "Park Forest"[17] and "Northrup,"[18] small-town Jews have fervent hopes that their children will keep the faith, marry Jews, and have contact with Jewish people.

They do not want to be Christian. Yet in good American fashion, they seem to want to retain some religious affiliation. Will Herberg has said: "It becomes virtually mandatory for the American to place himself in one or another of these [Protestant, Catholic or Jewish] groups. It is not external pressure but inner necessity that compels him."[19] And Herberg goes on to say:

> Being a Protestant, a Catholic, or a Jew is understood as the specific way, and increasingly perhaps the only way of being an American and locating oneself in American society. It is something that does not in itself necessarily imply actual affiliation with a particular church, participation in religious activities, or even the affirmation of any definite creed or belief, it implies merely identification and social location. . . . By and large, to be an American today means to be either a Protestant, a Catholic, or a Jew, because all other forms of self-identification and social location are either (like regional background) peripheral and obsolescent, or else (like ethnic diversity) subsumed under the broader heading of religious community.[20]

David Riesman phrased it well when he said that Americans are all "afraid of chaotic situations in which [we] do not know [our] own names, [our] 'brand' names."[21] Such is the case for small-town Jews.

For them, the need to affirm identity is particularly poignant. Perhaps it is because of this very need to belong that small-town Jews are anxious for their children to remain within the fold. Parents feel that without some reinforcement from the home (the only source of Jewish identification for the youngster in such circumstances) it would seem that *here* the Kaplan prediction might begin to bear bitter fruit.

In an effort to have their children meet Jewish people, most Jewish parents encourage them to leave the community for extended periods. Holidays are spent visiting relatives in the city; summers are spent in Jewish summer camps. As noted above, many encourage youngsters to attend universities where Jewish men and women make up a large part of the student body. Few small-town Jews want their children to return to the small community for precisely the same reasons that they encourage them to leave.

From conversations with parents it was learned that, in many cases, their hopes were being realized. Some parents with adult children reported that they had become *more* Jewish than their parents after leaving the rural community.

> My son was becoming a regular *goy*. He never dated a Jewish girl, there weren't any. He never had a Jewish friend. He then went to college in New York and met lots of Jewish youngsters. In his senior year he married a Jewish girl from Boston. She comes from a conservative home. Today they live in Providence, where they manage to keep a kosher home, go to synagogue and associate almost exclusively with Jews.

Another small-town Jew said:

> Our daughter never knew any Jews except her cousins. Now she's in college. At first she hung around with a totally Gentile group. After a while she found they didn't accept her as completely as did Jewish girls. Now her best friends are Jews and consequently she dates more Jewish boys than Gentiles. We're letting nature take its course. We're not worried.

The parents seemed much more concerned about the Judaism of their children than with their own religious convictions.[22] A high degree of satisfaction with rural living on the part of small-town Jews was noted. This is directly related to *their* feelings of acceptance in the small community. It is not the strength of Jewish identification that makes small-town Jews different from their urban counterparts, but rather the patterns of association and the nature of socialization they experience in their community. Small-town Jews, unlike urban Jews, become active participants in *all* phases of community life and engage in a degree of intimate socializing with Gentiles unknown in the city.

As members of rural villages Jews are subjected to the folkways and culture of small-town living. To a great extent they appear to accept many of them as their own. While they maintain more than remnants of their urban lifestyle and thus are more apt to consider themselves (and be seen) as more urban than rural, they generally feel that the small town is home, that their friends live there, that they are warmly accepted by others in the community.[23] Most significantly, they find it is not necessary for them to give up their Jewish identity.

Warner and Srole, in discussing the ethnic minorities of "Yankee City," cited the statement of one of their informants who said:

> The young men have found out that even to have the Christians like us, we should go to the synagogue. A Jew who is an honest Jew and takes an interest in his synagogue, that is, in his community, is really liked better by the Gentiles. A Christian who is a customer of mine told me that he would have more faith in one who was an observing Jew than in one who denied his religion.[24]

While small-town Jews are rarely participating members of Jewish communities, Jews who do not become apostates but maintain their religious ties and identity are as likely to be accepted in the Gentile community as those who try to deny their lineage or heritage. One of the respondents put it this way:

> To hide the fact that I am a Jew would be ridiculous. Who respects the person who turns his back on his own people? We have a rich heritage, one I'm proud of. People know I'm a Jew, that Jews are different in their beliefs from others . . . they respect me for my convictions.

Altering Images

It was suggested that the very success of small-town Jews led to a fulfillment of many stereotypic images held by other community leaders, especially those who occupy lower socioeconomic statuses. In the discussion of the study of non-Jews it was reported that despite generalized images of Jews, small-towners who get to know Jewish residents tend to like Jews better than those with no opportunity to have contact with Jews and those with limited opportunities for association. Those with a high degree of generalized prejudice (ethnocentrism), and especially people with a high antipathy toward Jews, were most apt to indicate that their closest Jewish contacts differed from other Jews. They employed the "exemption mechanism."

To the non-Jews certain "Jewish traits" were apparently more acceptable than others. As indicated, the religious Jew is more often accepted than the one who flouts his faith. On the other hand, those who conform to negative images of what Jews are supposed to be like are far less apt to elicit friendly feelings than those who differ from such sterotypes. The comments of a scientist *and* community leader, who lived in a village of under 2,500 where there were few Jews, is a case in point:

> Some years ago, the first Jewish people came, and I had the opportunity to observe the first contacts between this community and two different types of Jewish people, almost simultaneously. (1) One Jewish couple (orthodox Jews) who were unobtrusive, helpful, and sociable; the husband was a physician. They maintained their contacts with friends and neighbors on a perfectly natural and un–self-conscious basis and were universally well-received and loved by everybody, and have thus remained for the whole twenty years they have been here. (2) A Jewish schoolteacher from metropolitan New York, who was aggressive, impolite, and pushy, came here about the same time as the couple cited above. She was soon disliked by her colleagues and by almost everyone in the village.
>
> It could be observed that this community was disposed to adopt all of these people without regard to the fact of their race, which was largely forgotten until things began to be unpleasant personality-wise. The teacher's unpopularity was due to her own personality and to the "herd" instinct acquired in New York's ghetto, rather than to this community's antipathy to Jews, which was practically nonexistent until she came here and stirred it up. My conclusion, therefore, is that it was the individual rather than the race that was the real crux of the issue. The contrast was striking.

The respondent's suggestion that antipathy was stirred up indicates that hositility was latent in the minds of citizens. The physican apparently did much to allay such feelings while the teacher brought them to the surface.

It was found that those who were of equal status to Jewish residents (in income, occupational roles, education, and "urbanness") tended to be more favorably inclined toward Jews as a group. This is particularly evident in the case of the younger generation. Attending the same school, living close to one another, growing up together, the lines of differentiation did not seem to be drawn as sharply by children compared to adults. As we found that intimate contact lead to a reduction in prejudice, we noted that the Gentile children were more amiable toward Jewish children living in their own communities than their parents were to adults. It seems that this would tend to shape *their* future images and stereotypes.

The isolated minority member appears to play a significant role in changing attitudes of community members toward Jews as a group. Despite the fact that older-generation Jews (the parents) were more often exempted from commonly-held sterotypes, the younger generation were often viewed by children of small-towners as "regular guys." It seems that the children of the small-town Jews were most effective in changing generalized images of Jews, at least in the small community. One 19-year-old Gentile respondent, the head of the volunteer firemen, told us:

> I grew up with the [Jewish name] kids. I knew they were Jews but it didn't make any difference to me or to the others in our gang. They were all very nice and very friendly. When I hear some of the old-timers around here talk about Jews in a bad way it makes me sort of mad. If they really got to know some Jewish people they wouldn't feel the way they do. I'm sure of it.

There were others who had grown up with the chidren of small-town Jews who expressed similar sentiments. One man in his early twenties said:

> A Jewish family has been here as long as I remember. They're fine people and a real part of this community. Some folks still are not so friendly toward them. This is particularly true of those of their own generation. The younger people who knew their children in school, as I did, have nothing but the best to say for them. They did a great deal to change the minds of those who thought they knew what Jews were supposed to be.

Increasing contact with Jews, especially those who have spent their early years in the rural community, would probably have a marked effect on changing the overall attitudes of Gentiles toward Jews. A study of the children of small-towners living in communities where Jews also reside would provide the information needed to test this prediction. But any such research would have to be conducted in the very near future.

The Future of the Small-Town Jew

This exhortation is related to another prediction that is, unfortunately perhaps, in order. With the tremendous rate of postteen emigration on the part of the offspring of Jews living in rural communities, one wonders whether the small-town Jew is a disappearing type in the spectrum of American Jewry. Most Jews who settled in small villages did so prior to World War II. Since that time few have chosen to live in such communities. Now their children are grown and rapidly leaving the nest to live in large cities. Although some children will return to "run the business," the studies suggest that small as it now is, the population of American Jews living in small communities will increasingly diminish in years to come. Levinger sums up this situation:

> Young people are constantly leaving the small town for the city, in consonance with one of the established patterns of American life, and these small-town Jews may then be reabsorbed by the body of organized Jewry. . . . So the village Jews disappear before our eyes. Their only chance for survival lies in the growth of their town, in its transformation into a suburb by the spread of a metropolitan community.

> Thus, as time passes, it seems that we shall soon have to write off most of the 150,000 village Jews from the roster of America Jewry.[25]

Based on my limited study, I am inclined to agree. In time to come it will be hard to find isolated Jews in small-town America.

Notes

1. See Toby Shafter, "The Fleshpots of Maine," *Commentary* 7 (January-June 1949):60-67; Earl Rabb, "Report from the Farm," *Commentary* 8 (July-December 1949):475-79; Harry Golden, "The Jews of the South," *Congress Weekly* (31 December 1951); Lee J. Levinger, "The Disappearing Small-Town Jew," *Commentary* 14 (July-December 1952):157-63; Louise Laser, "The Only Jewish Family in Town," *Commentary* (December 1959):489-96; letter to the Editor from Gerald M. Phillips, "Jews in Rural America," *Commentary* (February 1960):163.
2. This research was sponsored by The Anti-Defamation League of B'nai B'rith, New York. The original manuscript is entitled "Strangers in Their Midst: A Sociological Study of the Small-Town Jew and His Neighbors," (Cornell University, 1959). The project title was Cornell Community Studies. (Permission to use Cornell's name was granted by Vice-President for Research Theodore P. Wright.)
3. Approximately 25 percent of those who did not respond were randomly selected and attempts were made to interview each. Of this group two persons claimed they were no longer Jews and refused. Both were German refugees and had married non-Jews prior to their immigration to America. Two persons were deceased. The remaining group all identified themselves as Jews. Four permitted themselves to be interviewed and the information gathered was consistent with that of the less reluctant respondents. One individual refused to be interviewed and expressed the general feeling that such a study could do little to enhance Jewish-Gentile relations.
4. That slightly less than two-thirds responded suggests the possibility of a selective bias in the second part of the study. Time and budget did not permit the personal follow-up of nonrespondents similar to that in the first study. At present efforts are being made to gather data from a selected number of these reluctant participants.
5. The Coefficient of Reproducibility is .98.

6. Everett V. Stonequist, *The Marginal Man: A Study in Personality and Culture Conflict* (New York, 1937); Robert E. Park, "Human Migration and the Marginal Man," *American Journal of Sociology* 33 (1928):881-93.
7. Georg Simmel, "The Stranger," in *The Sociology of Georg Simmel,* trans. Kurt H. Wolff (Glencoe, Ill., 1950):402-8; Robert E. Park and Ernest W. Burgess, *Introduction to the Science of Sociology* (Chicago, 1921):286.
8. Park, p. 891.
9. The scale itself breaks down in the following manner. Those "high" on ethnocentrism have a low faith in people and agree with the statements that America would be better off without so many foreigners and that some religious groups are inferior. Those "medium" were negative on one of the three items. Those "low" did not agree with the latter two and were of the opinion that "most people can be trusted." The Coefficient of Reproducibility is .96.
10. Mordecai M. Kaplan, *The Future of the American Jews* (New York: Macmillan, 1948):536.
11. Trude W. Rosenmarin, *Jewish Survival* (New York: Philosophical Library, 1949):185-86.
12. Ben Kaplan, *The Eternal Stranger: A Study of Jewish Life in the Small Community* (New York: Bookman, 1957):147.
13. Will Herberg, *Protestant, Catholic, Jew* (New York: Doubleday, 1955), pp. 52-53.
14. Nathan Glazer, *American Judaism* (Chicago: University of Chicago Press, 1957), pp. 106-26.
15. See Marshall Sklare's response to Isador Chien's challenge in defense of a paper written by Marshall Sklare, Marc Vosk, and Mark Zborbowski, "Forms and Expressions of Jewish Identifications," *Jewish Social Studies* 17 (3):205-18.
16. Loc. cit.
17. Herbert Gans, "The Origin and Growth of a Jewish Community in the Suburbs: A Study of the Jews of Park Forest," in *The Jews: Social Patterns of an American Group,* ed. M. Sklare (Glencoe: Free Press, 1953).
18. Evelyn N. Rossman, "Judaism in Northrup," *Commentary* 24 (no. 5, 1957):383-91.
19. Will Herberg, p. 53.
20. Idem. See also Henry E. Schultz, "Out of the American Experience," address at Annual Meeting of National Commission of the Anti-Defamation League of B'nai B'rith, 27 November 1956 (published by Anti-Defamation League).
21. David Riesman, *Individualism Reconsidered* (Glencoe, Ill.: Free Press, 1948):178.
22. See Nathan Glazer on Jewish revivals in *American Judaism,* pp. 106-26.
23. Most small-town Jews are more apt to feel accepted in their communities than Gentile community leaders seem willing to accept them.
24. W. Lloyd Warner, *The Social Structure of American Ethnic Groups* (New Haven: Yale University Press, 1945):216.
25. Lee J. Levinger, "The Disappearing Small-Town Jew," *Commentary* 14(July-December 1952):1961-62.

4.
City Lights: The Children
of Small-Town Jews

(1977)

When you get around to studying the effect of survey research methods on minority group life in isolated settings, perhaps you will take into account my experience 18 years ago. I was 16 years old when my mother filled out the questionnaire from Cornell and in either reading it or discussing it with her, I learned, for the first time, that she would prefer for me to marry a Jew. I was totally surprised. Here were my parents, so completely accepting of the non-Jewish world we lived in, so it seemed, and yet they harbored the same longings for their children Jewish parents do everywhere. Yet imagine that I was being spared the "boogeyman" approach to interdating. There was never a controversy, as there was never a choice. There was interdating or no dating. Ours was the only Jewish family in the community and in my school. And so, this revelation through the questionnaire had a profound effect on me. The subject of research was changed in some ways by the research itself.

Whether the original study I conducted many years ago had as much of an effect on others as it apparently had on the daughter of the woman interviewed in 1958, and who was herself interviewed in 1976, is difficult to say. What she described about her parents and their anxieties does, however, accurately portray what I had learned.

The small-town Jews studied in 1958 seemed caught in a peculiar dilemma. Despite their own firm belief that they had found "the best of both"—the opportunity to retain their identity as Jews and to enjoy the amenities of small-town living—they worried about their children. Over and over individuals who had carried their childhood memories and ethnic ties into the hinterlands felt they had to validate their identity for their children. These youngsters, born and raised in small towns, had little sense of the larger Jewish community. The parents tried to fill the void in experience through holiday celebrations at

home, travel on special occasions to synagogues in nearby (and sometimes distant) cities, by sending their children to Jewish summer
camps, and encouraging them to look forward to urban colleges and
universities where they would meet other Jewish young people. Yet the
same parents were anxious to provide their children with normal small-
town childhoods and urged them to take advantage of the quiet and
healthy life they themselves had sought and enjoyed. They permitted
their children to fully participate in their communities' necessarily non-
Jewish social offerings and, unlike their urban counterparts, approved
of a degree of informal social interaction with non-Jewish youngsters
that was far more extensive and intensive than that experienced by
nieces and nephews and the children of childhood friends in the city.
They did so with mixed emotions, "ever aware," as one person
succinctly put it, "that it was risky business." The small-town Jews did
not want their children to become apostates. And they worried about
it. They need not have worried. Their children did not become *goyim*.

This terse statement summarizes what was learned in a follow-up
study conducted with my student, Liv Olsen Pertzoff, eighteen years
after the original research was completed. That new study sought,
among other things, to find out the extent to which mixed parental
signals of pressure to "keep the faith" and permissive approval of
interaction with non-Jewish children resulted in involvement in or
detachment from Judaism among the first generation of *native-born*
small-town Jews.

During the almost two decades since the first studies were conducted, most of the children of those interviewed and questioned by
mail had grown, married, and begun to establish families themselves.
We decided to find out what we could about them and to see if an early
prediction—that the population of American Jews living in small
communities would increasingly diminish in the years to come—would
prove accurate. To do this it was necessary to find the children.

The Follow-up Study

The projected follow-up study of the children of the 1958 respondents provided a chance to become reacquainted with participants in
the original study. I had lost track of many of them. I wondered how
they had fared over the years. How had their lives changed? Were they
still content with village life? Had their religious attitudes been modified over time through continued isolation from a Jewish community?
It was decided to seek answers to these questions and those about the
children by making the 1976 follow-up study a two-part survey: the

first part directed to the 1958 respondents and the second to their children.

Fortunately I had saved the original research materials. Several large cartons, mildewed from storage in a sequence of attics and cellars, disclosed the rough notes, first drafts, and early statistical marginals of the 1958 studies. The real treasure of its contents, however, were the bits of correspondence and lists of names from which the original "snowball" of informants was composed. We were able to reconstruct a mailing list of 107 of the original respondents to the detailed questionnaires mailed in 1958.

For the first part of the study, a new questionnaire was designed, incorporating a number of questions from the old schedule, measuring satisfaction with village life, group membership, socioeconomic levels, as well as religious attitudes and practices. Some new questions were also included to assess parental transmission of religious traditions and values to children. And, explaining that we wanted to contact their children, we asked for their names and addresses.

Examining the reconstructed mailing list, it was necessary to delete nine names of people known to have died since 1958. A first mailing of covering letter, questionnaire, and postage-paid envelope, was sent to 98 people from the 1958 study. Seven envelopes were promptly returned unopened. They were stamped "deceased." In addition we received a steady stream of unopened envelopes marked "unknown," or "no forwarding address," or "forwarding time expired." Efforts were made to trace the 35 people whose envelopes were returned to us by village post offices. Letters were sent to some postmasters explaining the nature of the survey and its importance to us and to other students of minority life in America, and asking for their help in locating addresses. Letters were also sent to the few 1958 respondents on our mailing list who shared surnames, asking if they were related to the missing respondents, and if they could tell us how to locate them. Neither of these efforts was successful.

In time we learned that 21[1] of the original 107 respondents had died. Since some of the 1958 respondents would have been well-advanced in years by 1976, it was not impossible to assume that as many as 30 or more of the 54 missing informants were deceased.[2] Thus, 24 or less of the first respondents were unaccounted for. These may have chosen not to answer either of our appeals, or they may not have received either mailing. Within six weeks we had the final return: 46 percent of 91 mailings (107 minus 16 known deceased, not represented by widows), or 42 completed questionnaires.

Respondents were given the opportunity to send back their questionnaires anonymously, but only two were returned unsigned. Despite the fact that many of the original respondents had died, that we could not locate some people who were presumably still alive, and that there were 21 percent more women respondents than in 1958, those from whom we did hear were comparable to those in the first study. A nearly identical representation of countries of origin, immigration periods, occupations, and socioeconomic self-ratings was found in the first part of the follow-up as compared to that of 1958. Table 4.1 indicates this in terms of two "background" items.

Table 4.1   Representativeness of the 1976 Jewish Respondents as Compared to Those in the Original Study

Period of Immigration	1958 Respondents	1976 Respondents
Before 1850	1%	2%
1850–1880	10	15
1880–1925	64	57
1925–1940	19	21
Since 1940	6	5
	100%	100%
	(107)	(42)
Country of Origin		
U.S.	62%	69%
Russia	4	2
Poland	–	–
Germany	22	22
Rumania	–	–
Other European	11	2
Canada	1	2
No answer (not U.S.)	–	2
	100%	99%
	(107)	(42)

Continuity and Change

One man wrote at the end of his questionnaire: "It doesn't seem possible that eighteen years have passed since the other questionnaire." And yet those eighteen years saw a number of changes: nearly half the villages increased in population, and while over two-thirds of them were described in 1958 as a "rural town" or a "farming center," today only a few of the villages were so classified by the *same* people. New descriptions, such as "suburb" or "industrial community," are attributable to the urban sprawl of the last two decades.

Of the 42 respondents, two had retired to live in Florida. Six others had moved to nearby larger communities to improve their business or professional opportunities, or for "better scenery." One lawyer moved forty miles away in 1968 "to be part of a Jewish community." Another lawyer's widow said: "I feel more secure in a small town—but it has nothing else to offer; my husband died in 1968, and why I stay here, I really don't know."

Some of the other respondents expressed dissatisfaction with small-town life, even after two, three, and four decades of it. "Too much closeness with people you'd rather not be close to," said one housewife. An industrial consultant said he preferred a small community "because city life is so dangerous," but said that even in the small community "personal contact is still restricted; social life is within the churches." A merchant expressed concern about the "lack of cultural activity" in his small town, and pointed out the "small-mindedness and unworldliness" of its population.

A teacher described her town as "the smallest city in New York State, slowly dying as small and large industries move out." She added: "There is little to do here and one's resources are now limitless. As part of a couple it was fine. As a widow tied here by responsibilities and need for my job, it is unsatisfactory."

Several explained that many of the towns' young people (Gentile and Jews) with opportunities to go away to college, found that their home towns had little to offer them. One said: "There is very little opportunity for them here unless they go into their family's business, and the social life is very poor." Another noted: "Limited employment opportunity; no movies except outdoors in the summer." Yet, as a teacher in a quiet village commented: "They try to leave—but many do come back—those who can't cope with the larger progressive world. A few remain because of the fact that life in a metropolis has become more hazardous."

Two-thirds of those who responded to the request for information reported that the young people in their towns did leave, mainly for better educational and occupational opportunities. Two told us unequivocally that in their towns "the upper-class children leave; the working-class children stay." And as one merchant said frankly: "If they have any ambition or background, most leave." (Later we will see the implications of such ambition and background in the lives of small-town Jewish children.) After twenty, thirty, or even forty years in small towns, half the small-town Jews contacted still considered themselves more "urban" than "rural." They viewed the cultural limitations of their villages with some impatience but persisted in claiming that this was compensated by the security and safety their small towns offered.

They were obviously ambivalent. Although more than half of the respondents in 1976 said they would very happily begin life all over again in a middle-sized city or a metropolis, nearly all were at least "somewhat satisfied" with life in their small town, and half were "very satisfied." An attorney said succinctly: "No noise, traffic, pollution, violence, crime." And a physician wrote: "Have made a good living, have a good relationship with our community, have good close friends here, have been honored and respected here, besides having continuing personal, family, religious, and educational contacts in [nearest city]." Another lawyer, from a small academic community, said: "Raised a family in an education-oriented atmosphere; made a place for myself and earned a comfortable living in the process." A housewife listed the advantages of small-town life as "security, familiarity, friends, no industry, no pollution." And a third lawyer summed it up: "It was a good place to raise our children."

The trend of all the comments seemed to reflect the ex-urban small-towners' continuing appetite for particular cultural amenities: if there were any educational or aesthetic opportunities in or near their small towns, they were perfectly content; if there were not, they longed for the offerings of even middle-sized cities.

In the 1958 study I had concluded that in the small community the Jews were active participants in all phases of community life. Their associations were almost wholly with non-Jews. As a result of repeated contact with Gentiles, they enjoyed a degree of intimate social interaction unmatched in the urban context. Yet they maintained that they remained ever-aware of their Jewishness. We wondered whether this sense of Jewish identity had weakened. We asked again: "When are you most aware you are Jewish?" And heard echoes from their own earlier commentaries:

- When I walk the streets of this 100 percent Christian town.
- When a [Christian] clergyman gives an invocation.
- When "blessings" are given and Christ is mentioned at meals, benedictions, etc.
- I am always aware that I am Jewish, especially when I am practicing medicine.
- My attitudes, opinions, my social life (or lack of it!) always have that awareness very much in the forefront.
- When showing pictures of my trip to Israel to a non-Jewish group.
- If Jews are in trouble, anywhere.
- When helping with Jewish projects (Temple, UJA, Hadassah) or when being hurt by anti-Semitic utterances and actions. I felt proud to be Jewish when I saw the accomplishments in Israel.
- All the time.
- With questionnaires like this!

This banquet of answers to the question about consciousness clearly bore out another conclusion reached in 1958: *Being alone in a small town increases a Jew's consciousness and awareness of being Jewish and different from the rest of the community.* Time did not mitigate the sense of "differentness." For nearly everyone reinterviewed, Jewish identities remained salient after two or more decades of being residents in a Gentile milieu. Only 6 of the 42 respondents said they practiced no religious observances in their homes (and only 5 said they were "not religious at all"). Some said they had become less observant of ritual because the children had grown and moved away, or because it was more difficult to attend services at distant synagogues or to "keep kosher" as they grew older.

Few regrets were expressed for having chosen to live in small communities and having reared their children in the country. They still feel they had had good lives in their rural towns, and the best of both worlds. Such sentiments are noted in the following commentaries:

> I always wanted to be Christian when I was a teenager in [the city]—it seemed easier, more acceptable than being Jewish. However, now I feel quite differently. I find many doors open to me and those that are not are not important. I don't feel shy or embarrassed being Jewish.

> The expression "loner" is often applied to my wife and me by people in the community. Perhaps it is our outlook on people that has kept us satisfied in a non-Jewish community all these years. We are very self-sufficient, don't enjoy people in large groups, and avoid being involved with the "in" groups. We've tried them and found them distasteful. We have some good friends in town—both Jews and non-Jews—but take people in small bunches. We enjoy a respected position in town and feel pretty generally accepted by the community.

> I find that as I get older I miss more Jewish contacts and would like to have more contact with Jewish people and religious groups, but on the other hand have many friends in this small town and would not like the faster pace or dangers of larger communities. . . . Advantages outweigh the disadvantages of a rural small-town life.

> You well know that we chose our way of life before most people felt it was a good life and we still think it is and has been. We've had the best of two worlds: Our grandchildren love to come to [name of town] and our sons come home as frequently as possible.

> The community has been wonderful to us. They have shown their gratitude to my husband for having stayed with them in many wonderful ways. But we always were the only Jewish family in town.

> These questions are very difficult to answer when you have lived a lifetime among the same families and friends. My son's three children are all doing well and growing up. My daughter's three are also wonderful. She is married to a Yemenite boy and they belong to an Orthodox synagogue and are much more religious than I ever was. And very happy.

Finding the Young Adults

At the end of the follow-up questionnaire the small-town Jews were asked if they would give us the names and addresses of their adult children. We explained that a questionnaire, similar to the one they were returning, would be sent their children to make general comparisons between the views of their generation and those of their offspring. We assured them that no attempt would be made to correlate or match up their individual responses with those of their own sons and daughters.

Five respondents said they had no children. Eleven answered questions concerning their children but did not send us their names and addresses. Twenty-six included names and addresses totaling 58 offspring. One daughter was traveling in Europe; we made an attempt to locate her but were unsuccessful. Of the remaining 57, we heard from all but 5 (or 92 percent) in two appeals. Among the 52 young adults whose stories follow, there is at least one from each of the 25 families who gave us enough information to contact their children.

The questionnaire designed for the children who grew up in small towns included many questions asked of their parents in 1958 and 1976—about education, socioeconomics, satisfaction with community, as well as those measuring religious attitudes and observances. In addition, they were asked about childhoods spent in small communities where many had been the only Jewish children in town.

We wondered whether these children, born and reared in small towns, would have Jewish identities significantly weaker than their parents'. We knew that it was impossible for many or most of these youngsters to have received any sort of formal religious training because of the long distances to the nearest synagogues. And we knew that the dominant membership groups for these children were the small-town non-Jewish social (school and play) organizations of their home towns.

Thirteen of our 42 "parent generation" respondents were immigrants to the United States from Hitler's Europe. We wondered whether their children would feel the strain that historians and sociologists had often suggested as common among second-generation Americans—the pressure to assimilate quickly into the dominant value system around them, to deny their parents' European culture, behavior, and depredations. Would these children be the sorts of sons and daughters described by Marcus Hansen, who wish "to forget"?[3]

Twenty-five women and 27 men returned questionnaires. The median age of the children of the small-town Jews was 32 at the time of the follow-up study (the age range is 20-48). Two-thirds were married and three-fourths of these families had children of their own. Forty percent of the young adults were living in major American metropolitan centers (New York, Philadelphia, San Francisco) and one in Jerusalem. Twenty-five percent lived in areas surburban to metropolitan areas and 20 percent in "middle-sized" cities. *Only six of the children lived in small communities.*

None of these children's parents reported a growth in the Jewish population of their small towns (including those towns reclassified as "suburban"), and only two of the known children were residing in their childhood towns. My earlier prediction, in accord with Lee Levinger's, that the population of American Jews living in small communities would increasingly diminish, was proving to be quite accurate.

Almost all the children said they were as satisfied with their new communities as their parents were in the small towns. While 84 percent of the parents[4] who were interviewed in 1976 said they were "very satisfied" or "somewhat satisfied" with country life, 82 percent of their children were equally content in their cities. Three children, satisfied metropolites, wrote the following testimonials:

> One reason I like living in New York City is the personal relief I feel here at not having the responsibility for everything Jewish on my back.

> I see a large city as permitting a freedom to choose friends and lifestyles. Being Jewish in a small town gave me a sense of being special and proud, but I felt I could not share this secret with Gentile friends. I tried hard to be accepted by all and on the surface merged my identity with the community. Yet I felt I was living a lie. I feel a sense of relief in living now in a city where being different is acceptable. I still think of myself as special—but now my pride comes from having more hay in my shoes than my city friends. Now I can speak about being special. In my home town, I felt it was dangerous to feel special.

> Although not reared with any formal Jewish training, I did attend services on the High Holy Days and because of having been born and raised in Germany and having fled with my parents to this country in 1939, I felt that Judaism had meaning for me; that I could not actively pursue my Judaism unless I moved to a community where this was possible.

In contrast to some of those whose comments are printed above, over half of all the children say they prefer middle-sized cities whether living in them or not.

> I feel one is able to benefit the most from [a middle-sized city]. One may grow with a company, or socially not feel as isolated as in a small community or as lost as in a big city.

> There are enormous opportunities in daily life in New York City, but it takes enormous economic and physical strength to take advantage of what the city offers.
>
> I like the religious and cultural aspects of [a metropolis], but dislike the pollution and rush of a big city.

Most of the children reported living in urban areas to benefit from the very same advantages their parents had wished for them: greater job opportunities, cultural offerings, affiliation with other Jews, and participation in a Jewish community. More striking is the finding that only one in five of the young urbanites said they would happily begin their adult lives all over again in small towns like the ones in which they grew up.

On the plus side, a housewife said she preferred a small town "basically for roots and lifestyle, including proximity to nature's recreations; it is what I grew up with." And a dietician said: "I enjoy the cultural, educational, social, and working opportunities, but I have never been able to fully adjust to some aspects of city living—crowded slums, dirty streets, heavy traffic, not being able to know many people who live on my block." A high school teacher said she still preferred village life "because I was raised in the country on a farm and I love it. There's a special peace to be found in nature and in God. I find it in the country." "A small community," wrote an industrial artist, "would be best for my general aptitude, but at this point it cannot offer me the type of stimulating job I presently have."

For all the general satisfaction with urban life, over a third of the children considered themselves more "rural" than "urban." One young woman who returned to a small community, wrote:

> The community in which we live has 152 people, no restaurants, theaters, stores, etc. We enjoy this life, choose it, but do find it isolated at times. I have lived abroad and would prefer to live in London, or a city in Asia; but as it is no longer financially possible, I would choose living in a small American community. American cities are overcrowded, dirty, unsafe, expensive, and anonymous.

She sounded like some of the members of her parents' generation who, in 1958, explained why they had settled in some tiny upstate hamlet far removed from the hustle and bustle of the metropolis.

The young adults who responded to the latest questionnaire were more frequently registered Democrats than their parents (44 vs. 36 percent), less often Republicans (8 vs. 21 percent), and slightly more children than parents were "independent" (46 vs. 43 percent). A few of the children said they were Socialists. "Like," said one, "my grand-parents."

The children rated themselves somewhat lower in socioeconomic status than did their parents in 1958. This difference between children and parents may also be a reflection of the fact that 77 percent of the parents were self-employed in 1958, while only 21 percent of their children were. Less children (34 percent) entered the high-income medical or legal professions, whereas fully half the parents had been among the few professionals in their towns. The children's occupations represented a far greater diversification than their parents'—far more career choices requiring higher education are available in metropolitan areas, but they are generally salaried, and financially limited by competition.

Of the urban young adults, 35 percent claim not to belong to any formal organizations compared to only 12 percent of their small-town

Table 4.2   Occupations of Small-Town Jews and Their Adult Children

Occupations	Total 1958 Respondents	1976 Respondents (Parents)	1976 Respondents (Children)
Medical Arts: physician, nurse, dentist, veterinarian, podiatrist	36%	36%	13%
Entrepreneurial: merchant, sales manager, salesman, clerk, dealer, manufacturer	20	17	18
Professional (nonmedical): attorney, accountant, engineer	15	14	21
Education and Social Service: teacher, professor, social worker, graduate student	10	12	29
Agricultural; farmer, cattle dealer	10	7	–
Skilled or Semi-skilled: carpenter, electrician, plumber, tailor	1	–	–
Unemployed: housewife, retired	8	12	19
No answer	–	2	–
	100% (107)	100% (42)	100% (52)
	90%-M 10%-F	67%-M 31%-F	52%-M 48%-F

Table 4.3   Educational Levels for Three Generations

Level of Education	Fathers of Small-Town Jews	Small-Town Jews	Children of Small-Town Jews
More than college	12%	62%	69%
College graduate	2	14	21
Some college	5	10	8
High school graduate	7	5	2
Some high school	12	5	–
8th grade or less	33	4	–
Other (technical school diploma, etc.)	10	–	–
No answer	19	–	–
	100%	100%	100%
	(42)*	(42)*	(52)

*Figures are those given in 1976 follow-up by original small-town Jews.

parents. Thirty of the 42 parents reported belonging to at least one organization in which he or she was the only Jewish member, a situation reported by only 7 of the 52 children. Four of 5 parents said, in 1976, that they belonged to a synagogue, compared to half of the children. Of the children who were members of synagogues, only a few reported belonging to sisterhoods, fraternal orders, or Jewish philanthropic organizations as well. (This does not indicate a rejection of Judaism but perhaps a lack of need for institutional support for those now living in predominantly Jewish communities or neighborhoods.)

Twenty-one percent of the parents who belonged to local organizations said their community service clubs were their most satisfying affiliations. Their urban children, however, belonged to less than half as many community service organizations, and even members often claimed these among the least satisfying of all the organizations to which they belonged. (Half of the—admittedly few—children who belonged to Jewish organizations of a religious or service nature found these their "most satisfying" affiliations, whereas such memberships were ranked as high by only a quarter of the parents who belonged to them.)

Schooldays

In 1958 I found a high rate of Jewish parental approval of social interaction between their children and the non-Jewish children of the community. It was predicted that the attitudes and behavior of the children would necessarily reflect this social intercourse—that they would feel full membership in their school and play groups. It was suggested that small-town Jewish children, unlike urban Jewish children, would be quite comfortable within the Gentile milieu and would not feel outside the community mainstream.

In 1976 we asked the adult "children" about the nature of their contact with others during their childhood, and nearly all (92 percent) said it was almost exclusively with non-Jews; the rest said it was "mixed"—Jews and non-Jews. Only two said their closest childhood friends had been Jewish. In answer to the question "Do you think your Gentile friends considered you "different" from themselves?" more than half (62 percent) answered "no." From some of those who answered "yes," we heard:

> I was always absent from school on High Holidays and usually questioned about it. I did not believe in Christ, making my Jewishness a subject of discussion. Later, from 7th grade up, friends asked why Hitler considered Jews only fit for slaughter. I sang in and accompanied the Methodist Church Choir, and sometimes was asked how I felt about using Christian music.

And:

> My close friends just figured I celebrated different holidays, but they accepted this. Others stereotyped me as "rich and spoiled." People who didn't know Jews at all just considered us weird—they listened to what they heard from the church, etc., and avoided personal contact.

One man described his childhood peer group experience as one of "indefinable exclusion."

Other children remembered being perceived as different in terms of their socioeconomic status as much as their Jewishness. A real estate broker said: "As the son of one of the few professionals in town, we had special status. Being Jews reinforced this." An executive secretary recalls: "As a Jew, and as the child of a professional, I was considered to have a different home life and a different future than my generally less affluent friends." A museum registrar sums up some childhood experiences in this way: "Because I had more money; because I would go to prep school; because I had broader horizons."

Yet we found I had made too sweeping a generalization in 1958: not unlike their parents, many of the children felt the counterpulls of their communities and homes. More than half (56 percent) of the children said they remembered feeling different from their non-Jewish friends (regardless of social acceptance). A few felt different, again, because of their socioeconomic status in their small towns: "We had more money and traveled frequently, an opportunity not available to other children in our village." And: "I was more interested in cultural and intellectual activities than in sports cars." But for most of the children, the feeling of "differentness" was directly related to being Jewish:

- I didn't have a religious group to belong to—like *everyone else* did.
- Often uncomfortable at Christmas, Easter.
- Not having a church affiliation and religious identity in a town of 1,200 people and seven churches.
- I did not go to religious classes on release time at school. At the beginning of living in the community there was harrassment from the other children. I also felt my parents were being discriminated against.
- Only at Christmas and Easter, but my parents let me color Easter eggs and let me believe in Santa Claus in addition to Chanukah and Passover. That way, they lessened my feelings of being different at those times.
- I felt more attention was paid to my every daily action than was normal. I was made to feel responsible for the actions of every other Jew in the world. It was my duty to represent and explain Judaism for the adults and children of [the town].
- Growing up in a small town gave me a very precious awareness of "difference" that I would have taken for granted and perhaps lost in a larger city with a larger Jewish community.

Although 62 percent of the children felt they were not perceived by others as different, when asked later on if they had ever been called upon to represent "the Jewish point of view" at one time or other during their schooldays, 87 percent reported they had been. A college student remembered: "In class, when the teacher talked about anything related to Judaism, she always asked, 'Is that right?' It was annoying." Another wrote: "I don't remember being *expected* to, but always did take a box of matzoh to school for distribution to my classmates during Passover." For one woman, the pressure was relentless: "I had to be more moral, better behaved, etc., to adults (teachers, shopkeepers, baby sitters, etc.) because I was a representative Jew."

One-third of the children said they had gone to Jewish summer camps, one-fourth to nonsectarian ones (YMCA, Boy or Girl Scout camps), and five children had gone to primarily Christian camps. Fifteen percent of the children had left their childhood communities to attend high school or prep school. But it was not until they went away to college that three-fourths of the children were involved for the first time with a larger Jewish community. Over 65 percent of the children, as college students, participated in Jewish organizations (Hillel, sororities, fraternities, and other groups), some with enthusiasm: "While at college I was exposed to Orthodox Judaism for the first time. The more

I learned, the more I wanted to know and do. I am now a member of a Chassidic (Lubavitch) community. Although my religious views are very different from the rest of my family, we are on very good terms."

Some young students had reservations about joining in Jewish campus activities and mixing with other Jewish students whose only common ground with them was "tribal." A lawyer wrote: "Some Hillel participation. Closest friends and roommates were Jewish, but from upstate New York, not New York City." A college student asked rhetorically: "Do you know what a 'Jewish-American Princess' is? They are the vainest, most snobbish, and self-centered girls I've ever met. They are from New York City and Long Island and consider upstate people to be 'hicks.' Would you want to associate with people like that?"

Religious Training

When Americans move from one place to another, most of them may be confident that whatever religious support they need may be found in their new communities. For the urban Jews moving to small towns thirty or forty years ago, it was another story altogether. They knew they would have to provide whatever religious identity and education their children might need, without the support of synagogue, religious school, relatives, or Jewish friends. How concerned were the parents about providing their children with an understanding of, or background in, Jewish life? Half the children felt their parents were "very concerned." As for the parents themselves, in 1976 only 2 claimed they had been not at all concerned with providing a Jewish home life for their children. Only 7 children perceived this absence of concern in their homes and further reported receiving no religious education whatsoever. Nearly three-fourths of the children remembered having a Passover seder, and 80 percent of them remembered lighting Chanukah candles. In the homes of only 4 children were there no religious observances at all.

Half the children said they had received some informal religious training from their parents, and three-fourths reported having gone to Sunday school. Among urban Jewish children there is no question but that "Sunday school" refers to Jewish religious instruction. But among the small-town Jewish children, Sunday school included "playing the organ at Methodist Church" and other Christian church activities. Only 12 percent attended any kind of Hebrew school or took instruction. In such cases, as one wrote, "the rabbi visited town one time a week to teach five or six children."

The problems the parents faced in providing their children with some formal religious training are reflected in some of their sons' and daughters' recollections. Some of the parents' personal struggles with their own identities as "outsiders" are implicit in their childrens' remarks:

> If my parents' own "Jewish sense" had been stronger, I feel there were *many* more things they could have done to instill a greater sense of identity in their children. My father had knowledge enough to help, if mother did not.

> My parents, in my judgment, should have cared less about how our neighbors felt about us while we were growing up, and should have presented a less ambivalent face to us. That is, I needed, in retrospect, them to be stronger, more confident Jews—less concerned about what "they" might think.

Other children reported their parents' sacrifices and innovations in providing religious training for them:

> For a brief period, the rabbi (18 miles away) instructed us during Wednesday afternoon "Church school" sessions in the public school. The nearest synagogue was 50 miles. In my very early teens, my parents made a brief but rather unsuccessful effort to establish a sort of written weekly "correspondence course" for me with the rabbi. Without other Jewish children to relate to and no one to answer immediate questions, I was not motivated to keep this up for more than a few months.

> My parents did the best they could to provide me with a sense of Jewishness considering that we lived 50 miles from the nearest synagogue. My father was not a well man and although he drove my older sister to Sunday school and holiday events, when I was old enough to go, he was not able to take me. However, we did go every year for High Holy Day services—a great strain on my parents, financially, as it meant staying in hotels, restaurant bills, etc.

Despite their isolation, three-fourths of the male children did become bar mitzvah. For the rest, it was ignored due to the logistical impossibility of arranging for preliminary instruction (one man said he "was prepared twice monthly by the travelling rabbi") or due to lack of parental concern for the rite. A lawyer explained: "The nearest temple was 40 miles away, therefore religious instruction was minimal. Father decided it was unnecessary." Another lawyer said: "We lived too far from a synagogue for formal training and I believe my parents really didn't care that much."

Childhood religious education (at *cheder,* Sunday school, or home)—or its lack—seems to have had little effect on the choice of marital partners. Sixty-one percent of all those we contacted were married, and three-fourths of these were married to Jews. Among the 7 who claimed not to have received any religious training, 5 married Jews, 1 married a non-Jew, and one was unmarried.

In a similar vein, we found that the lack of childhood religious education bore little relationship to adult religiosity. Of 21 young adults who reported having received no religious instruction from their parents, 5 said they were "not at all religious" in 1976; another 5 said their religious identities were stronger than their parents'. In all, three-fourths described themselves as moderately religious children of parents who had been moderately concerned with their religious education.

The Strength of Jewish Identity

The adult children of the small-town Jews were asked: "Do you think you would have developed a stronger Jewish identity had you lived in a larger Jewish community as a child?" Forty-two percent said "yes," a third said "no"; 23 percent said they "didn't know." One man wrote: "I find all these questions of Jewish identity to be very slippery and difficult—and no doubt some of my attitudes on this questionnaire appear to be inconsistent. However, I certainly feel closer to Judaism now than when I was a child." A young mother said:

> I might not have become so involved with Jewish life had it not been for my marriage to a man with strong Jewish background and education. . . .I believe I would be more assimilated were I living in a rural area—it's easier to be "more Jewish" in areas of large Jewish communities. Also in or near metropolitan areas where one is exposed to speakers such as Meier Cahane [sic] and Elie Weisel, one's Jewish consciousness and conscience is heightened.

Looking back, more male children (56 percent) than female (32 percent) felt they would have developed a stronger religious identity had they grown up in a larger Jewish community. On the other hand, more than twice as many women (28 percent) as men (11 percent) claimed a Jewish identity stronger than their parents'. This cannot be positively correlated to early childhood training, because 6 of the 25 women (compared to only 1 of the 27 men) had received no religious instruction. What accounts for the heightened religious identity among the children, particularly the daughters, of small-town Jews?

We noticed that many of these religious daughters mentioned their own children in marginal comments they wrote on the surveys. We wondered whether there was a connection between enhanced religious meaning and the roles they, as Jewish mothers, were fulfilling in urban Jewish communities. All the women who reported a religious conviction stronger than their parents' and, similarly, 66 percent of the men, had children. One possible reason for their reportedly heightened religious identity is the support these young parents receive from others like themselves within large urban Jewish communities. They are "learning" urban parenting, Jewish style, with its emphasis on the transmission of tradition and heritage, in practice and belief.

Table 4.4   Religiosity: Affiliation, Attendance, and Self-Assessment

	1976 Respondents (Parents)	1976 Respondents (Children)
Religious Affiliation of Parents and Children		
Orthodox	2%	4%
Conservative	45	34
Reform	41	33
None of these	12	29
	100%	100%
	(42)	(52)
Religious Service Attendance		
At least once a week	2%*	4%*
At least once a month	24	19
On High Holidays	43	27
Rarely	19	33
Never	10	17
No answer	2	–
	100%	100%
	(42)	(52)
*Orthodox		
Self-Assessment of Religiosity		
Very religious	–	2%
Moderately religious	45%	37
Somewhat religious	43	36
Not at all religious	12	23
No answer	–	2
	100%	100%
	(42)	(52)

Most of the children professing themselves to be nonbelievers or unaffiliated observed many religious rituals in their homes. More observances were practiced by these young adults than their parents. This is especially noteworthy in that a third of the adult "children" were unmarried, and most of these single young adults reported an impressive frequency of religious observance. (A college student told

Table 4.5   Religious Observances Practiced in Own Home

Religious Observances Practiced in Homes of Small-Town Jews and in Homes of Their Adult Children	1976 Respondents (Parents) n = 42	1976 Respondents (Children) n - 52
	(Figures in Percentages)	
Candles on Chanukah	71	71
Seder on Passover	62	62
Fast on Yom Kippur	47	54
Lighting sabbath candles	35	37
Bacon or ham never served	28	33
Kiddush	26	25
Special dinner on Friday night	21	23
Kosher meat bought regularly	17	23
None of these	14	17
No answer	–	2

Table 4.6   Generational Differences in Strength of Religious Commitment

Religious Identity as Compared to Parents	1976 Respondents (Parents)	1976 Respondents (Children)
Stronger identity than own parents	17%	19%
Weaker identity than own parents	19	40
About the same as parents	62	37
Don't know	2	4
	100%	100%
	(42)	(52)

us it was difficult to observe dietary laws in the dormitory, but she was as strict as possible.)

Yet 40 percent of the children reported feeling that their Jewish identity was weaker than their parents'. Perhaps for many, paradoxically, this was because living in Jewish milieux their Jewishness did not have the same salience as that of their isolated parents. Interested in the meaning of being Jewish, we asked: "Do you think your life would have been more difficult (or less difficult, or the same) if you had been born a Gentile?" Ten percent of the young adults answered "less difficult," the same answer was given by 45 percent of their parents, a fourth of whom had fled Nazi Europe. On the other hand 71 percent of the children compared to half of their parents felt it would have made no difference.

The point of view reflected in the remarks made by the children who thought life would have been more difficult (or no different) had they been Gentile is peculiarly untouched by the anti-Semitism reported by some of their same parents. Rather they stressed the stimulation they might have missed not growing up in a Jewish household. A young housewife who said it would have been more difficult to have been born a Gentile wrote: "I doubt if I would have had any very strong ambitions." And a hospital administrator thought it would have been more difficult "by virtue of the emphasis on educational and intellectual stimulus which I believe is a part of the Jewish culture." A lawyer felt it would have made no difference, although "I feel that I would not have succeeded as I have without the pressure on me being a Jew. Also I would not have felt as different and privileged and entitled to success." One of the parents answered: "Where would the challenge be?" A young professional woman said: "Being female is a lot more of a raw deal!"

When we asked whether they agreed or disagreed with the statement "Jews are different in many ways from non-Jews," 56 percent of the children and 45 percent of the parents agreed. How does one reconcile this with what we found in the 1958 study—the special salience ethnic identity appears to have to the isolated minority group member? Perhaps there are different ways of being different. One recent respondent of the older generation put it: "Speaking as a Jew in a small town, I feel differently. Perhaps in a city the differences aren't so keenly felt." But this was countered by many others who described differences keenly felt even in the city. They prove to be markedly similar to the differences between Jews and non-Jews felt by parents and their children alike. Consider these parallel comments of children and parents:

Comments of Parents	**Comments of Children**
[Jews] don't want to work for someone else: more ambitious, more anxious for an education.	In general, the lifestyle, status, and drive to succeed is more evident in Jew than non-Jews.
I think they truly believe in more of a home and family closeness. Education is very important—but I think that as parents they are too submissive with their children.	There's a certain degree of family closeness and right direction. *Stability*—not found in non-Jewish family life.
More intelligent, more vivacious, more personality, more interested in the outside world, aware of cultural affairs in cities.	Smarter, more ambitious.

Comments of Parents	Comments of Children
They have to be, to be Jewish.	Attitudes toward family life, education, personal "sanctity."
They seem to have more *sechel!*	The rigors of being Jewish, and the feelings—often heightened—lead to a greater emotional core and reaction in many Jews.
With regard to charity and a feeling for his fellow man, I think that the average Jew is better.	Jews have a greater feeling of history and the responsibility to relate basic ethical principles to others, e.g., truth, justice.
Centuries of persecution leave their marks!	A very ancient history of persecution, a high moral and ethical code, a self-imposed separateness in community, an unusual degree of liberalism, humanity, charity, and respect for education and for Jewish life or other law, have created a people who *still* could walk into gas chambers believing others could not possibly be so monstrous and barbaric, who could *still* not believe such evil could exist.
As a minority they cannot always follow their own inclinations. They have to lead more exemplary lives, study harder, and work longer hours to be accepted by non-Jews and to progress in their chosen work.	I believe in a Jewish character represented by needs to be special; Jews aren't nice and self-sacrificing. Jews are not polite. Jews are more intelligent, creative.

Three-fourths of the children believed "a personal sense of Jewish identity is desirable in this day and age," and 81 percent agreed that "Jews personally benefit from a strong sense of their ethnic culture and tradition" (this last group includes some of the children who are "not at all religious").

Only 15 percent of the children as compared with 43 percent of their parents saw Jews appropriately labeled "a religious group." The majority of children preferred the label "cultural group" and yet when asked: "Suppose a person is born of Jewish parents, but does not believe in any religion. Would you consider him or her a Jew?" Twenty-one percent of the children said "no" (compared to 12 percent of the parents). When asked about a person born of Jewish parents who converted to Christianity, nearly a third of the parents and a fourth of the children would still consider that person a Jew. This includes those parents who feel Jews are best identified as members of a religious group, and far more children than those who perceive Jews as a religious group. Presumably for the other children who agree with the statement, Jewishness transcends religious affiliation. As one man wrote: "A state of mind and a people."

Metropolitan Grandchildren

Thirty-five of the 52 children were married—26 of the 35 were married to Jews, and 1 was married to a convert to Judaism. Of the 8 who were married to non-Jews, 5 reported that they were "not at all religious." (The other 4 respondents who said they were "not at all religious" were unmarried.)

Most of the married children of the small-town Jews we heard from now had children of their own. Of this group only the grandchildren of one of our original respondents had nearly exclusive contact with non-Jews; according to their parents the rest (65 grandchildren in all) had contact with either mixed school and neighborhood groups or "exclusively with Jews." This is a total reversal of their parents' experiences growing up in small towns (and more like their grandparents'). Of the grandchildren who attend them, half go to primarily Jewish camps and only one attends a camp that is seen as "Christian."

Seventy percent of the children of small-town Jews with sons say their own boys will be (or have been) *bar mitzvah;* 52 percent of those with daughters plan *bat mitzvah*.

Of all the parents of the 65 grandchildren, only one said there was "no concern" in the household to provide the children with an understanding or background in Jewish life. Sixty percent of the rest of the young parents were "very concerned" (compared to 51 percent of *their* parents about their religious education when they were children in small towns), and the rest said they were at least "moderately concerned."

Although many of the young parents said of their children that they were not old enough to have a measurable Jewish identity, nearly a fourth reported that their children (the grandchildren of our 1958 respondents) had a stronger Jewish identity than their own: "I felt I missed out on something very important to a child [as a small-town

Table 4.7   Maintaining a Jewish Commitment

How concerned have you been with providing your children with an understanding or background of Jewish life?	1976 Respondents (Parents)*	1976 Respondents (Children)**
Very concerned	51%	59%
Somewhat concerned	43%	37%
Not at all concerned	5%	4%
	99%	100%
	(37)	(27)

*parents only
**children of small-town Jews who themselves are parents.

Jew]—I was determined to have my children be surrounded by Jews and have basic religious schooling and they have!"

Many others, who do not yet have children, intend to see that they are raised to appreciate their Jewish heritage. Here are two comments:

> We don't have any children yet as my husband is attending graduate school. When we do, we hope to bring them up knowing and being proud of the fact that they are Jewish. . . . We hope they marry Jews!

> I probably suffer to some degree a Jewish identity crisis which related to my childhood and contrary parental religious attitudes. In terms of my own children, I would hope to reject my father's position and provide them with a far more complete Jewish education, as my sister is doing with her three children.

Conclusions

Thirty-seven of the 42 respondents from the 1958 survey list were parents, but 11 of these parents did not include any adult "children's" names and addresses for our follow-up study. Information on the questionnaires of the reluctant eleven discloses that only one of the parents was "not at all" concerned with providing his children with a background or understanding of Jewish life; the other ten were "very" or "moderately" concerned with this. Fifty-six percent of their children were reported by them as having "weaker" religious identities than their own (only one of these eleven parents was "not at all" religious). Of the twenty-six parents who did provide us with the names and addresses of their children, less than a third were reported by them as having weaker religious identities, and nearly one in five reported having stronger religious identities (compared with the children of only one of the eleven parents who did not supply their names).

A reasonable speculation from this analysis of the questionnaires is that some or most of the eleven parents felt their children would not be interested in participating in our follow-up study. The children of the parents who did feel comfortable submitting their names and addresses were almost totally cooperative. The congruence between these parents' rating of their children's religiosity and their children's own self-designations demonstrates the mutual understanding between the two generations represented in the follow-up study. This understanding may be projected onto the eleven respondents mentioned above, and thus we may conclude that all the parents knew their children and their interest in things Jewish very well.

While there is a drop from parents (the original small-town Jews) to children (their offspring) in identifying themselves as *religious* Jews (in affiliation and self-designated religiosity), this is not paralleled in terms of any decline in ethnic pride (as read in their comments), religious attitudes (as high as their parents'), and concern for their own children's religious training (higher than their parents' concern for theirs). Furthermore, while none of the parents registered themselves higher than "moderately religious," several of their children did.

Quantitatively, those children who felt a stronger religious identity than their parents, did not statistically compensate for those who felt a weaker religious identity (19 percent stronger, 40 percent weaker). But qualitatively it may be that the more religious of the children were *much more* religious than *any* of the parents. All ten children who designated their religiosity as higher than their parents' gave evidence to this in the high frequency of religious observance in their family lives—8 of the ten observing the Sabbath, and all of them fasting on Yom Kippur. With only one exception, the parents of these very religious young adults kept only three or fewer such observances. We found that of the 21 children who rated their identities as weaker than their parents', only 2 practiced no religious observances, and 2 others practiced as many as six, with the remaining 17 children practicing a range of observances similar to their parents', from one to five. Thus we read of a professed weakening of religious identity among some of the children, but we see strong evidence of the Jewish tradition that colors their lives today. In summary, this is the childrens' story:

1. They felt "different" as children, because they were Jewish, wealthier, had broader horizons than many of their non-Jewish friends,

and had no church affiliation. They felt, however obscurely, the absence of religious group membership in their lives.

2. The children were satisfied to live in urban centers because of the occupational, cultural, and social advantages cities offer; and the opportunities they found within the larger Jewish community in which they were able to shed their childhood sense of "different-ness."

3. However the children defined themselves as Jews, they were for the most part, proud of their Jewish heritage and firm in the conviction that it was their obligation and privilege to transmit it through their own children, the grandchildren of the small-town Jews we studied in 1958.

Epilogue

The small-town Jews studied in 1958, those urban émigrés who moved to New York villages during the thirties and forties, contributed a valuable perspective to the portrait of American Jewry. Yet their section of the portrait is on fading canvas, to be preserved in the controlled light of historical archives. Their stories have told us that a generation or two of life as strangers in the midst of non-Jewish American communities has not resulted in the extinction of their sense of Jewishness. The cultural pluralism they enjoyed, those "two cups of life," enhanced and reinforced their Jewish identities.

Growing up in Gentile communities did not seem to cause a psychological disorientation among their children. Most remained self-designated Jews and were living in large Jewish communities. In the next few years, these young parents might be asked the same questions we asked their parents in 1958, concerning their approval of social interaction between their offspring and children of other faiths and races. This generation of young parents, a "skip generation" having grown up without communal Jewish identity, may have lingering, if subliminal, questions about the validity of their own Jewishness. The question which may only be answered by the course of *their* children's lives, is: Is the newly urban generation, the children of small-town Jews, a generation of marginal members of the continuous metropolitan Jewish community? We know they were "different" from their Gentile school-mates in small country towns. Might they not also be "different" from their Jewish peers who grew up in metropolitan communities? If they are, they will have carried a cultural pluralism peculiarly their own into their urban lives.

Notes

1. Nine known personally to the author; 7 returned by post offices marked "deceased," and 5 represented by widows in this follow-up study.
2. We queried employees in village post offices near our own small city to ask if the "forwarding time expired" stamp would be affixed to mail addressed to deceased residents, and were informed it would be probable after one year.
3. See Marcus Lee Hansen, *The Immigrant in American History* (Cambridge, Mass.: Harvard University Press, 1940).
4. All references in tables and text to "parents" are *inclusive* of the total (42) 1975 respondents of that generation—37 parents, 5 nonparents.

Part II
Red, White, Blue—and Black

5

The Black Experience: Issues and Images

(1969)

History is often written in terms of the images people, or peoples, wish to project. American history, for example, was long recounted as if the English, Scottish, and Irish Protestants—and a few Dutchmen—were the only ones to have had an impact on the growth and development of the country.

The Future as Guide to the Past

Early books and classroom lectures dealt almost exclusively with the "Anglo-American tradition" or "our Christian heritage." Throughout most of the eighteenth and nineteenth centuries, newcomers from Northwestern Europe (whom Fletcher Knebel named the "out-WASPS") were encouraged to forget about the customs of Germany or Scandinavia and to adapt to those eminently superior American life-ways. Other immigrants were most often considered beyond the pale of social acceptance. In story and song the Irish Catholics, Poles, Italians, and Russian Jews—to say nothing about those who came from China or Japan—were referred to as "unassimilable aliens." Many politicians expressed serious doubts about whether such immigrants would ever have the makings of *real* Americans. Many noted social scientists went so far as to endorse the Dillingham Commission reports and the restrictive legislation of the 1920s.

In time, most scholars changed their views, and their histories changed as well. Pluralism came in vogue and schoolchildren and college students were then told that "our differences make us strong," that "America is a multiplicity in a unity," or, as John Dewey once said, in this country "the hyphen connects instead of separates." It even became fashionable to teach about the "Judeo-Christian heritage" and to consider Catholics as Christians, too. As if to bear public witness to such a revisionist view, the single Protestant preacher who had always intoned opening prayers at official gatherings was supplanted by a ubiquitous triumvirate: minister, priest, and rabbi, representatives of "our three great religions." (Sociologists even gave expression to this new phenomenon and America became known, at least in the parlance of the classroom, as a "triple melting pot.")

Now it is time to include yet another figure on the dais—and add another "culture" to the heritage. Behavior rises to meet expectations and the behavior of academic historians and social scientists seems no exception. Today bookstores are flooded with a thousand volumes on "the Negro problem." The problem is not new. It is as old as America. But, worried about the future, we have once again begun to look at, and to some extent rewrite, the past.

Textbooks being prepared for the 1970s will indicate that there is much more to "Black history" than the slave blocks, the old plantation, Emancipation and "the grateful darkies," Freedmen's Bureaus, the Hayes-Tilden compromise, *Plessy vs. Ferguson,* Booker T. Washington, race riots during the two world wars, Marian Anderson, Jackie Robinson, Ralph Bunche, Thurgood Marshall, and the Supreme Court decision of 1954. Rather, to judge by the advertising copy of books already under preparation, they will dwell on the role played by Black Americans who, "under the most adverse conditions, fought and died to gain their own freedom" and who (paradoxically it seems) "were enlisted in every major battle to save this Republic."

The new texts will continue to tell a story of life in the antebellum South, but readers will learn that things were not so tranquil beneath the mimosa trees, that not all Negroes sought to emulate the ways of their masters, and that none ever had good relations with them (no matter what the romantics say). They will also learn that Blacks did not really move North to freedom but exchanged one kind of hell for another.

As more and more new histories appear, a far different picture of Black Americans will emerge. It will not be limited to celebration of the martyrdom of Crispus Attucks (the Black Colin Kelly) or the achievements of George Washington Carver (the Black Jonas Salk). The new books will include discussions of Black soldiers who fought in the Union Army; they will tell of Black politicians in the turbulent days of Reconstruction; they will praise the Black cowboys who helped open the West; the Black troopers who rode with Teddy Roosevelt; the Black workers who toiled along railbeds, in factories, and farms. Some will go farther, extolling the virtues of blackness and the solidarity of "soul," and exposing the pallid character of "White culture" in contrast to "Black."

The motivation for this latest attempt at reexamining American history and giving the Blacks an honored place along with other "minorities" has come about as a consequence of the civil rights movement and the campaign to eliminate segregation. The demand for an entirely new view of the Afro-American is an offshoot of that larger struggle.

Feeling that many of the hard-won victories of the 1950s and 1960s have not made that much difference, angry Black spokesmen have begun to challenge a number of basic assumptions of the reform-minded civil rights advocates. First, they argue, liberal White leaders (whatever they wanted personally) have rarely offered much more than palliatives often viewed as programs to keep *their* cities from erupting rather than being expressly designed to help poor Blacks. Second, they say that traditional *Negro* leaders have never been much better. They were either out of touch with the people for whom they claimed to speak (as many felt about the late Martin Luther King) or were too willing to play the Establishment game (as was often said of Roy Wilkins). Arguing that their people have always been deluded by Whites who had taken up the "burden" and Negroes who were trying to lighten it, the new militants wanted to turn them "blackward," wanted them to have an identity truly their own. They began their campaign by excoriating White liberals, "Uncle Toms," and especially "Honkie society." They are carrying it forward with appeals to Black nationalism. They may end by making (and in some cases making up) history itself.

Since no group has a monopoly on ethnocentrism, it should not be surprising to find that many of the new views of Black history will be similar to most paeans to a cloudy past: compilations of vague memories which have become legends, of vague legends which have become memories, of isolated incidents swelled to monumental significance, and a good deal of hard evidence of what actually happened and, for any number of reasons, has been overlooked or purposely ignored. The history of Afro-Americans, like that of those from Europe, is almost by necessity going to turn out to be a potpourri of fancy and fact. What makes it different is that it has to serve a double function of helping to strengthen communal ties among Blacks while having other Americans learn that those who came from Africa also had a noble past and are a proud people.

To tell it like it really was is a difficult and frustrating task. It is difficult because there is so little data untainted by the biases and romanticism of those who captured the oral tradition or the written record; it is frustrating because even the sketchy story that does emerge is so ambiguous—not in terms of the patterns of oppression so much as their effects on the oppressed. But one thing is fairly clear: much of the old heritage was replaced by a new orientation. Western ways and Southern values were absorbed and, for good or ill, countless thousands of Black Africans became American Negroes.

W.E.B. DuBois once suggested that "there is nothing so indigenous, so made in America, as me." And yet, as is too well known, few Negroes came to enjoy the freedoms that other Americans could take for granted. Few ever got away from the stigma attached to the color of their skins. As DuBois and others repeatedly pointed out, every Black child has always asked "Who am I?" "What am I?"

Self, Segregation, and Soul

Not very long ago, James Baldwin wrote an essay entitled "Nobody Knows My Name."[1] In a sense, it dealt with only half of the problem. White people did not know what to call him and *he did not know himself*. Baldwin's people—variously called Blacks, coloreds, Negroes, and Blacks again—had little to look forward to and even less to look back upon, or so it seemed.

Still, saying they had little is not to say they had nothing. There is such a thing as Afro-American culture and every Black person in this country knows it. Like all cultures it is made up of many things: memories, moods, and myths. What makes it different is that the memories, moods, and even the myths "remembered" are unique: slavery and its aftermath; spiritual uplift and over-Jordan imagery;[2] continued subjugation by those who claimed and repeatedly tried to prove that "white" was always right.

Against (and in some ways in response to) these debilitating aspects there was resilience, richness, and romance. The Negro world had (and has) its cuisine (now called "soul food"), its old-time religion, its rules of conduct, its lingo, its literature, its sounds. Those who now study the Blacks' experience in America contend that it has left them with different conceptions of time, space, property—and life. (Today, it is even fashionable in certain liberal circles to celebrate the unique characteristics of Negro people in this country. A mere five years ago such contentions, traditionally made by many segregationists, would have been called "racist" by the very same liberals—and by many Negro leaders too.)

Resistance was another matter. Being frozen into the rigidity of a caste system and unable to become partners in the society from which so much of their own customs, beliefs, and values were derived.

Negroes often lacked the organizational apparatus characteristic of that possessed by many other minority groups in America—the very groups to which Black Americans have long been compared and have often compared themselves. For years Black people had talked about organizing and fighting their tormentors, but faced with retribution from large institutions and powerful men, they usually had no recourse but to adapt to the system which kept them in servitude.

Segregation kept many Blacks humble, and sometimes their own leaders aided and abetted "The Man." Both Black preachers and White segregationists spoke of their children; both tended their "flocks." (Not all White men and not all leaders of Negroes acted in such a manner. But the point is that *these* were the most significant role models available for the vast majority of Black people, especially in the Old South.)

There is a parallel to be drawn between the plight of many Black Americans and that of mental patients. Some psychiatrists have recently reintroduced the notion of reality therapy. Crudely described, reality therapy is a technique used to shock patients into the realization that the world *is* cruel and if they are going to make it, they are going to have to do more than play out the sick role which "enlightened doctrine" has ascribed to them and which, quite understandably, they have internalized. For years now, few well-educated people have said that Blacks are innately inferior; they know better. Rather the conventional wisdom sounds strikingly like that of the old planters and ministers of God. Saying, "only we know what's good for them," many social workers and schoolteachers have held to this view to the present day. Disadvantaged Black people are viewed and treated as victims or patients or some sort of unfortunates in need of care and succor. Many of them, in turn, like the inmates of one asylum after another, have internalized the roles ascribed and acted accordingly.

This is not to say that most Black Americans are (or perhaps ever were) simple "Sambos." But many did and continue to learn to act out the stereotypes others held of them and many, even in putting the White man down by seeming to play along, came to believe—in spite of themselves—that they *were* inferior. The late Malcolm X understood. He said: "The worst crime the white man has committed is teaching us to hate ourselves."[3]

Perhaps one can understand the bitterness of those who now claim to speak for the Negro, those who say there has really been no progress, only expanded "welfare colonialism." And one should be able to understand why young Black radicals choke on that noblest of all words in the lexicon of human relations: *brotherhood*. Brotherhood, to too many has meant: "When you become like me, brother, *then* we'll be as one." They have a point. Time and again Negroes have found there was always one more river to cross. White people would offer the boats if the Black rowers did not rock them too hard.

What a choice for a potential leader. Tell your people to remain supplicants in the hope that someday the White man will overcome his prejudices, lower the barriers, and welcome you into his big *White* house; or become a firebrand in the hope that you might force his capitulation. And once having made the decision—where were you left? Dead on the inside or dead all around.

It is no wonder that the civil rights movement was always white-ward-oriented—no matter what is being said about it today. To solve the dilemma of supplication versus rebellion, most efforts to redress the grievances of the past have been channeled into campaigns for integration (not quite supplication and not quite rebellion). Most Black people, it seems, wanted to give the impression (and many wanted to believe) that someday, somehow, color would really be overlooked. Those the angriest Black spokesmen hold in contempt today—the White liberals[4]—helped perpetuate this myth without realizing what they were doing nor having much personal contact with those they claimed to accept as equals.

Attention has been focused on "most" Negroes and "many" Negroes, but not all. There are those who have made it; some by the very same techniques used by other members of minority groups, including the exploitation of those whose identity they share; some by becoming athletes, soul singers, or jazz musicians performing for both their own and a "wider" community; some—the largest group—by sheer determination to overcome the barriers of segregation, often by entering government service as postmen and clerks, secretaries and soldiers, and as teachers, working their way up. Together, these members of what has come to be called the "Black bourgeoisie," the "colored entertainers," and the "Negro respectables" represent to Whites (especially the middle class) living evidence that Black people can make it if they try hard enough and are willing to thicken their skins (often fairly light skins) whatever abuses the "system" and its agents mete out. Perhaps. It is true that many such people have prided themselves on their progress and, for all their difficulties, have seemed quite stable, even happy in American society. They have belied the claim that Negroes are characteristically lazy, ignorant, or walking phallic symbols,[5] and seemed to be the essence of middle-class respectability: friendly, hard-working, religious, and community-minded.

Many of their children who are now in college think differently.

They, and not just the poor people in Watts, know what Ron Karenga means when he decries: "There are only three kinds of people in this country: white people, black people, and Negroes. Negroes? They are Black people that act like White people."[6] The message is not lost. Those Negro college students, particularly at Northern schools and the larger Southern ones, know that part of Karenga's rhetoric is addressed to them and concerns their parents. ("Which side are *you* on?") Those who have suffered least from the stigma of color are beginning to suffer the most. Many are reacting by forming Afro-American organizations on campus and by going "home" to Harlem or Hattiesburg to work, teach, and organize. Some, to resolve their race/class schizophrenia, have begun to join the ranks of the most militant members of the Black community and provide the copy for the spokesmen and the plans for the revolution. Stressing both poverty and race, the disorganized "Black lumpen" have become their cause. With the poor, one can put to use some of the direct and fringe benefits of a college education. For them one can try to offer a new and different view of the Americans who came from Africa.

Yesterday, Today, and Tomorrow

The young Black militants are, as one said recently, "a new breed of cat." They see themselves as the vanguard of a movement to erase once and forever the stigma imposed by White slave masters and perpetuated by segregationists over the last hundred years. They want everyone—parents and peers, White liberals and conservatives—to know that times have changed and that they are Black *men* not Black *boys*. Often using the future as a guide to the past, they have called for a new view of the Black experience, "in which the real truth about Black people will finally be known."

In response to mounting pressure, colleges and universities (and some public schools) have introduced Afro-American programs and curricular innovations geared to the special needs of Black students. From amongst the welter of proposals and pronouncements requesting (or more often demanding) such programs, one message has come across loud and clear: "We will be *Negroes* no more."

This mood, its strategy, and its rhetorical style, has signaled the end of an old era and the beginning of a new phase in Black-White relations in the United States. With the benefit of hindsight, one can say it was inevitable that such a shift in character, focus, and leadership should have come to pass. The new ideology is a culmination of years of struggle and crisis during which Black people were trying to come to grips with their unique problems and their constantly thwarted desires to become full-fledged Americans.

Among the various techniques of protest, two types of action were most prevalent from the time of emancipation to its centennial. One centered on Blacks themselves and was concerned with "uplift": learning useful skills, instilling pride in self and neighbor, and such Puritan virtues as thrift and practicality. The other focused in integration and gaining civil rights. In the first instance, the underlying notion seemed to be that Black people would show the White man that they were responsible, upright, and talented citizens and that in time they would be ready to take their place beside anyone. In the latter, the argument was that the problem was not the Negro's but the White man's and he should be made to change. Thus the seeds were sown.

Booker T. Washington was the best-known advocate of the uplift philosophy. At Tuskegee Institute, which he founded, he put into practice his bootstrap operation. A generation later a West Indian, Marcus Garvey, was to turn Washington's accommodationism into strident Black nationalism. But with all the fervor and pageantry, Garvey, like Washington, exhorted his followers to prove to the world that Blacks were truly respectable. In time those who were to lead the many mosques of the Temple of Islam were to go beyond even Garvey, claiming Black supremacy and rejecting Christianity. Yet even the Black Muslims could not and did not reject Puritan values. On the contrary, they built them into the basic credo of everyday life.

The reaction against Washington's accommodationist plans were publicly voiced by but a few Negro leaders. Two who did speak out were Monroe Trotter and W.E.B. DuBois. DuBois was one of the founders of the integrated and, for its time, militant National Association for the Advancement of Colored People. In time, other organizations were to be added to the NAACP: CORE, SLCC, SNCC—each more militant, more "engaged" than the one before. Still, until 1964, most of those who followed the banner of integration were possessed with a sense of mission that would ultimately culminate in that grand day, the Golden Jubilee, when color would no longer matter when the dream of the Reverend Martin Luther King and a thousand other Negro preachers would no longer have to be deferred. "Free at last," they would cry out, "Free at last." "Lord, God Almighty, we're free at last."

Black Power

By the time of emancipation's centennial (and for some, before), it was evident to many outside observers and to many field workers that neither ethnocentric blackwardness nor soullness militancy could turn the tide of racism, so deep did it flow.[7] Since there was little likelihood that they could really go it alone and even less that they could (or would) ever "turn white," Negroes were going to have to learn (or relearn) sooner or later that to make it, they had to take pride in themselves *and* become politicized. They had to harken to what Frederick Douglass had prescribed a hundred years before the Student Non-Violent Coordinating Committee was born:

> Those who profess to favor freedom yet deprecate agitation are men who want crops without plowing up the ground; they want rain without thunder and lightening. They want the ocean without the awful roar of its many water. . . . Power concedes nothing without demand. It never did and it never will. Find out just what any people will quietly submit to and you have found out the exact measure of injustice and wrong which will be imposed upon them, and these will continue till they are resisted with either words or blows, or with both. The limits of tyrants are prescribed by the endurance of those whom they oppress.[8]

Black Power did begin as a movement of words, impassioned words exhorting poor sharecroppers to get out and exercise their franchise. But this was not enough. Intimidation and threats raised the ire of the civil rights workers and turned many Black pacifists into soldiers while turning away many White allies. The code of Thoreau and Gandhi was being replaced by the law of Hammurabi—much as Frederick Douglass had suggested.

For years, Negro and civil rights White leaders had counseled patience and fortitude. Until quite recently their authority went unchallenged, for it was widely felt that the liberal integrationists (Black and White) were on the right path. The civil rights campaign in the late 1950s and early 1960s, and the bills passed by Congress in their wake seemed positive proof of the efficacy of nonviolent direct action. But, as many of the victories proved Pyrrhic, as tensions mounted between Black field workers who saw radical pacifism as a tactic and Whites for whom it was a way of life, as the Vietnam war syphoned off funds that (it was said) would have been earmarked for ghetto reconstruction, and most of all, as the relative deprivation of Black people become more apparent, the climate shifted. The movement went sour and the old coalitions began to break apart.

The urban riots were an exacerbating factor. Many Whites who had begun to feel some empathy with the embattled civil rights workers, or at least were talking of "giving Negroes their due," grew increasingly fearful—and hostile—as they saw the flames of Harlem, Rochester, Watts, and Detroit on their television sets or in some cases from their upstairs windows. Charges and countercharges. Cries of duplicity on the one hand and corruption on the other. Shouts of "Burn, Baby, Burn" and "Get the Honkies" mixed with "Send them back to Africa." Frontlash. Blacklash. A litany of curses filled the air—and the airwaves.

Given the disillusionment and fear, the persistence of institutionalized segregation, and especially the fact that little was being done to satisfy those poorest Blacks whose expectations had suddenly begun to rise, it is little wonder that the hymn "We Shall Overcome" was replaced, literally and figuratively, with "Black Power." The new mood began to reach out and envelop the unorganized masses of Negroes, particularly in the Northern ghettos where few meaningful communal institutions existed around which people could rally and where even the oratory of Dr. King could not arouse. The focus began to shift away from integration and toward the more basic matter of "getting it together."

In the early 1920s, E. Franklin Frazier had said that "if the masses of Negroes can save their self-respect and remain free of hate, so much the better. But . . . I believe, it would be better for the Negro's soul to be seared with hate than dwarfed by self-abasement."[9] Again it was being argued that there was a psychosocial need for Black people to call "The Man" to task rather than accept and internalize second-class status and all it means. As William H. Grier and Price Cobbs have recently shown, there has long been (and remains) an almost desperate need to find a sense of positive selfhood and meaningful peoplehood.[10]

To accomplish this meant that the leadership would have to change as well. And it did. Whites began to be eased or pushed out of positions of dominance to make room for those who could more easily identify with, and be identified with, the Black masses. The new leaders sought to prove to their followers that Black was the symbol of light at the end of their tunnel.

As Black Panthers gained a certain amount of notoriety, those in the "traditional organizations" changed too. SNCC became more militant. CORE turned away from its original stance of integration in favor of Black consciousness. The Urban League and the NAACP sounded more militant even while trying to assuage the anxiety of White liberals who did not understand what was happening. The Southern Christian Leadership Conference continued fighting its battles for jobs and freedom, but also began forming uneasy coalitions with other embattled minority groups. Despite many differences in symbol (the clenched fist or the double bar of "equality"), in slogan, and in style, pride and protest were joined and, for many, it had become a time to be Black.

The Second Reconstruction

There is a real question as to whether the new turn of events will facilitate the growth of genuine and relevant organizations with power to effect both psychological and political changes in the Black communities and to make the need of those communities apparent to the rest of society, or whether the "Second Reconstruction" will end in tragic failure like the first. Those who take the former position are quick to invoke the model offered by other minority groups. They say that Black Power is not an attempt to destroy society but to provide a basis for pride and representation to those lacking it; the same kind of pride and recognition that the English, Italians, Irish, Jews, and the others have had in themselves, using, among other things, the same sort of "creative distortion" of history. It is also seen as the basis for the formation of institutions that can implement organized action to aid in the ascent up the ladder. Those who believe this suggest that the "ethnicity" that *already* exists among Blacks must be strengthened and embellished; and that once again ethnic power must become a factor to reckon with. They say that this is really nothing new; it is "as American as apple pie." Others argue that the zeal to have everybody listen to the rage boiled up inside may well be self-defeating, for few Black leaders will be able to translate their language of estrangement into a meaningful remedy that will cure the disease of racism without killing the patient.[11]

There is no easy way out of the present dilemma. Old techniques have failed because they never reached those who needed help most. New techniques (as advocated by the Black militants and others) will fail, it is said, because they will inevitably alienate the very peole who are most needed in abetting the transition—those concerned liberal people in the schoolrooms and universities, in planning boards, in the government. Simon Lazarus goes so far as to suggest that many well-meaning liberals, ignoring the innuendos of a genuine separatist rebellion, often tend to give Black Power a familiar, pluralistic face and, believing their own propaganda, have begun to offer Black Power (or their version thereof) "both to whites on their right and to blacks on their left." He goes on to say that "convinced that black leaders *should* not adopt systematic violence as a tactic, liberals have assumed they *will* not adopt it."[12] The point is well taken, especially given what is now known about the tensions in American society—on the campuses and particularly in the ghettos. But it should not be exaggerated either. The majority of Black Americans, including many in the slums, still want to join the society, not turn it upside down. And for many, Black

Power (read "bloc power") is still seen as a way to get in. How long they will feel that way is highly speculative. The potential for independence movements to break out of the colonized status, as Robert Blauner suggests, is very great—and very real.[13]

It is becoming increasingly difficult to predict what will happen on the racial front in the coming years. A few years ago the past was used as a fairly accurate guide to the future and the predictions made were based on a critical assessment of the data available to anyone bothering to sift through it. Among the evidence was a pretty clear picture that few White people were about to support any efforts to effect changes unless they were pressured into it. In celebrating the passage of the Civil Rights Acts of 1960, 1964, 1965, and even of 1968, it is easy to forget that these victories were the result of protest marches, boycotts, demonstrations, and threats of disruption. Such activities did more to bring about changes in the status quo than all the pious platitudes from segregated pulpits or the admonitions of the specialists in urban affairs and poverty.

The federal government dedicated to opening new frontiers, making a Great Society, and waging war on poverty, got itself so bogged down in Vietnam that it could only offer monumental legislation and modest programs for carrying it out—programs offered to show good faith but construed by many as proof of continued tokenism and contributing to the overall "minus-sum game," as Aaron Wildavsky has called it. Minus-sum games are those, he says, in which every player leaves the contest worse off than when he entered.

> Promise a lot; deliver a little. . . . Lead people to believe they will be much better off, but let there be no dramatic improvement. . . . Have middle-class civil servants hire upper-class student radicals to use lower-class Negroes as a battering ram against the existing political systems; then complain that people are going around disrupting things and chastise local politicians for not cooperating with those out to do them in. . . . Feel guilty about what has happened to black people; tell them you are surprised they have not revolted before; express shock and dismay when they follow your advice.[14]

Those who warned about the dangers of such "games" were often told that the problem was being exaggerated or that they were "nervous Nellies" inadvertently disrupting the cause of civil rights by trying to keep everybody's expectations within realisitic bounds. Now many other voices have been added to those who decry the sociologists and behavioral political scientists for their reluctance to take more radical stands. The entry of large numbers of such spokesmen—

mounting the stumps from Harlem to Watts, the campus stages from Boston to Berkeley, and writing in old Negro papers and the new Black ones—has brought about many changes in the Black mood and movement. The crystal balls are far cloudier ("Whitey doesn't know what we're going to do next"—and he doesn't) and the emanations from the computers are consequently less reliable. Given what was known before, the Black Power movement was an almost inevitable next stage for those who were called "darker Brethren" but treated like hired hands by most Americans.

Now that many Black Americans have begun to question the way their past has been handled, and now that they have begun to claim that no White man can ever speak for *them,* it is difficult for anyone, Black or White, to separate fact from fancy. But perhaps this is the way it has to be (it was even one of the earlier predictions). A real dilemma faces compassionate historians and sociologists who feel that there is a psychological need for Black Americans to discover a past at which they can look with pride and the necessity to continue probing and searching for the truth about race relations, whatever may be revealed.[15] One thing is clear: as David Riesman has suggested, "To understand black narcissism is one thing. To feed it in a gesture of white masochism is dangerous for blacks and whites alike."[16] It is, in the vernacular of the moment, to go from one "bag" to another.

Still, in the gloomy present there are few hopeful signs. One of them, perhaps the most important, is a growing realization that the grievances of Black Americans are legitimate: the schools are poorer, the neighborhoods are shabbier, the rents are higher, the jobs are scarcer. At least some teachers, community leaders, landlords, and businessmen are coming to recognize that they have a critical role to play in abetting the transition from dependence to independence. They know that the road is rocky and the risks are great. But failure to act now means even greater dangers in the future.

In addition to support given to experiments in community control of the educational process, in neighborhood participation, in commercial involvement, and in the learning of technical skills, there must also be clear recognition of the need of Black Americans to say and *believe* that they are somebody too. This means a willingness to accept that the demand for equality means "equal time" as well. The "Black experience" must be seen as part and parcel of the American experience which is itself filled with tales of heroic achievements, resurrected "fests" from far-off nations and the echoes of a hundred cultures resounding in an oratorio of rhythm—and blues.

Notes

1. James Baldwin, *Nobody Knows My Name: More Notes of a Native Son* (New York: Dial, 1961).
2. See for example James Baldwin, *Go Tell It on the Mountain* (New York: Knopf, 1952).
3. *The Autobiography of Malcolm X* (New York: Grove, 1964).
4. See Eldridge Cleaver, *Soul on Ice* (New York: McGraw-Hill, 1968): 46.
5. Norman Podhoretz, "My Negro Problem—and Ours," *Commentary* (February 1963): 93–101.
6. This sentiment was expressed by Ron Karenga at a Human Rights Conference at Brotherhood-in-Action (New York, 5 May 1967). He has made similar statements in Los Angeles and elsewhere.
7. James Farmer, *Freedom, When?* (New York: Random House, 1965); Stokely Carmichael and Charles V. Hamilton, *Black Power: The Politics of Liberation in America* (New York: Vintage, 1967).
8. The quotation is from a West Indian emancipation speech delivered by Douglass in 1857. It appears in Carmichael and Hamilton, p. x.
9. This is also expressed most poignantly by Richard Wright. See his "Foreword," in St. Clair Drake and Horace Cayton, *Black Metropolis* (New York: Harcourt, Brace, 1945).
10. William H. Grier and Price M. Cobbs, *Black Rage* (New York: Basic Books, 1968): esp. 152–67.
11. See for example Lewis M. Killian, *The Impossible Revolution?: Black Power and the American Dream* (New York: Random House, 1968), esp. ch. 7.
12. Simon Lazarus, "Domesticating Black Power," *New Republic* 8 (June 1968): 37–38.
13. Robert Blauner, "Internal Colonialism and Ghetto Revolt," *Social Problems* 16 (Spring 1969): 393–408.
14. Aaron Wildavsky, "Recipe for Violence," *New York* 1(May 1968): 28–36.
15. Melvin M. Tumin, "In Dispraise of Loyalty," *Social Problems* 15 (Winter 1968): 267–79.
16. Personal conversation with David Riesman (Amherst, Mass., 18 May 1968).

6
Race and Education in New York: The Challenge Moves North*

(1964)

The New York City school system is in the midst of a crisis, the full impact of which is likely to be far more serious than any it has yet faced. Here, as well as in other cities, Black people have finally developed sufficient cohesion to engage in extended action directed toward political ends. Having arrived at a stage where the achievement of equality of opportunity seems only just beyond their grasp, where every victory brings them closer to total victory and every defeat heightens the desire to upset the status quo, they have become increasingly attracted to proposals involving a radical break with the past. They can no longer abide the promises of change. They want immediate action. And they are expressing in political form the intense hostility so long contained.

Those leading the revolt in the North feel a particular sense of urgency because a number of changes in the structure of American society have placed them in the position of many of those living in developing nations. No matter how fast they run, the horizon seems to recede even more rapidly. Since World War II, increasing numbers of Southern Blacks have been entering Northern cities—economically handicapped by a lack of adequate training and education, and socially rejected on the basis of racial discrimination. New York was one such place where many thought they would finally find the economic security which had always been so elusive. But as the city became their new home, it also became their new jail.

*With Stanley Rothman.

De Facto Segregation

Denied opportunities, treated gratuitously, and made more bitter by the progress of others, many of the new migrants—and Harlem's children, too—began to reflect in their attitudes and actions the stereotypes others held of them. For many of these newcomers, unlike the European immigrants to whom they are invariably compared, failure became a *modus vivendi*. Their culture of poverty maintained and fed on itself, there was a pervasive condition of anomie, a seeming inability to find stabilizing influences in the ghetto community.

Various attempts were made to break the cycle from within the Black community and from outside agencies. But the road has been rough. Unlike other minority groups, Black Americans had rarely in the past been able to develop those institutions which could provide a sense of cohesiveness while preparing their members for concerted social action to significantly alter their collective plight. Even the few well-established organizations, such as the NAACP and the Urban League, were unable to generate a groundswell of popular political activity among the masses. New movements in the South, such as Martin Luther King's Southen Christian Leadership Conference or other direct action groups like CORE, provided some sense of the possibility of fighting back but, by and large, Northern Blacks (like Northern Whites) saw such activities as challenges to *de jure* segregation, not the kind they knew. As for the community at large, New York City and its welfare agencies have tried for many years to make an intolerable situation tolerable. Money has been poured into schools and a wide array of remedial programs have been instituted. But the money has been far too little and the programs too inadequate to begin to turn the tide.

Thus many Blacks were trapped in this situation with little room to maneuver. They could not help themselves (or each other); nor—it seemed—could anybody else. The only alternative was concerted political action. Until very recently, partly because of the nature and character of Black leadership and partly because of the general failure of the Black community to create the institutional bases for such action, this appeared to be a most unlikely prospect. Yet the postwar economic boom, (in which Blacks partially shared), the emergence of African independence movements (in which they took pride), and especially the Supreme Court decision of 1954 (in which they found new hope), seemed to signal the beginning of a new era. Still, the disillusionment that resulted from the fact that changes were slow in coming finally triggered the rebellion that ricocheted around the country and through the cities and college towns. It was then that the unexpected occurred.

The Black Revolt

New leaders emerged in the city and others came from outside; and Blacks began to mobilize (sometimes joined by other minority groups and Whites too). The dominant group was caught off guard. It soon became apparent that the traditional liberal forces (both White and Black) which had been working to eradicate segregation and its legacies in some systematic fashion had let time run out.

Events in the South served as the catalyst for the Northern revolt and Northern Blacks followed the example of the Southerners and took to the streets in increasing numbers. The movement has grown with such force that many who for years have been too frightened to speak out have been caught up in the new mood of revolutionary fervor.

All at once a wide variety of social institutions have come under the attack of those organizations and individuals leading the Black revolt and their growing numbers of followers. Business firms and labor unions have been besieged with demands to open more jobs to Blacks. Rental offices have been picketed and rent strikes have been held to protest against continued inequities in housing. Churches have been subjected to the demands of those who are appalled by their reluctance to speak out in defense of the revolution. But nowhere have the battle lines been drawn more clearly than in the realm of education. In New York, the school system, above all others, has become the focus of the protest movement. The reasons for this are clear.

First, in this period of rapid technological advancement, automation is steadily and inexorably eliminating the need for unskilled laborers. Those who are poorly educated find themselves increasingly cut off from the mainstream of opportunity and relegated to the ranks of the unemployable (though they would welcome work were it available). Given these facts of life, many Blacks believe that only a white-collar career of some kind can satisfy the desire for job security. As for so many immigrants, education is seen as the one avenue of access to such careers, and thus part of the claim being made is for improved programs within the present system.

Second, the school system is particularly vulnerable because, more than any other target, schools are in the public domain and subject to the demands of the citizenry. New York's schools contain at least half a million children willing to stay out of school (as they did on February

3, 1964) to dramatize the urgency of their demands. The demands being made are perfectly logical: for *better* schools to combat social deprivation and to increase job opportunities, and for *integrated* schools to combat second-class citizenship inherent in segregation.

Taken separately, these are not revolutionary requests; but the new leaders have insisted on joining them, declaring that schools cannot be better so long as they are not integrated. This is the source of the greatest rift between the White and Black communities. For a time, any plan for school improvement which did not include *full* integration was seen by many Black leaders as tokenism and was thereby rejected. As one civil rights leader repeatedly said: "We want the whole loaf!"

Painful Realities

Between the dream of a new world of true integration and the realities of life in the city yawns a wide chasm. The demands of those leading the boycotts are more clearly understandable if one examines the situation in the slum schools. So are the anxieties of opponents of the program, which they see as "integration at the expense of education."

Both teachers and students in slum schools become victims of the culture around them. In part, this is because many lower-class Blacks themselves (in contrast to those leading the revolution) regard the school system with considerable ambivalence. On the one hand, they do want to learn; on the other, schools are frequently associated with a society so deeply resented that they cannot bring themselves to accept its rules. Unable to attack the real source of their difficulties, resentments are sometimes taken out on school buildings and individual teachers, natural scapegoats for the despair and hostility built into their lives.

In families in which no father is present (and there are many) this hostility is compounded by the lack of any male figures to provide young boys with a model to imitate and a masculine source of authority. And even where the family situation is more stable, the problems are serious. Many parents and children have little understanding of what education involves; many find the teachers' value system incomprehensible. (This condition is made worse where teachers are incapable of using the pupil's own world—different though it is—to aid in bridging the gap.) Some tend, as in the case of developing nations, to regard education as a kind of magic while being intellectually and emotionally unaware of the kinds of self-limitations required. The net effect is that initial antipathy to the system is heightened by failure in it.

But even when these things are not true, when parents want their children to succeed and the children want to as well, they are often entrapped by the unavoidable norms of their world. To their most embittered peers in the schoolroom and in the neighborhood, these children are the White man's "bootlickers," without real status and often the objects of intimidation.

Many teachers who come to these schools fight this atmosphere, at least initially. But all too many are defeated by the system. Many new teachers soon discover that even five or six sullen boys or girls in an adolescent class of thirty are enough to take effective control away from them—however imbued they may be with all the "proper" teaching methods—if they have not been adequately trained for the kinds of situations they encounter. For such persons, it does not take long to become discouraged (even with the best of wills) by an inability to communicate with students. It does not take long to develop a concern for personal safety when they are taunted and sometimes attacked or see other teachers and students molested. And it does not take long to realize that if they try to discipline children, they are in danger of being accused of racism.

For too many, these factors tend to destroy whatever effectiveness they might have had. They flee these schools when they can or leave the system. If neither is possible, they effectively retire from the profession while still practicing it. In some cases, a group of exceptional teachers and an exceptional principal, plus some neighborhood *esprit de corps*, enables them to overcome the environment and make progress. But too many teachers have become increasingly embittered as they find that every attempt to describe their difficulties with some honesty is interpreted by their audience as a sign of lack of sympathy or competence.

It is fashionable today to speak of teachers as being prejudiced because they are narrowly middle class, because they are reluctant to abdicate their own values and principles. It is true that many are inflexible and become discouraged too rapidly because the children they try to teach do not live up to their conceptions of proper decorum. Even experienced teachers of considerable understanding and flexibility frequently find themselves overwhelmed by a situation which they see as a cul-de-sac of daily frustration.

These realities have important consequences for the integration movement. The increasing pressures brought to bear on school officials to lower the bars of neighborhood restrictiveness succeed in depleting the small number of good students without which the old system (bad as it is) becomes intolerable. For many upwardly mobile individuals, the only escape from slum schooling has been actual flight, and those who have sought (and won) the right to bus their children to distant schools have operated under the assumption that only by getting out will their children have a chance. Under present conditions, they are usually right. Those who do leave often find better schooling and a more congenial academic atmosphere in schools beyond the ghetto.

Reactions to Change

The children brought in from outside have been greeted with mixed feelings by their new classmates. In some schools they remain a separate group; in others, every attempt is made to fit them into the program. Yet not being residents of the immediate area, each day they must make the long trek back to their segregated neighborhoods while the Whites return to theirs.

The situation is one of strain but not turmoil. Many parents of the predominantly middle-class children who attend schools into which Black pupils are bused have come to accept the inevitability of integration, especially of children who are quite like their own. (Parents of the famous P.S. 6 in Manhattan have called on the Board of Education to place more minority pupils—including Blacks and Puerto Ricans—in the school.)

Yet experiences with middle-class Blacks who have been able to leave the ghetto or with a limited group of transients have not offset concern about the sudden influx of socially and economically deprived Black children who enter the school because the neighborhood is changing or because school boundaries have been rezoned. It is here that the argument shifts from race to class.

The turmoil begins when the ratio in the school reaches a certain point at which the students (both White and Black) feel that the school is about to become overwhelmingly Black even though the actual percentage may be 25 to 30. Then the fear of invasion supplants the idea of integration, and children (and their parents) begin to develop concerns about the behavior patterns the newcomers bring with them. White students find themselves under attack because they are White; and the Black minority already in the school find themselves trapped between the group toward which at least some aspire and those whose racial identity they share.

Frequently middle-class White parents become frightened at the possibility of violence directed against their children. (This is often exaggerated, but given the nature of recent events, is understandable.) They also become concerned that their children will respond to temptations which they fear the lower-class children offer. (Many Black parents share these views.) They know that children's attitudes are shaped in part by their peers and that the orientation they wish to provide for their own is threatened in a peer environment where the values of repression are sharply challenged. The result is that many White (and some Black) parents take their children out of the public schools or leave the neighborhood. Often, too, the result is a sharp reaction against their own former "liberalism" and increasing hostility toward lower-class Blacks—expressed (at the moment) only among themselves because it is not the thing to say, but quite sharp nevertheless.

For many of those involved it is only another phase of the constant effort to break out of the ghetto only to find themselves back in it once again, and it only confirms their own suspicions of and hostilities toward the White world around them. There is some evidence that rapid integration of the type just described can heighten the sense of alienation of lower-class Black children and the sense of superiority of Whites. In many "integrated" schools administrators, attempting both to reassure middle-class parents and to deal effectively with wide divergencies in preparation, have established special classes for "advanced" and "culturally deprived" students. Black children of slum backgrounds almost invariably find themselves in the lower levels. In the rapidly integrated schools the result is often classroom segregation.

Thus the lines are drawn. Slum schools do not and cannot, in their present state, hope to provide the kind of education so desperately needed for those who are seriously deprived. All-out crash-programmed integration without commensurate preparation for adjustment on the part of *both* White and Black students will not solve the Northern Negro's dilemma either. Such a claim would be a gross distortion of reality.

What's Ahead?

In New York the situation has reached a critical impasse. The boycotts of February and March 1964 will most certainly be followed by others (and more extreme forms of protest) unless the School Board is willing to give in to some of the demands of the boycott's leaders. Should this happen (especially if it involves an attempt at the compulsory two-way busing of children as demanded), there is a good chance that members of the once apathetic, now anxious White community will react in a way which will seriously undermine the possibility of securing badly needed additional funds for public education, without which practical programs cannot be supported. Those who believe this to be the case argue that the civil rights movement (particularly the militancy directed against educational institutions) will have succeeded in destroying the New York City school system without attaining the ends it seeks, and that the unrelenting pressure will have produced a boomerang effect—the so-called White blacklash.

Black leaders (and their White confederates) are not unaware of these arguments. Some dismiss them as rationalizations, as further evidence of White reluctance to give Black people their just due; and some are so bitter that they are willing to use any means short of violence to attempt to bring about the redress of grievances they so desire. Others, whatever their personal feelings, consider that they must go along with more radical demands for a variety of reasons. There is, perhaps, the unconscious fear that if they do not they will lose their position in a movement to which they have given their lives and which has given their lives meaning. There is also the feeling that if they do not move with their constituency, it will only fall under the control of irresponsible elements.

Whatever the motivation, Black leaders agree that the only way to make the White community take on responsibility is to make it listen to the angry voice of protest. Many believe that while boycotts and demonstrations will produce a certain amount of anxiety, Whites will more readily come to accept the changes which will inevitably ensue and, in the long run, will add their votes and voices to those of Blacks for a massive effort to handle the problems they have inherited.

Finally, responsible civil rights leaders are banking heavily on the belief that many Northern Whites, whatever their anxieties, are ideologically committed to equality and to making whatever adjustments are necessary to prevent the peaceful revolution from becoming violent.

The society into which many Blacks want admission is a middle-class society, and the values they hold and want their children to embrace are middle-class values. Unlike nineteenth-century revolutionaries they do not seek to overthrow the system but to join it; or to share in what is constitutionally guaranteed. But the embourgeoisement will not occur overnight. Discrimination and the culture of poverty have produced norms for many which run counter to those necessary to function in a world of affluence and opportunity. If the problem is not to be further exacerbated, it is here that the greatest effort must be expended.

Compensatory services must be provided. Children must be reached long before they attain school age and must be provided with compe-

tent instruction that will develop the necessary aptitudes for achievement. (It is known that waiting any longer may mean the loss of the
individual.) Teachers in the regular schools need more training in new
methods of teaching reading; more exposure to group work and case
work practice and to intergroup relations; and more pay. Students must
be assured that the education they receive will not be in vain; that jobs
are available and that they are employable. In addition to the nationwide effort to find a reasonable solution to employment demands, this
means that as jobs become available businesses and unions must be
prepared to alter traditional policies and open their doors to qualified
people regardless of race or creed.

Above all, the housing situation must be dealt with—both in terms of
cleaning up the ghettos and improving conditions, and by breaking
down the walls of neighborhood segregation through more forceful
ordinances. As for the schools, integration can work in those areas
where Black and White pupils can find a common meeting ground at a
nearby school. The "Princeton" system of pairing (taking two
schools—one "Black," one "White"—in contiguous areas and mixing
several grades in each), while not without difficulties, is the best plan
thus far devised. Pairing serves to maintain at least the spirit of
neighborhood schooling; it offsets racial imbalance; and it reduces the
social, psychological and economic problem of mass busing.

Even paired schools are bound to be characterized by a certain
amount of tension. Moreover, the possibility of more serious conflict
will be present so long as these schools—like any schools—contain
youngsters who are extremely difficult to reach in conventional ways.
For these children special restitutive services are necessary.

Civil rights leaders who know of these difficulties are averse to
admitting them publicly because they fear the use which might be made
of such an admission. Yet such refusal only militates against finding an
adequate solution to the problem. In New York today, even conservative groups accept the argument that the difficulties of Black children
are the result of their environment. Very few support the continuation
of a segregated school system on grounds of Black inferiority. At issue,
then, is the exaggerated fear with which lower-middle-class Whites
face the prospect of sending their children back (in many cases) to
schools in neighborhoods which they have left. To a large degree this
fear stems from the fact that what cannot be faced and discussed
openly takes on horrifying dimensions as it is passed on furtively from
neighbor to neighbor.

Any real progress toward the dual goals of *better* and *integrated*
schooling will require that both Whites and Blacks dispense with

slogans and air their anxieties—frankly talking *to,* not *past* one another. It will require that civil rights groups add to the dramatic work of promoting desegregation the new job of building a bridge between communities whose contacts have thus far been so limited. It will require that school administrators, naturally reluctant to share the running of their schools with nonprofessionals, come to recognize that the gains of such involvement are likely to be greater than the losses.

None of these suggestions is meant to serve as an excuse for impeding the pace of the desegregation movement. There is no question but that New York's school crisis (and the Black revolt itself) has served a most useful function. It has forced the White community to examine its own prejudices and fears and to begin to come to terms with social patterns it has permitted to exist. It has compelled the School Board to review its own policies and search for new avenues through the bureaucratic maze of red tape which has traditionally hindered or curtailed revolutionary innovations. And, most important of all, it has given Blacks a new lease on life.

The demonstrations will not abate—and should not. Yet one hopes that the movement will become as introspective as it has been militant and that responsible leaders of the various factions involved will recognize their role in abetting the transition to the kind of situation they desire. Whites in the power structure of the community are in a unique position to bring about dramatic changes. So, too, for the very first time, are Blacks.

7
Social Physics:
The Resurgence of Ethnicity

(1974)

One of the basic laws of physics is that every action has an equal and opposite reaction. The laws of society are not that simple. Yet it is safe to say that in "social physics" (a label Auguste Comte, the father of sociology, wanted to use for his new discipline) there are numerous examples of changes provoking reactions. This is certainly the case in the area of racial and ethnic relations. It was first evident in the responses of the American colonists to the increasing flow of new-comers to "their" country. Later on the children, grandchildren, and great grandchildren of those very "newcomers," began to echo the sentiments of the original nativists. Many were to back restrictive and racist policies. (Recently such views have been expressed within certain minority groups who have been troubled by the attention paid to refugees from Southeast Asia, while, they argue, their own people continue to struggle.)

Elsewhere I have discussed some of the principal sources of opposition that new Americans faced as they sought to deal with those who set the rules and often served as "gatekeepers." Many were members of that social category Seymour Martin Lipset refers to as the "once-hads"—persons who feared or felt they were losing control of "their" society.[1] Here I will concentrate on reactions to such movements as Black Power by those once removed from the centers of influence and control, the so-called White ethnics. The latter are not all "never-hads," although many make such claims; but they are people who have known subordination themselves. Many even consider that they, too, are minorities.

Feeding the Backlash

Placing Black people in a different light, giving them new models to admire and emulate, offering them the opportunity to say, "We're somebodies, too," certainly helped to change the self-conceptions of many Black Americans. Richard Wright once wrote, "White man, listen!" In recent years Whites were made to listen; and what they heard, saw, and felt greatly affected both attitudes and behavior.

Some welcomed the fact that Black Power advocates and Third World allies began to seriously challenge the system they felt kept many in servitude, perpetuated racism, and took a horrendous toll in human costs. Some were delighted that Black assertion resulted in the foreseeable end of old stereotypes and deference. Some were confused because they thought the struggle was for integration and began to see that goal thwarted by changed tactics and strategies advocated by many leaders. They could not understand why other Blacks did not call a halt to the draft apart. (Many Blacks were similarly confused.) Some were frightened because they simply could not predict what would happen next. ("Do they *really* mean guerrilla warfare?") Many became increasingly angry because they felt they were being asked or told to pay for damage they believed had been caused by others.

There are many indications of the changes to which those in each of the categories described above responded. All clearly recognized the profound differences between Blacks in the days before the post–civil rights shift in orientation and after. They had known about protest; they had known about Black nationalism. But the issues had not been joined until recently. Suddenly White Americans began to hear demands for a general reexamination of American history to put the Black experience in a more balanced light; to get rid of caricatured portrayal of Black people; to prove to others—and themselves—that Black is also beautiful. They saw a new swagger in the step, a new assurance in the swagger. They saw personal changes, both cosmetic and sartorial. "Processed" hair was replaced by the "Afro"; clothes associated with "Whitey" or with the ghetto were replaced by dashikis and other garb from Africa. (Ten years later shorter hair or corn-row braids were the style and few were wearing African-style clothing.)

The radio blared soul music at prime time. Television networks scrambled for more Black actors and actresses and presented more programs on "The Problem." The Black trend was evident elsewhere: in the streets, campuses, Black studies departments, Black cultural centers, political organizations—both local and national. The first Black political convention was held in Gary, Indiana in the spring of

1972, foreshadowing the implementation of the McGovern reforms during the Democratic Party's Miami convention the following summer. "Blacks," said one observer, "were suddenly everywhere." They got there through hard work, concerted pressure, and sometimes by demanding special and categorical treatment.

These developments, especially the last, had a profound effect, sometimes bringing about what appeared to be "an equal and opposite reaction." The new ground rules set up in response to Black demands, and the demands of other non-White minorities, significantly changed the basic premise that many liberals had long fought to establish and to which many other Americans, especially those of immigrant stock, subscribed: the idea that every individual must be judged on his or her merits "regardless of race, creed, color, or national origin."

As sociologist Michael Lewis has stated, this "individual-as-central" meritocratic creed has always been undercut by structural factors which inhibited genuine and open mobility. But, as Lewis suggests, this is not a phenomenon limited to any single group. All have been affected by endemic ideological contradictions. Many seem unaware of this fact of American life and continue to blame themselves (or those called "the victims") for failure.[2] Many of those who began to recognize the significance of cultural and systematic barriers were members of the non-White categories or their supporters. It was they, in particular, who began to demand group rights as recompense for past injustices. Equality of placement was sought to replace the idealized equality of opportunity for that placement. The complexity of the issue—involving, for example, the serious question of whether an altogether equal race is possible in the face of cultural, social, psychological, and political handicaps—did not lessen the important fact that the rules of the game had been changed. This change, at bottom, is where much of the current backlash focused.

Black Studies

One of the principal arenas of debate and conflict over the newly expressed sense of racial identity was the college campus. One of the most tangible signs of victory after the battles in the mid- and late 1960s was the establishment of Black Studies programs at many universities across the country and Chicano, Puerto Rican, and Native American programs in appropriate geographic areas. These were staffed by a mixture of highly trained academics who specialized in the study of ethnicity, race relations, history, and literature; militant activists whose professional skills were more often organizational than analytical; and assorted minority instructors whose main claim to expertise was their status as members of the group being studied and whose main staying power depended on the support of student claques. Arguments over whether Black Studies had a place in the academy gave way (once it was a *fait accompli)* to debates over what was being taught and by whom. Several studies were conducted which examined these questions. One of the most comprehensive was carried out by C. Wilson Record.

With grants from the Metropolitan Applied Research Center and the American Philosophical Society, in 1972 Record moved around the country visiting 70 campuses and interviewing 209 Black and White sociologists who "at the time or in the previous few years considered race and ethnicity as a teaching or research field."[3] Among this admittedly select sample, Record found that reactions to his questions could be grouped under four rubrics: (1) *Embracers,* who welcomed the innovation of ethnically-specific courses and programs (although they were sharply divided as to rationales for doing so); (2) *Antagonists,* who openly opposed Black Studies as a separate field and resented the tendency of its supporters to exclude *them* from participation or dismiss their prior contributions; (3) *Accomodators,* who reluctantly accepted what they saw as inevitable and tried to make the best of a dubious situation; and (4) *Dropouts,* who withdrew from the field under the fire of Black militants.

Each group had a motley array of members. The first was dominated by critics of the Establishment and included a number of Marxists. But also in the ranks were some conservatives who saw Black Studies as a device of both containment and decompression (much in the way that urban police forces had set up "human relations units" in the wake of the riots of the previous decade—and then went about business as usual). There were also those who saw Black Studies courses as a needed challenge to the traditional ways sociologists and others had addressed themselves to "the Black experience."

The Antagonists were a heterogeneous group too, but at its core were a number of White integrationists (and some Blacks) who saw themselves as part of the solution, not the problem. It was this subgroup more than any other that was caught between the rock and the hard place. For years many had studied race relations and tried to implement policies that would serve to make society more sensitive to discrimination and more open in all its aspects. Many had been civil rights activists frustrated by the slowness of change who saw the necessity for Blacks and other minorities to become more assertive. What they did not expect was that they would become targets and in many cases scapegoats for those who saw them as Establishment types. Some reacted with traditional academic arguments, thereby confirming the suspicions of their critics. Said one "antagonist" interviewed by Record: "They read Fanon but not Rustin; Malcolm X but not Kenneth Clark; Angela Davis and LeRoi Jones but not Roy Wilkins; the latter-day Du Bois but not Booker T. Washington; Marcus Garvey but not the mature Frederick Douglass. And a lot of time they don't read anything."[4]

Those in the third category, the Accommodators, seemed better able to ride the tide, many undoubtedly thinking that in due course it would ebb. Some tended to agree with the one who said: "Of course it isn't academically respectable, but there are a lot of things around here that aren't—physical education, home economics, social work, business administration."[5] In other words, Black Studies was something that had to be tolerated and even legitimized as part of the general offerings of a university.

Dropouts, roughly 20 percent of the sample, were older and more bitter than most of the others, including the Antagonists. Unlike the Antagonists whose members dug in their heels to fight against the separatist bent of the Black Studies supporters, those in this last category threw in the towel. Like all the others, this cohort included Black as well as White sociologists, often accused of being "Uncle Toms," whatever their skills or prior commitments. Most seemed to have dropped out only after having had a series of confrontations with militant nationalists or cultural revolutionaries who publicly denounced them, barred them from speaking, or blocked access to classrooms and offices. Included in this last group was a disproportionate number of old leftists (many of them Jewish) who were particularly troubled by two aspects of the protest. As Record explained:

> The direct or indirect challenge to academic standards that black studies programs posed, as they developed on most campuses, was particularly abrasive to the scholarly tradition of Jews. Denigration of the cognitive skills and insistence that nonblackness is an insurmountable barrier to understanding black experience clashed head on with the Jew's esteem for the traditional intellectual tools, in the use of which he had excelled, and with the classical academic perception of human experience as essentially universal. Black assault upon individual merit, traditionally defined as the single criterion for entry and achievement, rattled the age-old Jewish fear of quotas. Furthermore, the separatist thrust of the black studies movement offended a heavy Jewish commitment to integrationist ideology.
>
> Perhaps more pointedly, the rhetoric of the black militants who typically promoted the black studies movement was often openly anti-Jew and

anti-Israeli. The identification of some black militants with Africa bridged them emotionally to Muslims, to Arabs, and hence to oral attack upon Israel. Moreover, the focus of many black studies programs upon the black ghetto as subject matter as well as action arena has brought the old tension between the Jewish shopkeeper/landlord and the black consumer/renter into the classroom and onto the campus podium for fresh examination. Attempts to apply colonial theories to black-white historical experience in the United States leave little doubt that the "colonizers" include Jews.[6]

Demands for and the establishment of Black Studies programs were not the only manifestations of conflict between conservatives and radicals, integrationists and separatists, or Whites and Blacks. Campuses also came under increasing pressure to alter traditional standards for admission to facilitate the entry of more minority students. Sometimes the pressure took the form of demands for "affirmative action" and racial quotas.

Affirmative Action for Equal Opportunity

Many responded to the change of strategy and, in turn, of policy as it was responded to by sympathetic power brokers or vulnerable governmental agencies and frightened managers, principals, union leaders, politicians, and college administrations. Zeroing in on college admission boards, David Boorstin facetiously suggested that if the trend were to be followed to its logical conclusion, the I.Q. and other such tests would be abandoned as criteria for academic admission and would be replaced by an "E.Q." Ethnic Quotient.[7] This would mean that students, and eventually teachers and their subject matter, would have to be strictly apportioned according to background. There would be so many Blacks and so many Whites; so many Jews and so many Catholics—these to be further subdivided according to whether they were children or grandchildren of Italians or Irishmen, Slavs or Slovaks. ("Fractional men," as Vance Bourjaily once called people like himself,[8] would prove difficult to judge. What, for example, would one do with an application from a modern-day Fiorello La Guardia, that half-Italian, half–Jewish Protestant mayor of New York? Boorstin offers an answer: give him so many points for each of his traits in proportion to their representativeness in the overall population and make sure that his curriculum is balanced in similar fashion.)

What Boorstin lampooned was to become a real issue that went far beyond the campus. Many of the strongest advocates of *affirmative action,* the term used to denote weighting the balance in favor of the minority applicant, found it increasingly difficult to implement their new policies without exacerbating resistance by those who felt that special treatment, open enrollment, and the establishment of minima were designed only for certain segments of the population—which, for obvious reasons, they were. Even if what some call 'benign quotas" were applied across the board, it was argued that certain groups would have to lose. Many Jews were especially sensitive on this issue. They were overrepresented in university teaching, law and medicine, professions in which not long before they had often been limited by restrictive quotas. (To gain admission to colleges or universities they frequently had to have higher qualifications than other applicants.) They began to fear that in forcing institutions of higher learning to accept at least a minimum percentage of the members of all groups in the overall population, their own numbers would be severely cut. Many saw this trend as racism in reverse.[9] And some brought suit. In the spring of 1973 complaints were filed against several schools and universities.

The most celebrated case at the time was that of Marco DeFunis, a Jewish applicant to the University of Washington Law School who had twice been denied admission and brought suit claiming that his constitutional guarantee of equal protection by law under the Fourteenth Amendment had been violated. DeFunis charged that the law school used racial categories to admit less qualified minority students on a preferential basis. In time his claim was rejected by the highest court in the state but, in many ways, the die had been cast. A similar case, brought by Allan Bakke, a twice-rejected White applicant to the University of California Medical School, eventually made it to the Supreme Court where, in an ambiguous decision, the court ordered Bakke admitted since it appeared that the only grounds for his denial had been racial. Yet it also upheld the use of affirmative action measures in which the race of the applicant was to be one of a number of criteria admission boards might use in recruiting and selecting candidates.[10] Here is what was stated in the brief filed by the Office of the Attorney General of the United States as *amicus curiae* in October 1977.

> The judgment of the Supreme Court of California [which upheld the University's exclusion of Bakke] should be reversed to the extent that it forbids the Medical School to operate any minority-sensitive admissions.

> The remaining question is whether respondent is entitled to admission to the Medical School. We have argued that it is constitutional in making admissions decisions to take race into account in order fairly to compare minority and non-minority applicants, but it is not clear from the record

whether the Medical School's program, as applied to respondent in 1973 and 1974, operated in this matter.

The trial court found, and the University does not contest, that 16 places in the class were reserved for special admittees. The record does not establish, however, how this number was chosen, whether the number was inflexible or was used simply as a measure for assessing the program's operation, and how the number pertains to the objects of the special admission program. . . .

The deficiencies in the evidence and findings—which pertain to both the details of the program and the justifications that support it—may have been caused by the approach both parties, and both courts below, took to this case. They asked only whether it was permissible to make minority-sensitive decisions but that it is necessary to address, as well, questions concerning *how* race was used, and for what reasons. The findings with respect to these latter, critical questions are insufficient to allow the Court to address them.

Accordingly, the judgment of the Supreme Court of California should be vacated to the extent that it orders respondent's admission and the case should be remanded for further appropriate proceedings to address the questions that remain open. In all other respects the judgment should be reversed.[11]

In its arguments the majority made the following points which, to many, served as guidelines for future action:

A. This court has held that minority-sensitive decisions are essential to eliminate the effects of discrimination;
B. Both the legislative and executive branches of the federal government have adopted minority-sensitive programs for the purpose of eliminating the effects of past discrimination;
C. Minority-sensitive relief is not limited to correction of discrimination perpetrated by the institution offering admission; and,
D. Discrimination against minority groups had hindered their participation in the medical profession.[12]

Then stating that "the central issue on judicial review of a minority-sensitive program is whether it is tailored to remedy the effects of past discrimination,"[13] citing numerous cases, the Court concluded:

A. A program is tailored to remedy the effects of past discrimination if it uses race to enhance the fairness of the admissions process; and,
B. There is no adequate alternative to the use of minority-sensitive admissions criteria.[14]

All told, knowledge of racial group affiliation may be a necessary criterion but it cannot be the only one.

Many people followed these cases with considerable interest. Not a few were uneasy about the pressure to right recognized wrongs by accepting a change in the ground rules for "making it" into the university, onto public school faculties, or entering a profession. Many others felt a different sort of pinch. They worried more about jobs and neighborhoods than quotas in college placement, although here too there were White working-class parents who began to ask why their children could not obtain special scholarships to elite schools for which, like many Blacks, Puerto Ricans, Mexican-Americans and other non-Whites, they realized that their children were, as one put it, "equally unqualified" (at least according to traditional criteria).

The problem, as Allan Sindler has pointed out, is partially the differing perspectives (and understandings) of what "affirmative action" or "equal opportunity" means. Sindler summed up the traditional view by asserting:

> The traditional concept of equal opportunity, when applied, say, to jobs, emphasized a fair process of evaluation among the applicants competing to be hired. This involved assessment of applicants on an individual basis by use of nongroup criteria relevant to satisfactory handling of the job in question. The result of such a meritocractic process was the selection of the persons best qualified to do the job, judged in terms of the current performance abilities of the competitors. By definition, a genuinely meritocratic process was fair and, therefore, both guaranteed and defined a fair outcome and equality of opportunity. The elimination of racial discrimination in hiring thus represented a belated purification of the traditional concept, not a challenge to it. Hence both nondiscrimination and government enforcement of nondiscrimination have become comfortably incorporated within the prevailing notion of equal opportunity. . . .[15]

> At least one justification embodied an alternative view of equality. In contrast to the traditional concept, it stressed groups and outcomes, not individuals, and process. If all other things were truly equal, asserted this view, a genuinely fair and meritocratic process would result in roughly the same proportion of nonminorities and minorities gaining the school admissions, the jobs, or whatever the competition. Where disparate group proportions were the outcome, that indicated the existence of unfairness and unequal opportunity for the underrepresented groups, for which the selection process had acted simply as a "pass-through" rather than a corrective: The proper measure of fair process and equal opportunity was, then, proportional group results.[16]

Many poor and working-class Whites were wont to accept the first view, feeling (as suggested earlier) that their failures could be explained as bad luck or not having tried hard enough. Most likely they would not have accepted the second argument. They would doubtless have said that no one had ever given them special treatment just because they were poor even though they, too, knew the meaning and effects of discrimination. [17]

Looking Backward

It is sometimes forgotten that like non-White minorities, Jewish and Catholic ethnics also had to deal with special problems in this society. Many of them were among the wretched refuse Emma Lazarus described in her famous poem "The New Colossus."[18] They were not welcomed with equanimity. Many Americans, far from sympathetic, agreed with the sentiments of Madison Grant who in his racist tract *The Passing of the Great Race* (1916) wrote:

> These new immigrants were no longer exclusively members of the Nordic race as were the earlier ones who came of their own impulse to improve their social conditions. The transportation lines advertised America as a land flowing with milk and honey, and the European governments took the opportunity to unload upon careless, wealthy and hospitable America the sweepings of their jails and asylums. The result was that the new immigration . . . contained a large and increasing number of the weak, the broken and the mentally crippled of all races drawn from the lowest stratum of the Mediterranean basin and the Balkans, together with hordes of the wretched, submerged populations of the Polish Ghettos. Our jails, insane asylums and alms-houses are filled with the human flotsam and the whole tone of American life, social, moral and political has been lowered and vulgarized by them.[19]

Thus the newcomers found that many were hostile to them. They suffered from discrimination, often based on erroneous notions about their mysterious ways or their allegedly undemocratic tendencies. Even after the immigration laws of 1921 and 1924 had closed the "golden door" (largely in response to widespread antiforeign sentiment), the prejudices remained. "Old stock Americans have become restless," announced a Ku Klux Klan pamphlet in 1924. "They are dissatisfied with the denaturalizing forces at work in the country. There is something wrong and the American people know there is something wrong, and they are talking among themselves as to where the trouble is."[20] The tract continued: "They know the arrogant claims of the Papacy to temporal power and that the Romish church is not in sympathy with American ideals and institutions. They know that Rome is in politics, and that she often drives the thin edge of her wedge with a muffled hammer; they have seen the results of her activities in other lands."[21]

Even those who were themselves anathema to the Klan sometimes echoed their anti-Catholic sentiments. The Black educator Booker T. Washington is reported to have considered Sicilian sulfur miners deserving of their fate as human beasts of toil—"They are superstitious Catholics who eat garlic." According to Everett and Helen Hughes, "Mr. Washington passed upon them the judgment of a middle-class American Protestant; quite naturally so, for that is what he was."[22]

We are again reminded that the European immigrants were often victims of discrimination and subjects of prejudicial thoughts and sentiments that set them apart from the "WASPs" and sometimes, as one wag once put it, from certain "BASPs" (Black Anglo-Saxon Protestants) as well. (Of late, White Anglo-Saxon Protestants have found themselves victims of sorts, verbal targets of "ethnics" or, as Irving Lewis Allen suggests, of their intelletual or academic spokesmen who "perceive and perhaps reprove White Protestants as a category.")[23]

On Being an Ethnic

Hegel once said that "the eyes of others are the mirrors in which we learn our identities." A student of mine once put it even more pointedly: "I am," she said, "what others think I am." For many decades the eyes of others looked down not only upon Blacks, Chicanos, and American Indians, but also upon Jews, the Irish, and those other ethnics whom Michael Novak sardonically referred to as "PIGS": Poles, Italians, Greeks, and Slavs.[24]

Novak claimed to speak for many children and grandchildren of Eastern and Southern Europe whose relatives had left the Old Country to seek a better life in the new and often found it. They also found that they were outsiders and, in many ways, were to remain so despite the fervor of their patriotism and their willingness to prove it. They were, to many, "peasants," looked down upon not only by White Protestants who saw them as socially, religiously, even racially inferior, but also by more than a few intellectuals of varying backgrounds themselves who depicted them as unwashed, uneducated, uncouth—in general, culturally inferior.

The legacy of this kind of attitude still lingers, sometimes expressed in far from subtle terms. To Novak and many of those about whom he writes, there is more than a kernel of truth in former vice-president Spiro Agnew's remark about that "effete corps of impudent snobs." The latter are the kind of people about whom Ralph Levine writes:

> Those who appear most willing to sacrifice time and effort in a "good" cause, whatever the cause, prove invariably to be those who can retreat

to upper middle class sanctuary and rejoin the "establishment" whenever the need arises. Such [individuals] seem either unable or unwilling to recognize a simple truth; that people considerably lower (although not the lowest) in the class structure, lack a similar sense of mastery and freedom, but rather are fighting desperately to achieve the sense of economic and social security which these [people] accept as their birthright.[25]

David Riesman summed up this sentiment when he wrote that some intellectuals "espouse a snobbery of topic which makes the interests of the semi-educated wholly alien to them—*more alien than the interests of the lower class."*[26] Riesman's words are italicized here because they underscore one of the main points made by those who look with some skepticism at the seemingly selective sensitivity of some of those intellectuals and pundits who write about America in general and intergroup relations in particular. White as well as Black, they often appear to be unaware of differences in ethnic values, class-based orientations, and political concerns, especially of those who have not so long ago left the ghettos themselves.

While many White ethnics have been more sympathetic to Black aspirations than the controversy over equal opportunities might suggest, they have been primarily concerned with their own survival and success, concerns shared by most other Americans. What other Americans, at least those who lived in middle-class neighborhoods or suburban communities, did not share with many ethnics was the proximity to the Black ghettos, a situation that in time was to place the latter in a difficult doublebind. They often found themselves forced to choose between staying in the changing neighborhood or leaving their "urban villages." They had to face the fact that others in similar situations had become victims themselves in places where old neighborhoods, even stable slums, deteriorated into disaster areas marked by anomie and despair, by internal confusion and pent-up frustration, where the old-timers found themselves ready targets and convenient scapegoats for the newcomers.[27] In corner bars and coffee shops the ethnics remonstrated about "the squeeze," about the insensitivity of the people uptown. They also complained about those whom they saw as threats to their safety and security. But for a long time even what was said was voiced within the confines of the community.

In recent years, however, after decades of public silence, spokespersons for increasing numbers of angry, frightened, frustrated, and seemingly abandoned people have begun to express their feelings. They have done so by supporting conservative candidates for local and national political offices, by organizing neighborhood associations—

which some observers saw as Northern equivalents of White citizens' councils—by playing on the growing resentment others were feeling. Not only did all Americans hear what was being said, they began to read about the sentiments in a spate of articles and books on ethnic Americans.[28]

Common themes ran through many of these writings: the earlier immigrants faced great difficulties and obstacles, but they accepted the challenges and internalized the values of the wider society, values that were often alien to their own heritage. They knew camaraderie with kin and countrymen, their own people who understood them, respected them, and stood by them when others failed to do so. Many had become *more* pridefully Irish, Polish, Italian, or Greek than they had been "back home."[29] They knew what it meant to be helped by others in similar straits and how to use certain public institutions to advantage—especially the schools, political machines, and, eventually, the civil service. But what they also knew, and this is perhaps the most persistent theme, was that one could not ask for special favors because of background or by pleading "special conditions."

It is not surprising that many White ethnics reacted with astonishment at the seeming capitulation to demands by Blacks and other non-Whites for group rights and privileges. "Who in hell do they think they are?" they began to say. "Why can't they be like us?" A growing resolve to get their own share arose. A sense of righteous indignation at being put down by those above them to satisfy the demands from below became more and more apparent and annoying. Many argued that they were loyal, decent, hardworking, God-fearing, and patriotic Americans who had had nothing to do with slavery or segregation but were being forced to pay for the sins of other people's fathers.

The Challenge of the "Unmeltables"

The new situation provided many examples of the feelings of members of White ethnic groups. Let one illustration suffice. In San Francisco a new word entered the glossary of bureaucratic newspeak in the early part of the 1970s—*deselection*. To meet new government guidelines, certain school supervisors were removed from their positions and placed elsewhere in the system, to be replaced by members of "minorities"—such non-Whites as Black-, Mexican-, Japanese-, and Chinese-Americans. In the first month of the program many administrators, all White, were "deselected." The merits of this new system are debatable and one can argue that somebody has to begin to pay. But the furor created is also understandable.

Episodes of this kind encouraged one group after another to assume a position of defensive pluralism in which they began to reassert their old ties, stress their own earlier deprivations, and demand their own hearings and their own affirmative action plans. One of the many results of the ethnic protests was the establishment of campus centers for Irish Studies, Jewish Studies, Polish Studies, and so on. Another was the increased attention paid to ethnic programs on radio and television.

It often led to a gnawing sense of frustration and bitterness among many Americans who had been, at best, only moderately successful and had received no special aid. Many were especially upset by the fact that authorities seemed too willing to buy urban peace at their expense. They grew to resent the "kneejerk" liberal response of those who seemed to love the poor (often at a distance) and champion the underdog but condemn the average White ethnic or middle American for his complacency, his ignorance, his lack of compassion, even for living in a "ticky-tacky" house and liking it; those who proclaimed support for the Blackstone Rangers but had no sympathy for their victims Black or White.[30] They grew equally impatient with the "radical chic" displayed by many celebrities who appeared to kowtow to militants, especially when the latter, in their view, were satisfying their own needs to appear magnanimous at relatively little cost to themselves. The comments of a steelworker, Mike Fitzgerald of Cicero, Illinois, reported by Studs Terkel, are illustrative:

Terkel: Does anger get you, bitterness?

Fitzgerald: No, not really. Somebody has to do it. If my kid ever goes to college, I just want him to realize that when I tell him somebody has to do it, I just want him to have a little bit of respect, to realize that his dad is one of those somebodies. This is why even on [muses]—yes, I guess, sure—on the black think . . . [sighs heavily] I can't really hate the colored fella that's working with me all day. The black intellectual I got no respect for. The white intellectual I got no use for. I got no use for the black militant who's gonna scream about 300 years of slavery to me while I'm busting my back. You know what I mean? I have one answer for that guy: Go see Rockefeller. See Harriman. See the people who've got the money. Don't bother me. We're in the same cotton field. So just don't bug me. . . .

It's very funny. It's always the rich white people who are screaming about racism. They're pretty well safe from the backlash. You even notice it's always: go get the Klansman, go get the Honkies, go get that Polack. But don't touch me, baby, 'cause my name is Prince John Lindsay, Park Avenue, Lake Shore Drive. They're never gonna get at 'em, baby, uh-uh.[31]

People like Mike Fitzgerald feel and express a backlash sentiment most strongly. They are old ethnics who, for a time, had begun to move up and away from seeing themselves solely in terms of their hyphenation. Since such people were often the first to be affected by the new policies, we began to witness a forceful reassertion of ethnicity in many White commuities, even at the expense of class-based allegiances. As Glazer and Moynihan noted:

> Ethnic identities have taken over some of the task of self-definition and in definition by others that occupational identities, particularly working-class identities, have generally played. The status of the worker has been downgraded; as a result, apparently, the status of being an ethnic, a member of an ethnic group, has been upgraded. . . . *Today, it may be better to be an Italian than a worker. Twenty years ago, it was the other way around.*[32]

The New Pluralism

Andrew Greeley has written that "the new consciousness of ethnicity [among White ethnics] is in part based on the fact that the blacks have legitimated cultural pluralism as it has perhaps never been legitimated before."[33] This legitimation has significantly altered a number of other aspects of American life. Not least is the fact that, once again, the issue of assimilation versus pluralism is being hotly debated in universities, journals of opinion, government circles, and, in some communities, in the streets.

There are those like Andrew Greeley and Murray Friedman who, despite certain misgivings, believe that the resurgence of ethnicity is highly functional for our society because, in the end, America must remain what it has always been: a tissue of primordial ties.[34] Some writers, such as Peter Schrag and Michael Novak, go further. They argue that not only will Blacks benefit from their newly found sense of consciousness but so too will White ethnics, those who have suffered far too long under the cultural hegemony of "the WASP Establishment."[35]

Still other observers contend that reality is simply catching up with the dreamers, especially those who see things in class terms. Irving Levine and Judith Herman suggested that there has not been much important change, save for the fact that the strains and divisions that have always existed began to be acknowledged both by social scientists and ethnics themselves.[36]

> In most of the cities where the white working class is ethnic—in the Northeast and Midwest particularly—common origin is reflected in

distinctive neighborhoods. People tend to live near one another according to ethnic background, even "unto the fourth generation." For some, the choice is a conscious one, influenced by the presence of such institutions as the church. For others, the ethnic neighborhood is a convenience, maintaining some features of the extended family, lost (but yearned for) in more heterogeneous neighborhoods.

Even suburbanization has not diminished the intensity of many ethnic neighborhoods. In many cases, what looks like an economics-based blue-collar suburb is in reality a community consisting of several ethnic enclaves. For instance, Long Beach, a Long Island town, has been described as "three worlds," Italian, Black, and Jewish—though to the outsider it may seem a typical lower income surburban community.[37]

Before accepting these views, I should note several disclaimers focused on the sympathy expressed for the tendency to advocate further mobilization or separation along ethnic lines. The first is that alluded to by both Glazer and Moynihan and Levine and Herman—the extent to which ethnicity may become a mask to hide greater differences based on social class.[38] Critics believe that too much attention is being given to ethnic feelings and too little to the sense of alienation of all who are relatively powerless in the context of the larger society. Their position is that fostering ethnicity—of Blacks *or* Whites—serves mainly to keep minorities and poor Whites from uniting into a coalition of opponents to a repressive system. Many Marxists use this class-based coalitional argument. Others do too. Foremost among those who take this stand is the venerable social democrat, civil rights leader Bayard Rustin, who opposes both Black separatism and White ethnic or nationalistic recrudescence. Rustin wants the people to have power and believes that they will not achieve it by putting their special racial or ethnic interests above more basic social and economic needs.[39] [In one sense, this is close to the position of William J. Wilson whose recent book, *The Declining Significance of Race*, puts forth a forceful (and highly controversial) thesis concerning internal responses to the widening gap in Black America. Wilson argues that middle-class Blacks (or those who have crossed the threshold from poverty to affuence or, at least, have steady employment and respectability) often align themselves more with those they seek to emulate than those whose racial identity they share. The Black poor are left behind to fend for themselves or to become putative wards of the welfare state. While Black consciousness may help them, Black separatist ideas may only add to the misery of their plight.[40] Abandoned by their "brothers," they need to identify with those who share their *other* status, their lower-class status.]

The second critique comes from those liberal integrationists who have stood firm against the winds of change and challenged the Black militants and the new pluralists alike, if for somewhat different reasons than those of Bayard Rustin. Most notable is Harold Isaacs who condemns what he sees as a "retribalization."[41] Reviewing Murray Friedman's volume *Overcoming Middle Class Rage*, which seeks to explain backlash politics and ethnic insularity, Isaacs writes: "The two themes—on the Middle American as a harassed man and as an ethnic—are presented . . . as if they harmonize. They are in fact tunes beaten out by separate drummers who march down quite different roads. In effect, the appeal here to the Middle American is to depolarize on social issues and to repolarize ethnically."[42] Referring to the older pluralists, particularly Horace Kallen and Randolph Bourne and their imagery of symphonic harmony, Isaacs warns against too high expectations. Modern symphonies often sound cacophonous: "This [repolarization along ethnic lines] may make beautiful music in the heads of some of these composers, but it has to be played out loud to hear what it actually sounds like."[43] In years to come, Americans will find out how it sounds—and, more important, what the new pluralism will mean.

Notes

1. Seymour Martin Lipset, "Prejudice and Politics in the American Past and Present," in *Prejudice U.S.A.* ed. Charles Y. Glock and Ellen Siegelman (New York: Praeger, 1969): 17-69.
2. See Michael Lewis, *The Culture of Inequality* (Amherst: University of Massachusetts Press, 1978).
3. Wilson Record, "Responses of Sociologists to Black Studies," in *Black Sociologists: Historical and Contemporary Perspectives*, ed. James Blackwell and Merna Janowitz (Chicago: University of Chicago Press, 1974): 368-401.
4. Ibid., p. 381.
5. Ibid., p. 386.
6. Ibid., p. 398.
7. Daniel Boorstin, "Ethnic Proportionalism: The 'E.Q.' and Its Uses," in *The Sociology of the Absurd* (New York: Simon & Schuster, 1970): 25-35. See also Martin Mayer, "Higher Education for All? The Case of Open Admissions," *Commentary 45* (February 1973): 37-47; "An Exchange on Open Admissions," *Commentary* 45 (May 1973): 4-24.
8. Vance Bourjaily, *Confessions of a Spent Youth* (New York: Dial, 1952), esp. "The Fractional Man."
9. See e.g. Pierre van den Berghe, "The Benign Quota: Panacea or Pandora's Box?" *The American Sociologist* 6 (June 1971); Murray N. Rothbard, "The Quota System, in Short, Must Be Repudiated," *Intellectual Digest* (February 1973): 78, 80. See also Earl Raab, "Quotas by Any Other

Name," *Commentary* (January 1972): 41-45; Bart Barnes, "Reverse Bias Alleged in College Hiring," *Washington Post* 5 (March 1973).

10. See Allan P. Sindler, *Bakke, De Funis, and Minority Admissions: The Quest for Equal Opportunity* (New York: Longmans, 1978).
11. *The Regents of the University of California, Petitioner v. Allan Bakke,* Brief for the United States as *Amicus Curiae,* 76-811 October Term, 1977, pp.28-29.
12. Ibid., pp. 30, 33, 38, 41.
13. Ibid., p. 50.
14. Ibid., pp. 55, 63.
15. Sindler, *op.cit.,* p. 12.
16. Ibid., pp. 14-15.
17. See Ralph Levine, "Left Behind in Brooklyn," in *Nation of Nations*, ed. Peter I. Rose (New York: Random House, 1973): 335-46.
18. Emma Lazarus, "the New Colossus," in *Poems* (Boston: Houghton Mifflin, 1889): 202-3.
19. Madison Grant, *The Passing of the Great Race* (New York: Scribner, 1916). Quoted from the 3rd ed., 1944, pp. 88-92, passim.
20. *The Fiery Cross* 8 (February 1924).
21. Ibid.
22. The statement attributed to Washington was made by his friend and associate Robert E. Park. See Everett and Helen Hughes, *Where Peoples Meet* (New York: Free Press, 1952): 10.
23. Irving Lewis Allen, "WASP—From Sociological Concept to Epithet," *Ethnicity* 2 (June 1975): 153-62.
24. Michael Novak, *The Rise of the Unmeltable Ethnics* (New York: Macmillan, 1971).
25. Levine, p. 342.
26. As cited in Novak, p. 149.
27. See Winston Moore, Charles P. Livermore, and George F. Galland, Jr., "Woodlawn: The Zone of Destruction," *The Public Interest* (Winter 1973): 41-59; Norman Podhoretz, "My Negro Problem—and Ours," *Commentary* 35 (February 1963): 93-101; Paul Wilkes, "As the Blacks Move In, the Ethnics Move Out," *New York Times Magazine* 24 (January 1971): 9-11, 48-50, 57.
28. See Ben Halpern, "The Ethnic Revolt," *Midstream* (January 1971): 3-16.
29. Nathan Glazer and Daniel Patrick Moynihan have pointed out that in many ways the American ethnic groups are a new social form having no counterpart anywhere. See *Beyond the Melting pot*, 2nd ed. (Cambridge: M.I.T. University Press, 1970): 16.
30. Michael Lerner, "Respectable Bigotry," *The American Scholar* 38 (Autumn 1969): 606-17.
31. Studs Terkel, "A Steelworker Speaks," *Dissent* (Winter 1972): 12-13.
32. Glazer and Moynihan, pp. xxxiv-xxxv (italics added).
33. Andrew Greeley, *Why Can't They Be Like Us?* (New York: Dutton, 1971): 13-19.
34. Andrew Greeley; Murray Friedman (ed.), *Overcoming Middle Class Rage* (Philadelphia: Westminster, 1971).
35. See Peter Schrag, *Out of Place in America* (New York: Random House, 1970); Michael Novak.

36. Irving M. Levine and Judith Herman, "The Life of White Ethnics," *Dissent* (Winter 1972): 290.

37. Ibid., p. 290. The reference is to Bob Wyrick, "The Three Worlds of Long Beach," *Newsday* 18 (October 1969): 6w.

38. See Dennis H. Wrong, "How Important Is Social Class," *Dissent* (Winter 1972): 278-85.

39. See e.g. Bayard Rustin, " 'Black Power' and Coalition Politics," *Commentary* 42 (September 1966): 35-40; "The Failure of Black Separatism," *Harpers* 240 (January 1970): 25-34. See also Orlando Patterson, *Ethnic Chauvinism: The Reactionary Impulse* (New York: Stein & Day, 1977).

40. William J. Wilson, *The Declining Significance of Race* (Chicago: University of Chicago Press, 1977). For a critique of this view see Charles V. Willie, "The Inclining Significance of Race," *Society* (July-August 1978).

41. Harold Isaacs, "The New Pluralists," *Commentary* 53 (March 1972): 75-79. See also Robert Alter, "A Fever of Ethnicity," *Commentary* 53 (June 1972): 68-73.

42. Ibid., p. 75.

43. Ibid.

8

Blacks and Jews: The Strained Alliance

(1981)

The first Blacks arrived in the American colonies in 1609; the first Jews in 1654. The former were indentured servants; the latter, merchants and professionals. The relative status of those early representatives was, in a sense, prophetic, for regardless of how far some Blacks were to move up the ladder of social mobility in the centuries ahead, Jews generally would be on a higher rung.

Even the Jewish immigrants who arrived between 1880 and 1920, impoverished refugees from czarist pogroms and general economic blight, were still better off than most Black Americans who had been here for more than two centuries. While these new Americans had come from traditional societies where the serfs had only recently been emancipated, they had never been in peonage. Their marginal status, whatever its negative consequences—and there were many—meant that they had learned to care for themselves while having to cope with the others around them. They had survived in part by playing the classic role of the "middleman minority."[1] That was to carry over into this country.

Many Jewish immigrants began their new lives as peddlers and merchants or in the needle trades, struggling to survive and give their families a new lease on life. Despite a variety of obstacles, not least anti-Jewish prejudices and restrictive practices, they worked hard to prove themselves—and improve themselves. By the 1940s , the dramatic mobility of the Jewish segment was beginning to be noticed. Within another decade the Jews were to be rated as the most successful of all ethnic groups in the United States on a variety of measures, including financial attainment, academic achievement, and professional status.[2]

Black Americans had a very different history.[3] They did not choose to come, and their entire existence was shaped by the reason that they did. The mark of their oppression left a bitter legacy. Slavery was

147

replaced by segregation, and still Blacks remained beyond the pale of social acceptance, far down in the stratification hierarchy and outside the mainstream of American political life. Yet owing to the nature of their particular acculturation experiences, they were to internalize many basic American values regarding achievement and mobility. What most Blacks came to want was not very different from what Jews sought—a legitimate place in American society. But coming out of different social worlds, they saw themselves and others—and each other—through very different lenses.

Until fairly recently, most Jews thought Blacks were seeking acceptance via assimilation. Many Black leaders gave credence to such assumptions, arguing that the idea that others should regard them as different was tantamount to racism. To White supporters the key word was "integration."[4] To a marked degree it was used to mean that Blacks should be helped to overcome those traits that signified their cultural deprivation. They should try to become like everyone else.

Jews had long maintained that what they wanted for themselves was the right to be different, to enjoy the pluralistic promise of America. Horace Kallen's metaphor of this society as a symphony orchestra in which each section has its own timbre and tonality was much more to their liking than any ideas of white washed Anglo-conformity.[5]

It is ironic that during the early 1960s when numbers of young Jews began to eschew their hyphenated identity in what some called a process of deracination, Blacks began to undergo a sort of ethnogenesis.[6]

This recognition led to the charting of a different course. Many liberal Jews were among those most alarmed by the increasingly strident assertions of militant Blacks in their ethnosyncratic quest for identity. They seemed unable to understand that what the new Black leaders were after was what Jews already possessed: a chauvinistic sense of their own collective worth, a pride in the uniqueness of their past. Perhaps part of the problem was that, for all their concerns, American Jews knew very little about Blacks.

To most Jews of German and Eastern European background, Black people were a mystery. They knew little about Africa or its cultures, or about the American South.[7] By contrast, Jews had long been an integral part of the Afro-American *Weltanschauung*—not America's Jews or Europe's, but the biblical Jews who followed Moses out of Egypt and into the Promised Land. The widely held sense of affinity with the children of Israel was part of the socialization process Blacks were exposed to in the Protestant parishes of the American South. Evidence of the linkage is abundant, but nowhere is it clearer than in the Negro spirituals and in gospel music. The lyrics reveal a litany of over-Jordan imagery and of deliverance from bondage.

That so much is derived from the fifth book of the Pentateuch is not to say that Blacks have been unaware of the protrayal of Jews in the New Testament, nor that as listeners to evangelical circuit riders or radio crusaders they could have avoided hearing about "the perfidious Jews," "the Christ-killers." Still, Blacks know that like Moses, Jesus was a Jew, and most have difficulty reconciling the wholesale dismissal of his parentage because of the acts of a small group of betrayers. While it has been argued that "if blacks are anti-Semitic, it is because they are Christian," most evidence belies such a claim.[8] One must look elsewhere for roots of whatever Black anti-Semitism exists. One place is the economic nexus where Blacks and Jews have often found themselves in an interdependent relationship since the early decades of this century.

The Old Ghettos and the New

The years 1910 and 1920 bracketed a new phenomenon in American social history: the steadily accelerating northward migration of Blacks. Prior to that period, over 90 percent of Black Americans lived south of the Mason-Dixon line. But in that decade alone Detroit experienced an increase in the Black population of 600 percent; Cleveland, 300 percent; Chicago, 150 percent; and the Black populations of Cincinnati, Philadelphia, and New York doubled.[9] That rapid influx was to change profoundly the pattern of intergroup relations in the country.

Not only did old Americans find themselves confronted with a new reality; new Americans, including Jews, did too. Many Jews learned of Black suffering through the Yiddish press, which began to draw comparisons between their own experiences—as slaves in Egypt, as ghettoized pariahs in the Middle Ages, and as victims of the Spanish Inquisition and of czarist pogroms—and the painful history of Afro-Americans. The diatribes of populists, the rampages of Klansmen, the frightening spectacle of race riots in the Midwest, and the growing nativist sentiment that was at once antiforeign, anti-Semitic, and anti-Black, served to further make Jews aware of the extent to which prejudice abounded in their new Promised Land. Yet while Jews became alerted to the discriminatory treatment of Southern Blacks and began supporting causes to redress their grievances, many Northern Blacks felt the Jews were part of the problem.

For many years, those Jews with whom most Northern Blacks had direct contact were not only a step or more ahead of them—as foremen in garment factories, teachers in public schools, or social workers—but were also apt to be those Whites on whom they had to depend for many goods and services and for housing. The old-law tenements and brownstone apartment buildings into which migrating Blacks moved were often owned by Jews:

> When we were growing up in Harlem our demoralizing series of landlords were Jewish, and we hated them.
>
> The grocer was a Jew, and being in debt to him was very much like being in debt to the company store. . . . We bought our clothes from a Jew and, sometimes, our secondhand shoes, and the pawnbroker was a Jew—perhaps we hated him most of all.[10]

James Baldwin, who wrote those bitter words, has argued that, unlike those he knew personally (good Jews?), those who were so distrusted epitomized for Blacks the evil agents of repressive White society.[11] Still, he and others acknowledged that Blacks did distinguish between "White oppressors" and Jewish ones, between Mr. Charlie and Mr. Goldberg. It was said that if Jews exploited you, they could also be exploited—or at least appealed to for assistance. They were middlemen in more ways than one.

Black folklore has long been filled with jokes and parables that begin: "Once a White man, a Jew, and a Negro. . ."[12] In those stories the leitmotif is that the White man has the real power, he runs the plantation and the society, but on the street it is the Jew who is the clever conniver, always taking advantage of the poor folk who are but innocent victims of the overall system of oppression.[13]

In many ways, the symbiotic relationship of urban Jews to the rural Blacks in their neighborhoods may be described as a kind of Russian Redux with Blacks playing the role of *muzhiks* (Russian peasants) and Jews playing themselves. Milton Himmelfarb once set up the parallel. He explained that in the Old Country the "muzhik was the Jew's external environment and more often than not, his livelihood."[14]

Substitute "urban America" for "the Old Country" and "Blacks" for "muzhiks," and Himmelfarb's description gives a fair reflection of how many American Jews felt about Blacks: "The Jews of the Pale of Settlement thought themselves superior to the muzhiks, feared them, felt guilty about them, pitied them, envied them, and, while distrusting them, wanted to see their lot bettered. The Jews did not hate the muzhiks. In general, we are poor haters—partly, I suppose, because we have had so many enemies that hatred is pointless."[15] Fear, guilt, pity, envy, distrust.

Numerous Jews, poor and working-class, spent their own lives struggling to get out and keep out of poverty, survive in the urban jungle, make something of themselves, and provide their children with a way out. Many made it, but some were left behind.[16] They saw their friends leave, their synagogues close down, and the neighborhoods undergo profound changes. They were troubled at the seeming lack of communal concerns on the part of many who moved in. When they tried to understand when others, including their educated and liberal children, explained that rising crime rates and deteriorating conditions were the legacy of segregation, neglect, and anomie, they would often counter by saying that after all they, too, knew what it meant to be poor, and they had never acted in such a manner.[17]

The accusations of Jewish exploitation, which were to grow even more vituperative in the years ahead, often overshadowed the fact that many upwardly mobile, blue-collar and middle-class Blacks—in the North and in the South—saw Jews rather differently than did those who remained in the underclass of society with little chance of escaping. They, too, knew the folklore. They knew the stereotypes. They knew the shopkeepers. They knew that "Jews are sharp," "Jews are smart," "Jews always help their own." But instead of saying, "That's the trouble with them," the Jews were often seen as models, exemplars of success, as allies in the struggle, even benefactors. As the late Dr. King once suggested:

> Jews progressed because they possessed a tradition of education combined with social and political action. The Jewish family enthroned education and sacrificed to get it. The result was far more than abstract learning. Uniting social action with educational competence, Jews became enormously effective in political life. Those Jews who became lawyers, businessmen, writers, entertainers, union leaders and medical men did not vanish into the pursuits of their trade exclusively. They lived an active life in political circles, learning the techniques and arts of politics.
>
> Nor was it only the rich who were involved in social and political action. Millions of Jews for half a century remained relatively poor, but they were far from passive in social and political areas. . . . Their life raft in the sea of discouragement was social action.[18]

Whose Brother's Keeper?

King was right. Jews had long been involved in social action, not least in the cause of civil rights. Not only did wealthy philanthropists like Jacob Schiff, Felix Warburg, Louis Marshall, and Julius Rosenwald feel a deep commitment to ensuring the rights of all Americans and to giving time, energy, and considerable amounts of money to the cause, but thousands of less affluent Jews contributed as well. The National Association for the Advancement of Colored People (NAACP) and the National Urban League were two of the most prominent Black-oriented civil rights and social service organizations to which Jews gave considerable financial support and in which they worked closely with Blacks.[19] In addition, many Jewish defense agencies, such as the Anti-Defamation Leage of B'nai B'rith, the American Jewish Congress, and the American Jewish Committee, were engaged in attempts to reduce intergroup tension and educate Americans as to the multiethnic character of the country.

From 1910 to the early 1960s, the principal thrust of Black activists and their Jewish allies was to challenge this society to honor its own vaunted ideals. This often meant taking the case to court—if need be, all the way to the Supreme Court. One of the most significant of the groups working toward constitutional justice was the NAACP Legal Defense and Educational Fund, which prepared briefs, planned the strategy, and pleaded cases that eventually were to overturn the famous *Plessy* ruling that had declared the legality of segregation. The staff included Blacks, such as Thurgood Marshall, and also a number of Jews. Its director was a Jewish lawyer, Jack Greenberg. Together they and their colleagues won a number of crucial cases in the struggle for justice, culminating in the *Brown* decision of 1954 in which the Supreme Court unaminously struck down the "separate but equal" doctrine.

The coalition of Black, Jewish, and other White liberal integrationists held sway for over fifty years. Even the Congress of Racial Equality and the Southern Christian Leadership Congress, two organizations that had far fewer Jews in positions of leadership, or as "angels" or staff members, still relied heavily on the support of Jewish activists. And during the periods of the most intensive campaigns in the Southern United States, the late 1950s and early 1960s, reports from the field cited over and over the disproportionate representation of Jews.[20]

Jews were numbered among the freedom riders, the voter registration teams, and those who demonstrated in Washington, Chicago, Birmingham, Selma, and throughout Mississippi. Jews were also prominent on the stage and behind the scenes in the last great display of integrated élan: the 1963 March on Washington. A quarter of a million Black and White Americans gathered on the Mall to hear

Martin Luther King say: "When we let freedom ring . . . we will be able to speed up that day when all of God's children, black men and white men, Jews and Gentiles, Protestants and Catholics, will be able to join hands and sing in the words of that old Negro spiritual, 'Free at last!' "[21]

A Harris poll of 1157 randomly selected Black men and women was conducted in 1963. Upon examination of the data, Celia Heller and Alphonso Pinkney noted that, "In general, the opinion of Negroes on the stand of Jews [regarding civil rights] is more favorable than unfavorable."[22] Jews were more apt to be seen as "helpful" (42 percent) than as "harmful" (9 percent) to the cause. A significant caveat was noted with regard to the helpful/harmful question: almost half (49 percent) of the respondents answered that they were "not sure." Heller and Pinkney suggests that this may not have been a result of the question's being improperly or ambiguously phrased or of the respondents' intentional evasion[23] (a similar "problem" had appeared on other nationwide polls).[24] It was more likely that many Blacks were confused about their own feelings and uncertain as to how they wanted to express this confusion.

In a 1964 study, Gary Marx sought to explore the character of Black anti-Semitism. His analysis was based on interviews conducted with 492 Black adults living in a variety of metropolitan areas outside the South and with 527 others who lived in one of four selected cities: New York, Chicago, Atlanta, and Birmingham.[25] According to answers to stereotype-laden questions, Marx found that the extent of anti-Semitism differed considerably by region. High scorers—those most anti-Semitic—were more common among those living outside the South. In each of the non-Southern subsamples, "roughly three in ten appeared as anti-Semitic, that is, gave an anti-Semitic response to five or more of the nine items compared to less than one in five in the South."[26]

To test the assumption that anti-Semitism among Black Americans was on the increase in the fall of 1964, the period immediately following a long, hot, and violent summer in many cities, Marx asked respondents: "Thinking of Jews as a group—would you say you feel more friendly toward them now than you used to, less friendly, or have you always felt as you do now?" He reported that most said they felt the same. Among that minority who said their attitudes had changed, most indicated thay they were more positive than before. Here regional differences were slight.[27]

Marx's results agreed in large measure with those of Harris, who found that "a large proportion of Negroes perceive Jews as helpful to the cause of Negro rights."[28] But such findings did not rule out the existence of pockets of anti-Jewish feeling in certain sectors of the black community.

> This is especially true of the Negro city slums, such as New York's Harlem and Chicago's Bronzeville, where the tradesmen, rent collectors, and real estate agents tend to be Jews. (As is pointed out in *Black Metropolis,* in New Orleans, where Italian merchants predominated in the Negro slums, Italians were the targets of hate.) . . . And some writers claim that certain black nationalist groups are ready to arouse these antagonisms.[29]

This last statement by Heller and Pinkney proved to be most prescient. Things began to change as race relations entered a new phase when, as I have written elsewhere, the "soulless militancy" of the Black integrationists and the "ethnocentric blackwardness" of the nationalists were finally joined into a potent movement for Black consciousness, Black pride, and Black Power.[30] Among the first to feel the results of the change in outlook and orientation were Jewish members of the various organizations and other Jewish activists. But many other Jews felt it too.

Breaking Ranks

In 1966, Allon Schoener had organized a highly successful exhibition, Portal to America: The Lower East Side, 1870-1925, at the Jewish Museum in New York.[31] In 1968, he was invited to set up a comparable exhibition on Black life at the Metropolitan Museum of New York. *Harlem on My Mind* was equally striking, but it was far from successful. From the start many Blacks were incensed that Schoener, a White man, was given the responsibility for the show. Many Jews were to become infuriated over the text of the introduction to the catalogue, for it was based on a theme written by a 16-year-old Black student.[32] Among other things, it included the following Baldwinian reprieve: "Anti-Jewish feeling is a natural result of Black northern migration."[33]

In fact, many passages in the essay were "borrowed," but not from James Baldwin. They were paraphrases from a book considered at the time to be one of the most definitive assessments of New York City's ethnic groups, *Beyond the Melting Pot,* by Nathan Glazer and Daniel Patrick Moynihan.[34] Even knowledge of the source did not assuage Jewish anger, especially when the paragraph quoted also included the sentence: "One other important factor worth noting is that psychologically Blacks may find that anti-Jewish sentiments place them, for once, within a majority."[35]

The chasm was widening. The rhetoric was sounding increasingly ominous. The polarization was occurring against a backdrop of rapid changes on both the national and international scene. At home it was the Black Power revolt, the growing resentment against the war in Vietnam, and the various counterculture movements that were causing profound alterations in social and political relations. Abroad there were many matters of significance, not least the Six-Day War in Israel. What was predicted in those turbulent days seemed to begin to become true. In 1968 I wrote:

> American Jews, delighted at Israeli victory in the Six-Day War, have evinced much less enthusiasm for their own country's protracted conflict in Southeast Asia and its stalemated war against poverty at home. Other groups in American life share the sense of frustration. In the search for scapegoats that may soon ensue, Jews may find themselves most vulnerable to attack from right, left, and below. By seeking reform and compromise on most issues instead of radical change, they may come increasingly to appear too white for the black militants, too red for the white conservatives, and too yellow for their own children.[36]

Many Blacks did begin to see Jews as too white; many Whites did begin to see them, again, as too red; and for a time, many of their own children saw them as too yellow—or soft. Adult Jews themselves, motivated perhaps by prideful identity with the Davids of Israel who slew the Arab Goliath, began to reassert their sense of Jewishness. But almost as soon as the resurgence of Jewish ethnicity began to take place, the New York school strike occurred: "The 'liberal' establishment of the city—including the Jewish organizations—had supported an experiment in community control of Brooklyn's Ocean Hill-Brownsville school district. Most of the teachers in that school district, like most of the teachers in the rest of the city school system, were Jewish. Most of the community were black. In the fall of 1968, the new community school board fired thirteen teachers, all of them jews."[37]

Things reached a flash point when members of the United Federation of Teachers (UFT) were confronted by local groups and many outsiders who opposed "Jewish hegemony" over the educational establishment.[38] While there were a number of Jews who publicly argued against what they called "the Myth of Black Anti-Semitism,"[39] many others were convinced that they were being used as scapegoats in a larger struggle. Their fear—some called it paranoia—was fed by the anti-

Semitic antilocutions of angry Blacks, expressed over the public airwaves. Statements such as "Hitler didn't make enough lampshades," uttered by 15-year-old Tyrone Wood on Julius Lester's weekly WBAI radio show, typified the sort of diatribe that fed the Jewish backlash.[40]

Lester, whose own views have undergone a profound change in recent years,[41] sought to explain the position of Blacks who were so outraged by the reluctance of the UFT and other bodies to support their demands for control.

> When blacks consistently attacked the political position of the UFT, their response was to accuse blacks of being anti-Semitic and to point to their liberal record on race relations and the fact that Shanker [the Jewish head of the UFT] marched in Selma. Indeed, Jews tend to be a little self-righteous about their liberal record, always jumping to point out that they have been in the forefront of the fight for racial equality. Yes, they have played a prominent role and blacks always thought it was because they believed in certain principles. When they remind us continually of this role, then we realize that they were pitying us and wanted our gratitude, not the realization of the principles of justice and humanity.
>
> Maybe that's where the problem comes now. Jews consider themselves liberal. Blacks consider them paternalistic.[42]

The same sentiments began to be voiced in local meetings of the national organizations. They were deeply felt and reacted to. Many Jews pulled back. Many pulled out. Once gone, they left the civil rights houses divided over the issue of any White involvement.[43] Those militant groups that survived bent their energies and turned their depleted financial resources to ghetto reconstruction, community organization, and the furtherance of strong Black cultural identity. They also gave their approval to struggles already taking place on the college campuses and, to a lesser extent, in the boardrooms—the latter being left to such groups as the still-integrated National Urban League.

The campus revolts of the 1960s involved many issues, but there were two prominent factions—one White, often dominated by Jewish radicals,[44] and one Black. The whole scenario was played out almost as if iconoclast Paul Goodman had written the script. As in his *Growing Up Absurd,* there were the frustrated, upper-middle-class White rebels inside the closed room looking for ways to break out; and there were the frustrated Black militants outside the closed room trying to find ways to get in.[45] Even at the height of the revolt, most Black students when asked, "What do you want?" would reply, "What you've got."

The Blacks' campus campaigns were quite successful. Blacks made demands: more Black students. They received commitments to do more recruiting. They wanted Black studies. Faculties, even those opposed in principle, gave in, and new courses and programs proliferated. They said they needed Black cultural centers. They got them.[46] Soon it was not enough to offer greater opportunities; places had to be guaranteed. The signal words were "open enrollment" and "affirmative action." Their implementation was to further exacerbate the growing rifts between Jews and Blacks.

Open enrollment meant altering, lowering, or removing traditional standards for admission to institutions of higher public education. In New York, the city with the largest Jewish population and one that had long prided itself on the excellence provided in the several branches of the City University of New York, it meant a substantial change, not only in the composition of student bodies, but also in the character of education itself. A great debate raged over the issue, with faculties, many of whose members were Jewish, deeply divided. As in other struggles over what some defined as elitism and others as simply maintaining standards, old faculty members and those in the hard sciences tended to be the most conservative; the younger ones, especially in the social sciences, the most liberal. In the end, the open enrollment policies prevailed, and many "minority students"—the label that came to be used for Blacks and other non-Whites—entered the colleges with minimal qualifications. The record of their achievement was mixed. Opponents, even those willing to concede minor successes, saw the program as an unmitigated disaster for higher education. They felt the city colleges were no longer a place of learning and research, but holding pens for unqualified job seekers. In other cities open enrollment was put into practice, but because their municipal institutions had played different historic roles and had far fewer Jewish students and staff members, the issue seemed somewhat less contentious. Affirmative action was another story.[47]

For Blacks, affirmative action means getting a bigger slice of the pie, a slice more closely proportionate to their percentage in the overall population. For most Jews, who represent a fraction of the general population and who remember not only the Nuremberg laws but the *numerus clausus* used to restrict their numbers in American universities, it means a return to quotas. Statistically overrepresented in the professions and in academia, positions attained by acceptance of meritocratic principles and by hard work often in the face of discriminatory practices, many Jews feared that the supplanting of such individualistic ideas by "group rights" and class actions would harm them more than others.[48]

In the celebrated legal cases of DeFunis and Bakke, both challenging admission policies that favored minorities in what some called "reverse discrimination," several Jewish organizations entered pleas, *amicus curiae*.[49] To many Blacks this was further evidence of the softness of the Jewish commitment to Black advancement; to some it was a clear indication of Jewish duplicity. For such critics, the Jews' pleas that fairness dictated an absolutely open competition was disingenuous. "They of all people should know what it is to be discriminated against." To which "they" replied: "Precisely. Such selective treatment merely plays into the hands of those who would see you (or us) in categorical terms and not as individuals, who will say that the only way you can make it is with special assistance which, ironically, gives credence to the view that you are in fact unable to compete in an open arena."[50] That debate continues. So, too, does one over the most divisive issue of all, the conflict over support for Israel by Jews and, increasingly, for the Arab cause by Blacks.

Choosing Sides

In many ways, this last source of conflict is different from all others. Every issue on which Blacks and Jews disagreed in the past was based on their asymmetrical relationship. For historic reasons, American Jews have generally been in positions of greater control than American Blacks whether as employers, teachers, merchants, landlords, organizers, donors, or academic achievers. But when some prominent Blacks began attacking Israel and offering support to the PLO, Jews were hit with a chilling reality that whatever their motives, some Blacks had seized upon the one issue that could be most damaging to Jewish security.

It was feared that Blacks—including those who maintained their ties and, perhaps, their dependence through thick and thin—were willing to trade traditional Jewish support and patronage for the more powerful economic weapons of their newly found allies, the Arabs, and in doing so, played into the hands of those who, once again, had that old scapegoat, the Jew, to blame. As Candice van Ellison put it: "Our contempt for Jews makes us feel more completely American in sharing a national prejudice."[51] She was writing in another time, about another aspect of the problem, but to Jews the words had and have a frightening ring.

For these reasons so many Jews reacted as they did to the incidents of the summer of 1978 when the ambassador to the United Nations, Andrew Young, admitted to having made unauthorized contact with PLO representative. Nothing seemed destined to raise Jewish ire more than the specter of a sellout of Israel, regardless of how divided they were themselves over Israeli policies, especially with regard to Palestinians. Nothing hurt more than the fact that among the principal movers for a changed policy were members, often viewed as representatives, of the Black community.

The matter of Black support for the Arab cause generated a dialogue not only among Jews, but within the Black community as well. Until recently, most Black leaders had supported Israel while the nationalists and separatists had opposed the state and its policies. For a time, that seemed to be changing. It was infuriating to Jews when they asked: "Why can't you understand *our* vulnerability? Why can't you understand how much we fear that the Arabs will carry out their threat to destroy Israel in another Holocaust?" to be told: "We're tired of hearing of your suffering."[52] It was shocking when such views were expressed by former civil rights leaders who marched with Martin Luther King and were endorsed by men such as Jesse Jackson, Wyatt Tee Walker, and Joseph Lowry, the head of the Southern Christian Leadership Congress. But as it turned out, there was far less unanimity on the issue in the Black community than the Jews and the press were given to believe.

One of the strongest critics and eloquent defenders of Israel—and American Jews—was the Black writer Julius Lester, the same Julius Lester known in the 1960s as one of the most vehement challengers of the Establishment and of the Jews within it.[53] By 1979, he saw things rather differently.

> And so, Jews are being used as scapegoats again.
>
> I cannot interpret otherwise the recent positions taken by black leaders on the Mideast and black-Jewish relations. And I am angered by how self-righteous and arrogant black leaders sounded: "Jews must show more sensitivity and be prepared for more consultation before taking positions contrary to the best interests of the black community."
>
> While I understand that such a statement comes from years of anger at active Jewish opposition to affirmative action, and how deeply blacks were hurt by this opposition to what was in our "best interests," black leadership still seems to be ignorant of the fact that Jews have been hurt by black indifference to the fate of Israel. . . .
>
> Because blacks have been silent while Jews continued to be murdered, I am appalled that they dare come forward now to self-righteously lecture

Jews to "show more sensitivity" when black leadership is guilty of ethnocentric insensitivity. . . .

I am deeply sorry that black leadership spoke as it did, because my humanity as a black person was diminished. The differences and tensions between blacks and Jews are real, but the positions espoused recently by black leaders were not "our Declaration of Independence," as Kenneth Clark put it. They merely showed that blacks, too, can be Germans.[54]

Toward Reconciliation

A number of black commentators thought Lester had gone way too far. Still, stung by such charges, some began to speak out arguing that, of late, too much had been made of the rifts between the two communities and too little of the continuing bonds—and interdependence—and that, regardless of the very real divisions over central issues such as affirmative action and Middle East policies, Blacks and Jews in many areas continued to march to the best of a common drummer. They were partially correct in this defense. Recently Joyce Gelb reported that "attitudinal surveys taken after Young's resignation reflect a Black constituency which had little apparent sympathy with Black leaders' statements on Israel, the PLO, and Young. Replies to the Gallup poll indicated general indifference to Middle East policies, a feeling that relations with the Jews had been and could continue to be friendly, and a denial of the view that Jews were responsible for Young's dismissal."[55]

The results of 175 interviews Gelb conducted in 1976 and 1977 and analyses of subsequent studies indicate that those called "Black spokesmen" were not always speaking for the rank and file. However, even while the debate was raging over issues that divided the groups, there were many signs of continuing cooperation on matters of common concern such as fair housing, school integration, and reduction of intergroup tensions. There continued to be an eagerness to maintain ties between such old allies as the Jewish Defense Agencies, the NAACP, and the National Urban League. Throughout the troubled times these groups continued to work in concert lobbying against federal cuts in social programs and for such matters as continued Medicaid reimbursement for abortions.[56] Such private sector cooperation is more than matched at the congressional level where the formal Black caucus works closely with the informal Jewish caucus, most often voting the same way on issues of *both* foreign and domestic policy.

In a preface to Gelb's report, Irving M. Levine suggests that "the true facts are that the two communities still play powerful roles as mutual beneficiaries of each other's support. There is also a heartening tendency, among leaders of both communities, to move rapidly to stem the worst effects of public controversy."[57]

Hillel's Admonitions

At the present writing there is evidence that efforts are being made to heal the rifts and reopen the dialogues. Some, such as Arthur Hertzberg, see the attempt to forge an alliance between Blacks and the PLO as "a temporary aberration at a moment of anger,"[58] as punishment for Jewish opposition to affirmative action. Such spokespersons urge both Jews and Blacks to ignore the innuendos of separatists and Third World supporters and to get on with the task of reducing interracial conflict in this country. Their words and phrases sound strikingly like those heard just before the Black Power revolt:

> The issue is moral. There are concrete, aching, suffering, trapped, enraged human beings out there, in the ghetto and in the barrios, in the hundreds of thousands. They are not intellectuals who know how to use sociological jargon, to argue and confute. They know, on their own bodies and in the marrow of their bones, that a ruling elite structures the system to protect its privileges, and that the elite must be persuaded—or pressured—to move over.[59]

But the radical sounding phrases are tempered by the standard liberal argument: "Jewish historical experience points to the path in the political spectrum which is occupied by moderate reformers. Their views, and the actions to accompany them, are the true public interest of all America."[60]

Surely they are in the interest of Jews who still believe in the American system and both of its seemingly contradictory credos: strength in diversity through equal protection, and *e pluribus unum*. But they know it because they have made it and must hold their hard-won ground. They succeeded in large measure by standing up for their own beliefs and caring for their own kith and kin. They succeeded because they had internalized not only the promise of the American Dream, but Hillel's admonition: "If I am not for myself, who will be for me?"

Blacks have come to heed the same sentiment. But unlike America's Jews, they have not yet made it. Some Jews still worry that they will continue to look for assistance wherever they can find it. Others, seeing that once again Blacks and Jews are targets of reactionary forces, know that unless there are serious attempts to reason together and reforge the old alliances, both groups will be used by those who have little use for either.[61] Jews know this too. For Hillel also asked: "If I am only for myself, what am I? And if not now, when?"

Notes

1. Edna Bonacich, "A Theory of Middleman Minorities," *American Sociological Review* 38 (Oct. 1973): 583-94. See also Walter P. Zenner, "American Jewry in the Light of Middleman Minority Theories," *Contemporary Jewry* (Spring-Summer 1980): 11-30.
2. See Alice Kessler-Harris and Virginia Yans-McLaughlin, "European Immigrant Groups," in *American Ethnic Groups*, ed. Thomas Sowell (Washington, D.C.: Urban Institute, 1978): 107-37.
3. Harold Cruse, *The Crisis of the Negro Intellectual* (New York: Morrow, 1967): 482.
4. E. Franklin Frazier, *The Negro in the United States* (New York: Macmillan, 1957): 68.
5. Horace Kallen, "Democracy vs. the Melting Pot," *The Nation* (25 February 1915): 220. And see Milton M. Gordon, *Assimilation in American Life* (New York: Oxford University Press, 1964): 88-114.
6. See James Farmer, *Freedom—When?* (New York: Random House, 1965): 87.
7. It should be noted that in Irving Howe's monumental history of New York's Jews there are but few references to the immigrants' images of or contact with Blacks. See Irving Howe, *World of Our Fathers* (New York: Harcourt Brace Jovanovich, 1976).
8. Philip S. Foner once suggested that to some Black leaders the problem was not that Jews were Jewish but "that they had failed to live up to their own principles as exemplified by Moses and the Prophets." See Philip S. Foner, "Black-Jewish relations in the Opening Years of the Twentieth Century," *Phylon* (Winter 1975): 359-67.
9. Hasia R. Diner, *In the Almost Promised Land* (Westport, Conn.: Greenwood, 1977): 15.
10. James Baldwin, *Notes of a Native Son* (Boston: Beacon, 1962): 125.
11. James Baldwin, "Negroes Are Anti-Semitic Because They're Antiwhite," in *Anti-Semitism in America,* ed. Leonard Dinnerstein (New York: Holt, Rinehart, & Winston, 1971): 125-31.
12. C. Eric Lincoln, comment in *Negro and Jew,* ed Shlomo Katz (New York: Macmillan, 1967): 90.
13. See Lawrence Levine, *Black Culture and Black Consciousness* (New York: Oxford University Press, 1977): 306.
14. Milton Himmelfarb, "Jew, Negroes, and Muzhiks," *Commentary* (October 1966): 83-86.
15. Ibid. For a personal account reflecting the tensions discussed by Himmelfarb, see Normal Podhoretz, "My Negro Problem—and Ours," *Commentary* (February 1963): 93-101.
16. See Ralph Levine, "Left Behind in Brooklyn," in *Nation of Nations,* ed. Peter I. Rose (New York: Random House, 1972): 335-46.

17. See Peter I. Rose and Stanley Rothman, "Race and Education in New York," *Race* 6 (October 1964): 108-16. See also Murray Friedman (ed.), *Overcoming Middle-Class Rage* (Philadelphia: Westminister, 1971).

18. Martin Luther King, Jr., *Where Do We Go From Here: Chaos or Community?* (New York: Harper & Row, 1967): 154-55.

19. See B. Joyce Ross, *J. E. Spingarn and the Rise of the NAACP* (New York: Atheneum, 1972); Nancy Weiss, *The National Urban League, 1910-1940* (New York: Oxford University Press, 1974): esp. 53-54; Stephen Birmingham, *Our Crowd* (New York: Harper & Row, 1967).

20. See August Meier and Elliott Rudwick, *CORE: A Study in the Civil Rights Movement, 1942-1968* (New York: Oxford University Press, 1973).

21. Martin Luther King, Jr., "I Have a Dream," *SCLC Newsletter* 12 (September 1963): 8.

22. Celia Stopnicka Heller and Alphonso Pinkney, "The attitudes of Negroes toward Jews," *Social Forces* 43 (March 1965): 364-69.

23. Ibid, pp. 366-67.

24. See "The Nationwide Poll of March, 1959" (New York: Division of Scientific Research, American Jewish Committee, 1959).

25. Gary T. Marx, *Protest and Prejudice* (New York: Harper & Row, 1967).

26. Ibid., pp. 133-34

27. Ibid., p. 135.

28. Heller and Pinkney, p. 369.

29. Ibid. See Louis Lomax, *The Negro Revolt* (New York: Signet, 1963). For a review of studies of Black and White anti-Semitism see Harold E. Quinley and Charles Y. Glock, *Anti-Semitism in America* (New York: Free Press, 1979): esp. 54-72.

30. Peter I. Rose, *They and We,* 3rd ed. (New York: Random House, 1981): 162.

31. Allon Schoener (ed.), *Portal to America: The Lower East Side, 1870-1925* (New York: Holt, Rinehart, & Winston, 1967).

32. Candice van Ellison, "Introduction," in *Harlem on My Mind,* ed. Allon Schoener (New York: Random House, 1968): 2. For a further discussion of the controversy see Lenore E. Berson, *The Negroes and the Jews* (New York: Random House, 1971), esp. "Pictures at an Exhibition."

33. Van Ellison, p. 2.

34. Nathan Glazer and Daniel Patrick Moynihan, *Beyond the Melting Pot* (Cambridge: M.I.T. and Harvard, 1963): 71-73.

35. Van Ellison, p. 2.

36. Peter I. Rose, "The Ghetto and Beyond," in the *The Ghetto and Beyond: Essays on Jewish Life in America,* ed. idem (New York: Random House, 1969): 17.

37. Stephen D. Isaacs, *Jews and American Politics* (Garden City: Doubleday, 1974): 164-65.

38. Herbert J. Gans, "Negro-Jewish Conflict in New York City: A Sociological Evaluation," *Midstream* (March 1969): 3-15.

39. A full-page advertisement titled "How New York's Jews Were Turned against Black Men" appeared in the *New York Times* (16 March 1969): 7E. It was "reprinted as a public service by the Jewish Citizens' Committee for Community Control."

40. For a discussion of the episode see Julius Lester, "A Response," in *Black*

Anti-Semitism and Jewish Racism, ed. Nat Hentoff (New York: Baron, 1970): 229.

41. See Julius Lester, "Affirmations: All God's Children," *Moment* 5 (26 April 1980): 11-14.

42. Lester, pp. 231-32.

43. Berson, pp. 138-45. See also Murray Friedman, "The Jews," in *Through Different Eyes,* ed. Peter I. Rose et al. (New York: Oxford University Press, 1973): esp. 154-61.

44. See Stanley Rothman and Robert Lichter, *The Roots of Radicalism: Jews, Christians, and the New Left* (New York: Oxford University Press, 1982).

45. Paul Goodman, *Growing up Absurd* (New York: Random House, 1960).

46. See Ben Halpern, *Jews and Blacks* (New York: Heider & Heider, 1971): 18-25.

47. See Leo Pfeffer, "Quotas, Compensations, and Open Enrollment," in *The Politics of Confrontation,* ed. Samuel Hendel (New York: Appleton-Century-Crofts, 1971).

48. Nathan Glazer, *Affirmative Discrimination* (New York: Basic Books, 1975). See also Daniel Patrick Moynihan, "The New Radicalism," *Atlantic* (August 1968): 39.

49. See Allan P. Sindler, *Bakke, DeFunis, and Minority Admissions: The Quest for Equal Opportunity* (New York: Longman, 1978).

50. See Bertram H. Gold, "The Bakke Decision," *Civil Rights Digest* (August 1968).

51. Van Ellison, p. 2.

52. Harold Cruse once claimed that American Blacks had little interest in the suffering of European Jews. What was important, he argued, was that Jews had not suffered in America as Blacks had. See Cruse, p. 482.

53. See Julius Lester, *Look Out, Whitey! Black Power's Gon' Get Your Momma* (New York: Dial, 1968).

54. Julius Lester, *The Village Voice* (10 September 1979). For another view, see Amiri Baraka, "Confessions of a Former Anti-Semite," *The Village Voice* (17-24 December 1980): 1, 19-10, 22-23.

55. Joyce Gelb, *Beyond Conflict: Black-Jewish Relations* (New York: Institute in Human Relations of the American Jewish Committee, 1980): 4-5.

56. Ibid., pp. 6-9

57. Irving M. Levine, "Preface," in *Beyond Conflict;* Gelb, p. v. See also "Black-Jewish Relations," *Data Black Survey Results* (January 1980): 2-4. A poll of 1146 Black adults found Black Americans more favorable to Jews than other White ethnic groups.

58. Arthur Hertzberg, "Merit, Affirmative Action, Blacks, and Jews," *Present Tense* (Winter 1980): 28.

59. Ibid.

60. Ibid.

61. See Balfour Brickner, "Am I Still My Brother's Keeper?" *Present Tense* (Summer 1979):64; James Farmer, "On Black-Jewish Tensions," *Open Forum* 3 (February 1980): 4.

Part III
On Ethnic Studies and Other Matters

9

On the Subject of Race:
Thinking, Writing, and Teaching about Racial and Ethnic Relations

(1970)

Throughout human history people have set themselves apart from others, making clear distinctions between those called "we" and those called "they." The ties of kinship, faith, culture, and tradition, and real or imagined racial differences, separately or in combination, have often been responsible for the instigation and perpetuation of conflicts within and between societies; and they have long been recognized as such.

Chroniclers from the days of Babylonian civilization to the modern era have recorded and discussed—sometimes in great detail—patterns of intergroup relations, varying forms of subjugation of both mass subjects and minorities, and different kinds of pluralism: political, cultural, and social. The subject of race relations is very old, antedating by many centuries the emergence of anthropology and sociology, the two modern disciplines that have concentrated on the subject.

Any truly comprehensive review of studies of race would have to go back into antiquity and encompass the works of scholars from every quarter of the globe. Such a survey would help us see the legacy upon which many current ideologies have been built and would indicate the persistence of certain tendencies, not least the ethnocentric proclivities of observers. Recently several historians have attempted to collate this material, and their books offer fascinating background for study.

My concern here is more limited. This review concentrates on modern Western and, particularly, American perspectives and the studies that have been conducted by social scientists who (however they saw themselves) are now considered specialists in the field of race relations. A rather arbitrary point of departure has been chosen: the time when anthropological data began to be systematically accumulated and the word *race* began to have specific biological meaning in the vernacular of several European societies.

Eurocentric Backgrounds

Scientific research on "the races of man" did not begin until the early part of the eighteenth century. Then students of racial differences, whether they viewed Europeans as innately superior to others (as did Bernier, Linnaeus, and Buffon) or leaned toward a more egalitarian stance regarding the potentialities of all peoples (as did Blumenbach), favored the notion that all human types were subdivisions of a single genus, *homo sapiens*. This theory was to be challenged by those who argued that racial differences were attributable to separate origins and that not all men were the direct descendants of Adam and Eve. The foremost zoologists and naturalists of the first half of the nineteenth century tended to follow suit. Louis Agassiz, Samuel G. Morton, and his disciples Josiah C. Nott and George Robin Gliddon were such "polygenesists."

Whether they adhered to a single- or multiorigin doctrine, the number of races these protoanthropologists described most tended to equate biological characteristics with social attributes.[1] This relationship continued even after anthropology became a well-established scientific discipline, namely after 1859.[2]

The year 1859 is selected as the crucial watershed, for it was then that Charles Darwin's *Origin of Species* was first published. Darwinian theory gave legitimacy to the polygenesists' views, and many took the superordinate status of "Whites" as evidence of the fact that the fittest survive and that the aggressive, not the meek, inherit the Earth. While eschewing mere observation and description for the more sophisticated mechanical techniques of measuring racial differences, most anthropologists of the late nineteenth century concurred that their findings revealed the inferiority of non-Caucasians and continued to link biological and social evolution.

Following Paul Broca, the French anthropologist and founder in 1859 of the Anthropological Society of Paris, many agreed that the differences separating human groups were primordial. They argued that "Since racial differences find their expression in opinions and behavior, the brain has something to do with race and the measured shape of the skull is the best way to get at the contents of the brain."[3] Elaborating on earlier techniques, a variety of cephalic indices were devised to aid in the classification process. In time, other methods of dividing humankind "scientifically" were used. By combining certain skull types, hair textures, nasal forms, skin colors, and the like, general groupings were suggested—not, it seems, unlike those three- or four- or fivefold paradigms proposed for two centuries.

Inevitably, even such arbitrary pigeonholing proved difficult to justify, especially when it came to "placing" such people as the brown-skinned, straight-nosed inhabitants of India or the black-skinned but hairy Australian aborigines. Some opted for a sixfold classification; others for a tenfold one; and so on.[4] Although not all scientists agreed, many continued to claim that "colored" people were degenerate, simple-minded, untamed, and uncivilized. "Scientific racism" was used to justify the slave system in the United States and to support the exploits of colonialists as they continued to bear the White man's burden in distant lands, especially Africa.[5]

Anthropological and Sociological Perspectives

Gradually some began to seriously question the position of the "scientific racists." They moved toward conceding that "racial groups" are most properly defined simply as statistical aggregates of persons who share a composite of genetically transmissible physical traits. Eventually for most, the concept was to be clearly distinguished—both semantically and empirically—from such ideas as language, nationality, personality, and culture.[6] This particular change of attitude did not come about overnight. Some anthropologists, like many other observers of the passing scene, were confounded by indigent people of Southern and Central Europe who were moving across the continent and migrating to the United States in ever increasing numbers. Many wondered, especially in this country, whether the motley array of poor immigrants could ever be adapted to the American scene. Not a few contended that they did not have the makings of *real* Americans.

Franz Boas, the most important ethnologist after Edward B. Tylor, emphatically disagreed with the latter view. His perceptive scholarship here and abroad was chiefly responsible for the new departure in the study of races and nationality groups. In *The Mind of Primitive Man* (1911) and subsequent publications, Boas dismissed the hypothesis that race determines ability and performance. He and his students denied that culture was determined by biology and helped to dispel widely held beliefs about racial groups—that they are temperamentally different, that there are racial cultures or such things as racial moralities, that some races are biologically and intellectually superior to others.[7] Research findings tended to invert the assumed relationship, and Boas argued that even physical attributes (such as size and head form) might well be influenced by the social and cultural environment: "Heredity may explain a part of the pronounced mental similarities between parents and children; but this explanation cannot be transferred to explain on hereditary grounds the similarity of behavior of entire nations in which the most varied lines occur. These assume their characteristic forms under the pressure of society."[8]

Today many anthropologists continue to follow the general course set forth by Boas shortly after the turn of the century. In 1961, the Fellows of the American Anthropological Association reaffirmed the Boas statement: "All races possess the abilities needed to participate fully in the democratic way of life and in modern technological civilization." In one way this forceful statement denied the discreditors the notion that those categorized as members of a given racial group (such as the far from "pure" American Blacks) are innately inferior. In another sense it begged several questions that remain scientifically legitimate. As Theodosius Dobzhansky, coauthor of the well-known *Heredity, Race, and Society* (1952) and *Mankind Evolving* (1962), has written: "Faced with a revival of 'scientific' racism one is tempted to treat the matter with the silent scorn it so richly deserves. . . . [Yet] it may perhaps be useful to add a warning against exaggerations which some writers bent on combating racism are unwittingly making."[9] Specifically: "The contention of racists is that cultural achievements of different races are so obviously unlike, their genetic capacities for achievement are just as different. It is, however, a matter of elementary genetics that the capacities of individuals, populations, or races cannot be discovered until they are given an equality of opportunity to demonstrate these capacities."[10]

Putting it in somewhat different terms, Manning Nash makes a similar point: "The scientifically responsible student of race is at a distinct disadvantage in trying to confront the propositions on racial inferiority. He is in the unenviable position of trying to defend the null hypothesis."[11] Nash goes on to suggest that an elementary distinction is needed between the study of race (the pursuit of knowledge about phenomena) and the study of the "ideology of race."

Lately we have begun to see significant strides in the direction of clarifying these elusive distinctions. The discussion of race in the new edition of the *International Encyclopedia of the Social Sciences* is a good case in point. While stating that "raciological (biological) explanations of sociocultural differences and similarities have attracted the support of a large and not infrequently preponderant scientific consensus," Marvin Harris indicates that "the term *race,* or its various ethnosemantic glosses, is applied in vernacular contexts to human populations organized along an astonishing variety of principles."[12]

> Nation-states, such as the Irish, Japanese, or German; tribes such as the Scythian, Iroquois, Zulu; language families such as Slavic, Latin, Semitic; minorities such as Jews, gypsies, Puerto Ricans; and phenotypically distinct but genetically hybrid aggregates such as whites, Negroes, yellow, and Coloureds are cognitively equivalent in many ethnosemantic contexts. Social scientists have tried to diminish intergroup conflict by exposing the disparity between biologically acceptable definitions of race and those which are entertained at the popular level. Since none of the folk usages is informed by valid genetic principles, the lack of correspondence between social race and biological race should occasion no surprise. Social races encompass both phenotypically similar and phenotypically dissimilar populations; actual gene frequencies, the ultimate goal of infraspecies systematics, are obviously not desiderata in folk taxonomies. The cognitive substratum by which so many disparate aggregates are united cannot therefore be regarded as racial in the biological sense. . . . In distinguishing socially defined races, therefore, attention must be directed toward common sociocultural rather than common biological features.[13]

Elaborating further, Harris says:

> Social races are composed of subjectively significant groups, unrestricted by age and sex criteria, in which membership is sociocentric (i.e. appears the same to all egos), is established at birth, endures for life, and confers special behavioral obligations or privileges. Social races differ from other stratified groups (such as classes with low rates of out-mobility) in their methods of maintaining membership and group identity. Social races accomplish this by a special ideological device, the idea of descent. Although the members of a social race are replaced during each generation, the group maintains a continuing identity through varied applications of descent rules.[14]

The Dutch sociologist Harry Hoetink also argues that social scientists would do well to search for a concept that is the sociophychological complement of the biological term *race*. He suggests (and uses) the phrase *somatic norm image* defined as "the complex of physical (somatic) characteristics which are accepted by a group as its norm ideal." In a somewhat similar vein, the British anthropologist Michael Banton argues that norms are indeed critical and that, at bottom, "race is a role sign."[15]

So-called Negro Americans represent a social race influenced by a specific somatic norm image that requires the playing of particular roles. In one sense they are persons who are said to possess certain phenotypic traits that cause others to lump them together. Such a grouping exceeds the limits of apparent physical similarity, for many who are "mostly White" are called "Negroes" and relegated to a particular position in the status hierarchy of American society. Deemed inferior, they are expected to play particular subordinate (or at times specialized) roles. In turn, the categorical ascription to those called "Negroes" of an inferior or differential place has served to unite an amorphous aggregate into what has begun to take on the characteristics of a community. There are more than conceptual connections between personal attributes, cultural norms, and the patterns of social relationships.

Rather than dwell on the matter of racial similarities and differences (still of central concern to physical anthropologists) or on the reconstruction and description of the minutiae of life in small, nonliterate folk societies, increasing number of social anthropologists are turning their attention to the comparative investigation of intragroup and intergroup conflicts and tensions. With certain social historians (such as Oscar Handlin, John Hope Franklin, Frank Tannenbaum, Stanley Elkins, David Brion Davis, Eugene Genovese, Herbert Guttman, and Winthrop Jordan), they are beginning to explore the relation of racial and ethnic minorities to the wider social systems in which they are located and the cultural traditions that underlie patterns of race relations. The works of Melville Herskovits, Robert Redfield, and more recently, Marvin Harris, Charles Wagley, and Gerald D. Berreman are among the best representations of this orientation in the United States.

Recently, comparative anthropologists, historians, and sociologists concerned with race relations have found themselves cooperating in a variety of ways and using very similar frames of reference. Such was rarely the case in the past. Unlike anthropology, American sociology was, at least in the beginning, only partly an extension of the European tradition. Of the many reasons for this, two stand out as particularly significant. First, in contrast to their European counterparts, most American sociologists lacked both a historical and a comparative perspective. This is not to say that Europeans were not ethnocentric. They were (and many did reflect current prejudices). Still, macrosocial forces were their uppermost concern, and the comparison of various social systems in time and space was a principal *modus operandi*.

American sociologists, by contrast, were mainly interested in *endemic* problems. Meliorism played a major role in the work and thought of early American sociologists. With some exceptions, they were imbued with the spirit of the social gospel and possessed by a faith in progressive social change. In America, "Applied Sociology" became a fact of academic life before Lester Ward gave it a name. Most of America's early sociologists (including all but a few of the first twenty-four presidents of the American Sociological Society, founded in 1905) came from clerical families and from rural backgrounds which, according to some commentators, led to an antiurban stance in much of their work and to a special concern with the problems of city living.[16] Whether or not the allegation is correct, there is little doubt that a concern about "social disorganization" played a significant role in shaping the course of sociological inquiry from the turn of the century into the Depression years. At that time, the pendulum swung from Chicago to the Eastern seaboard and sociologists turned away, at least for a time, from a problem orientation.

The most influential of the early sociologists, insofar as the study of race and race relations is concerned, did not represent the major trend. William Graham Sumner abhorred the reforming bent of his colleagues. At Yale University, where he taught the first sociology courses in America, he inveighed against sociologists engaging in humanitarian activities, raising their voices against the privations of certain segments of the population or advocating social legislation. On the last point, Sumner once claimed the "stateways cannot change folkways," a statement still used by those arguing against the position that morality can be legislated.

Despite this view, some of Sumner's basic writing has had a profound effect on the understanding of racial and ethnic relations. Particularly influential are his classic distinction between in-groups and out-groups (the former providing its members with a sense of superiority in relation to the latter) and his now-famous definition of ethnocentrism, "the technical name for this view of things in which one's own group is the center of everything, and all others are sealed and voted with reference to it."[17]

In discussing the concept of mores, Sumner made the seminal observation that "modern scholars have made a mistake of attributing to race much which belongs to the ethos."[18] Although a social Darwinist, he was not entrapped by the rhetoric of the racists. Claiming that social behavior and attitudes (including group antipathies) are learned, not inherited, he (as well as such contemporary anthropologists as Franz Boas) signaled a decided shift regarding the relationship between race and culture, which, as will be shown, grew more pronounced in ensuing decades.[19]

Others contributed to the growing literature on race *relations*. W.I. Thomas, for example, wrote one of the first essays on "The Psychology of Race Prejudice."[20] He recognized the extent to which ethnocentrism played a role in the perpetuation of in-group solidarity and out-group antipathy and said that "in race prejudice we see the . . . tendency to exalt the self and the group at the expense of outsiders."[21] (Somewhat later, Sigmund Freud was to write that "in the undisguised antipathies and aversions which people feel toward strangers with whom they have to do we may recognize the expression of self-love— of narcissism.")[22]

Most sociologists of the period were interested in the social and cultural conflicts they saw around them, most noticeably in the collision of values, interests, and lifestyles of the native-born and the newcomers from Europe. In this particular sense, they were comparative. Their work reflected that they were also wrapped up in their own culture-bound prejudices. Eugenicists like E.A. Ross warned the Darwinists that the "fittest" were not surviving,[23] and went so far as to express fears over the consequences of unlimited immigration, which threatened to pollute the American blood. Franklin Giddings shared these views as did Thomas N. Carver, Jeremiah Jenks, and other prominent social scientists of the day. They gave academic legitimacy and at times aid and support to the activities of the Immigration Restriction League and similar organizations.

Although he would never go along with the tirades of the eugenicists or support restrictive immigration, even Robert E. Park, who was to become the guiding force behind the empirical study of racial and ethnic relations in this country, believed for a time that "it is evident that there is in race prejudice as distinguished from class and caste prejudice, an *instinctive* factor based on the fear of the unfamiliar and uncomprehended."[24] Park was to modify his position and eventually to say that "race consciousness . . . is to be regarded *like* class or caste consciousness, that enforces social distance."[25] His emphasis (like that of Sumner) was now on the fact that, while group antagonisms do exist, they are a result of social and cultural conflicts and tensions and not innate aversions. As such, they could be modified.

Sociocultural Theories of Intergroup Relations

The apparent shift in Park's thinking characterized or perhaps symbolized the changes taking place in the sociological treatment of race. There was a shift from a stress on the biological aspects of human differences, heavily influenced by the early physical anthropologists, to a sociocultural frame of reference. Sociologists became particularly interested in the study of the social rather than biological histories of various peoples to explain character and modes of behavior. Later on, a third change was to become evident. Sociologists turned attention to the effects of intergroup contact and the nature of relationships between those who differed from one another because of their cultural backgrounds.[26]

These changes did not come about abruptly. An examination of sociology textbooks most widely read during the early part of this century bears witness to the confusion regarding the bases of group differences, the meaning of social experiences, and especially the use of such basic terms as *race* and *nationality*.[27] Donald Young addressed himself to the last issue in particular and sought to deal with the semantic confusion once and for all. In 1932, in one of the first major texts to deal exclusively with the sociology of intergroup relations in the United States, Young wrote: "There is, unfortunately, no work in the English language which can with philological propriety be applied to all these groups which are distinguished by biological features, alike national traits, or a combination of both."[28] He suggested using the term *minority*. Some years later, Louis Wirth spelled out the new concept in detail:

> We may define a minority as a group of people who, because of their physical or cultural characteristics, are singled out from the others in the society in which they live for differential and unequal treatment, and who therefore regard themselves as objects of collective discrimination. The existence of a minority in a society implies the existence of a corresponding dominant group enjoying higher social status and greater privileges. Minority status carries with it the exclusion from full participation in the life of the society. Though not necessarily an alien group, the minority is treated and regards itself as a people apart.[29]

Stressing both internal characteristics and the relation to the wider social milieu, Wirth continued:

> A minority must be distinguishable from the dominant group by physical or cultural marks. In the absence of such identifying characteristics it blends into the rest of the population in the course of time. . . .
>
> Minorities objectively occupy a disadvantageous position in society. As contrasted with the dominant group they are debarred from certain opportunities—economic, social, political. . . .
>
> The members of minority groups are held in lower esteem and may even be objects of contempt, hatred, ridicule, and violence. . . .
>
> They are generally socially isolated and frequently spatially segregated. . . .
>
> They suffer from more than the ordinary amount of social and economic insecurity.[30]

Because of these attributes, "minorities tend to develop a set of attitudes, forms of behavior, and other subject characteristics which tend further to set them apart."[31]

Emphasis on dominant group/minority relations finally brought the question of whether groups are superior or inferior to their position in the minds of others and to their treatment by others—together with their own response patterns. Wirth was greatly concerned about the deleterious effect of placement in inferior status of particular ethnic groups. Still he and others, such as E.K. Francis, stressed the fact that most ethnic groups, including many of the so-called minorities, frequently shared a positive sense of unity or "we-feeling," an ideology (however vague and unreflective), and an interdependence of fate (whether based on religious, political, cultural, or racial characteristics). Ethnic group ties were seen as being maintained as long as individuals felt bound to the community—a community dependent as much on the idea of communality as on actual proximity; a community one could feel if not touch.[32] The Jews are a classic case in point.[33]

Wirth was among the many sociologists who worked with Robert E. Park at the University of Chicago in the halcyon days of empirical sociology. Beginning with the founding of America's first department of sociology by Albion Small in 1893, led to eminence by Robert Park, Chicago was for many years the center for sociological training in the United States. There, under the tutelage of Park and Ernest W. Burgess, a number of important studies of social structure and community organization were conducted—studies that described, sometimes in intimate detail, the experiences of immigrants, life in the ghettos, the social and economic gap between the "gold coast" and the slum, and examinations of the "other side" of urban existence.

"As sociological study approached the status of scientific procedure," wrote E.B. Reuter, "its emphasis shifted from the description of social structure to the study of social processes."[34] He continued: "The interest in differences was replaced by an interest in uniformities; the interest in traits, whether inherited or acquired, whether biological or cultural, gave way to an interest in relationships. Social traits were seen to form and change in the experience of living together."[35] This change in emphasis was abundantly clear in the work of the Chicago sociologists. In early as 1926, Park had suggested that "in relations of races there is a cycle of events which tends everywhere to repeat itself."[36] The process involved the coming into contact of different groups, a period of competition followed by a détente (accommodation), and ultimately, assimilation or amalgamation.

In time others proposed their own "race relations" cycles; more recently, some have sharply criticized the use of such rigidly mechanistic models.[37] Yet Park's sequential paradigm represented a new departure in the theoretical study of intergroup relations and stimulated new research into the similarities of groups undergoing the strain of confrontation and adaptation to new situations. Not least important were the studies on marginal man first conducted by Everett V. Stonequist and those of social distance by Emory S. Bogardus—both stimulated by the pioneering work of Park.[38] Stonequist and Bogardus, each in his own way, symbolize what may best be described as a bifurcation of directions in race relations research. One was essentially sociological, the other sociopsychological. Though there was to be much overlapping, the former followed the trend of emphasizing the behavior of peoples in varied social situations; the latter stressed attitudes and the behavior of individuals.

From the late 1930s on, studies on the nature of prejudice (considered as "a negative social attitude") and of the "prejudiced personality" paralleled those on intergroup relations. Although psychologists concerned themselves with cognitive, affective, and conative dimensions of prejudice and individual responses to certain social situations, while sociologists concentrated on group processes, the two trends were never entirely divorced from one another. Many of the most important studies in the field as well as most postwar texts illustrate this interdependence. Among the former are John Dollard's *Caste and Class in a Southern town* (1937), Gunnar Myrdal's *An American Dilemma* (1944), Bruno Bettelheim and Morris Janowitz's *The Dynamics of Prejudice* (1950), Melvin M. Tumin's *Desegregation* (1958), Robin M. Williams's *Strangers Next Door* (1964), Kenneth B. Clark's *Dark Ghetto* (1965), Gary T. Marx's *Protest and Prejudice* (1967), and Elliot Liebow's *Tally's Corner* (1967).[39] Each deals partly or exclusively with the Black in comparison to other groups in America as seen from outside and within the dark ghetto or rural sector. Each stresses both the social structure in which intergroup relations occur as well as attitudes and behavioral responses. Taken together they illustrate what Richard Schermerhorn has called the major thought patterns of American specialists: preoccupation with problems of prejudice and discrimination; the depiction of minorities or ethnic groups solely in the role of victims; and progress in research primarily concerned with updating previous studies.

Courses and Research on Race and Race Relations

The first courses in the United States concerned solely with "races and nationalities" were offered at the University of Chicago in the late 1920s. One of the most significant was an interdisciplinary seminar in which sociologists, economists, historians, and political scientists took part. Robert Park, Louis Wirth, Robert Redfield, and Herbert Blumer were the organizers. Members of other departments reported on multiracial and multiethnic societies in various parts of the world. During this same period, Louis Wirth began teaching "American Minorities" and helped organize the American Council on Race Relations, on which he served as chief officer. Hughes, Wirth, and their colleagues developed the Committee on Research and Training in Race Relations, one of the first of its kind anywhere. In summarizing the days when the subject of race relations was first regarded as a distinct field for undergraduates to study (in contrast to being an area only for scholarly research), two themes were evident. One was the place of minorities in this country—"Negroes and the various groups who came later." The other was the broadly conceived comparative study of race relations. "Park," says Hughes, "spoke of it as the study of the expansion of Europe."[40]

In a short time the first theme became action-oriented and focused on attempts to reduce intergroup conflicts, interesting social workers as well as sociologists. Summarizing the trend, Wirth noted the change "from the earlier preoccupation with the study of differential traits and capacities of various racial and cultural components of the human family to the present dominant interest in the processes of interaction between racial and cultural groups and in the development of effective methods for understanding and dealing with the problems of racial and cultural relations."[41] Yet, perhaps understandably, he underplayed the fact that preoccupation with the bases for prejudice and attempts to reduce the malaise of those with minority status portended a narrowing perception of intergroup relations, which for a time led to a somewhat myopic concern with America's racial and ethnic problems. Elaborating on the latter point, Everett and Helen Hughes wrote in 1952 (two years after Wirth's commentary was published):

> It is an odd thing to say, but a true one, that many of the people who are now studying racial and ethnic relations are doing so from an ethnocentric point of view. This is true sometimes in one, sometimes in both of the following senses: they show little or no interest in the contacts of people outside the United States, or at most do not get beyond North America. Moreover, they look at cultural and racial relations almost entirely from the point of view of what have come to be called minorities; often, indeed, from the point of view of some particular minority. . . . It is not the special interest of one, but the exclusion of the others from view that makes the point of view ethnocentric.[42]

The comparative approach, by contrast, was far more sophisticated. Attempts were made to examine examples of groups both in harmony and in conflict from various societies and cultures and to develop theories of race relations. It captured the imagination of some sociologists as well as political scientists and anthropologists. Yet it never seemed to have the same appeal as did the problem-oriented, parochial, and seemingly more immediate subject of American minorities, at least not until the postwar period and the time when the study of cultural change and of new nations came into vogue. The dominant and subordinate themes are most apparent in synopses of research and texts on race relations and in course outlines. There have been numerous attempts to review research in this field.[43] In addition, many post–World War II textbooks and "readers" have developed the findings of researchers and have provided certain guidelines for students concerned with the general topic.[44]

With rare exceptions, most books written or compiled by these social scientists have been concerned with the American scene. A nationwide study of the focus of over eight hundred courses in race relations taught in American colleges and universities conducted in the mid-1960s indicated a major emphasis on America's problems.[45] It was found that most courses, like many textbooks used in them, are highly eclectic overviews rather than theoretical explorations of basic social structural issues. Although they are marked by an aura of scientific objectivity, the courses (and many textbooks) seemed to be infused with a sense of moral indignation.[46] Discrimination is seen as a stain on the fabric of American society which, as one respondent put it, "must be understood, then eradicated."

Few can fault the passion expressed by most who teach these courses. Few can disagree with their desire to improve the character and quality of life in the United States. Yet, as Tamotsu Shibutani and Kian W. Kwan have written:

> Ironically, one of the major barriers to a better comprehension of these phenomena is the indignation of the investigators. Social scientists are human beings, and their emotional reactions to the injustices they see make difficult the cultivation of a detached standpoint. Men who are angry often look for a responsible agent to blame, and this search for culprits often vitiates research. . . . When difficulties are preceived in moral terms, there is a tendency to explain events by imputing vicious motives to those who are held responsible. Furthermore, moral indignation often blinds the student to many facts that would otherwise be obvious. All too often deeds regarded as reprehensible are assumed to be fundamentally different from those that are approved, and the moral dichotomy often prevents one from recognizing that both may be manifestations of the same social process. John Dewey once wrote that the greatest single obstacle to the development of the social sciences was the tendency to approach human problems in terms of moral blame and

approbation, and in no field is this more true than in the study of inter-ethnic contacts.[47]

This problem of "the limits of conscience" has inhibited much meaningful assessment of the nature and course of racial and ethnic relations. Fortunately such American writers as Shibutani, Kwan, Hughes, and Tumin, and such Europeans as J.S. Furnivall, Harry Hoetink, and Michael Banton have begun to speak out against the deleterious effects of these limits. Yet few have heeded their admonitions. Having avoided the pitfalls of early racist doctrines to which some of their predecessors subscribed, and having overcome the tendency to oversimplify complex social relationships by taking the view that "the folkways make everything right," they have not been able to come to terms with the liberal rhetoric that has become so much a part of the sociology of race relations. (Hoetink calls this "the sociologistic vision," especially pronounced in America.) As a result, the same platitudes about "good guys" and "bad guys" circumscribe many approaches to intergroup problems and underlie the majority of courses currently being taught (and texts being written) on the subject of race and race relations. Too many continue to reflect the writing and ethnocentricity mentioned by Hughes over fifteen years ago.

Ethnic Stratification

Tamotsu Shibutani and Kian Kwan are among a small number of American sociologists who have attempted to offer an alternative to that bias. Their work is very much in the tradition of Robert E. Park, Everett and Helen Hughes, and Herbert Blumer. Like Park and his colleagues, Shibutani and Kwan feel that race relations should be viewed not as social problems but as social phenomena that exist *wherever* ethnic groups meet. In their text *Ethnic Stratification: A Comparative Approach* (1965), Shibutani and Kwan set forth "to formulate generalizations concerning the characteristics of various social processes and the conditions under which they occur, regardless of where they happen."[48] The bulk of the volume is devoted to an elaboration of the social processes themselves: "differentiating processes" (how color lines come into existence); "sustaining processes" (including patterns of adjustment and accommodation); "disjunctive processes" (dealing with tension and conflict, political tactics, and the consolidation of power); and "integrative processes" (concerned with such matters as acculturation and assimilation). *Ethnic Stratification* contains a far more comprehensive (and up-to-date) treatment of these subjects than was to be found in any single text available for classroom use when it was published. It also offered an antidote to those who sought an alternative to the many books whose object seemed to be "resolving social conflicts." Nowhere is this more evident than in Shibutani and Kwan's discussion of the loaded term *prejudice*. Though offering no direct substitute, they present an elaborate discussion of "Popular Conceptions of Ethnic Identity,"[49] dealing with such issues as categorization, stereotyping, and ethnocentricism. Emphasis is placed on the relative positions of groups in the stratification of different societies and on the differential meaning of subordinate status. "As incredible as it may seem to most Americans," they write, "systems of ethnic stratification are upheld for long periods by the willing support and cooperation of the people who are being subjugated."[50] Extensive examples and "natural histories" drawn from the world literature on interethnic contacts lend some (but not conclusive) support to such generalizations. The volume ends with a tightly knit theory of ethnic stratification in which the authors, a social psychologist and a sociologist, assert:

> The population in most communities is heterogeneous, the people being divided along class, religious, and ethnic lines. . . .
>
> The relationship between such groups varies; it may be one of coexistence, stratification, or sustained opposition. . . .
>
> Those who occupy the same habitat . . . sooner or later become involved in a common web of life, in most cases they participate in common economy.
>
> Ethnic stratification is one aspect of community organization, individuals are placed in a hierarchical order, not in terms of their personal attributes but in terms of their supposed ancestry. [Here we note similarities to Harris's notion of "social races."][51]

Having defined an ethnic group as "people who conceive of themselves as being alike by virtue of common ancestry, real or fictitious, and are so regarded by others,"[52] Shibutani and Kwan go on to say that "where a color line develops the fate of an individual depends upon the manner in which he is classified. The color line is a particular type of social structure."[53] Since social structures are viewed here as patterns of concerted action, "ethnic stratification persists as long as people on both sides of the color line approach one another with common expectations of how each is to act in the presence of the other. The color lines consist of a set of conventional norms. Where there is a high degree of consensus, violations of norms elicit emotional reactions, deviating acts appear immoral, perhaps even unnatural."[54]

The consensus of which they speak is built up through a "communicative process" in which perspectives are shaped and reaffirmed through a succession of culturally relevant gestural interchanges. (Although they do not refer to him, Shibutani and Kwan's ideas are very close to those expressed by Edward T. Hall in his book *The Silent Language,* in which he describes "primary message systems."[55] Thus acculturation is seen as determined by the ease with which subordinates can communicate with those who are dominant, both in the political arena and in all phases of social life.

Institutionalized segregation may be effectively used to block communication channels, isolating dominant groups from subordinates and resulting in the development or continuation of separate "cultures." Thus efficient communication is viewed as an "inverse function of social distance."[56] Rather tautologically Shibutani and Kwan then assert that "as members of minority groups become acculturated, they become more like those in the dominant group and attempt to identify with them."[57] Here one might ask whether identification or even heightened aspiration is necessarily the path to domestic tranquility. The evidence in this country is not conclusive. Closing the cultural gap does not necessarily close the social one. Moreover, competition for scarce resources or limited rewards by those who have grown closer to the dominant group in terms of desires and goals may exacerbate tensions and cause the reinstitution of ethnic or racial barriers. Although Shibutani and Kwan are aware of these possibilities, they tend to handle them in a manner reminiscent of the previously mentioned period of social Darwinian sociology. They write that "if values are in short supply, individuals compete for them and *new patterns of concerted action emerge initially through natural selection.*"[58]

As it is developed the argument becomes Parkian as well as Darwinian: when competition is intensified, it is transformed into rivalry or conflict that becomes fixed and eventually institutionalized. Shibutani and Kwan have come full circle. While denying their intention to offer another cyclical theory, they exhibit a proclivity for doing precisely *that* time and again. The argument develops as follows: most societies are hierarchical and many are heterogeneous. In those that are both, ethnicity is a critical variable. Shutting out those who differ intensifies separatism; opening the door increases communication and may alter traditional norms on the part of the subordinate minority in favor of those of the "host" society. A demand follows for a greater share in power, which often results in a backlash that throws the minority back on itself and reasserts the hierarchical, heterogeneous character of the society.

No society that goes through such a process—and American society is, in a sense, going through it today with regard to its Black popula-tion—is *ever* truly the same again. Theoretically, the circle may close (as in the case of any self-fulfilling prophecy), but in real terms there is no "cycle of events that repeats itself everywhere," as Robert Park[59] and, to some extent, Shibutani and Kwan would have us believe. (If one wants to use a simile here, a spiral would come closer than a circle.)

Despite disagreements over certain critical assumptions, I think the Shibutani and Kwan volume is a significant addition to the literature and an important text. Not only does it offer a refreshing perspective; it also provides a rich compendium of information obtained from the authors' perusal of the available literature in related fields, a source of comparative data that has hardly been tapped by sociologists: the studies of social anthropologists, economists, and area specialists. As for American sociologists who have done their own field work abroad, one recent commentator has claimed that "by the 1960s . . . they could almost be counted on the fingers of two hands!"[60]

A brief digression is in order here. Since World War II a number of economists and political scientists concerned with development began to study nation building and to search for common patterns in societies undergoing reorganization. In many ways their work was far more sophisticated than that of the problem-oriented "race relationists." They turned to basic sociological categories and began to substitute such concepts as "political system" for "state," "functions" for "powers," "roles" for "offices," and to rely on the premises of functional analysis.[61]

Despite its breakthrough quality, particularly in working out ways of understanding the relationship between the anatomy and physiology of political life, it tended to avoid, overlook, or underplay the significance of the race factor as a critical variable in the comparative study of social change and international relations. As for the few sociologists and anthropologists who have worked on this race factor, Richard Schermerhorn has suggested that five approaches seem to dominate the field.

The first is the gathering of new data with little attention to theory. Some of the early descriptive work published by the Institute of Race Relations in London is an example. The second involves the theoreti-cal interpretation of new data. Three examples are Robert E. Park's posthumous *Race and Culture* (1949), Everett and Helen Hughes's *Where People Meet* (1952), and the recently published book by Harry Hoetink, *The Two Variants on Caribbean Race Relations* (1967). The third approach centers on organizing vast quantities of data collected by taxonomic means. Three well-known volumes characterize this orientation: Alain Locke and Berhard J. Stern, *When Peoples Meet* (1942); P.A.F. Walter, *Race and Culture Relations* (1952); and Brewton Berry, *Race and Ethnic Relations* (1958).

Shibutani and Kwan's volume is a good example of the fourth approach: the attempt to pull together vast quantities of collected data by means of a unified or a specially constructed theory. Hubert Blalock's *Toward a Theory of Minority Group Relations* (1967) illustrates the latter. Finally, there is a very limited series of comparative case studies dealing with particular societies and utilizing the same theoretical framework for each. One of the first books using this approach is Charles Wagley and Marvin Harris, *Minorities in the New World* (1958). A more recent example is Pierre van den Berghe's *Race and Racism* (1967).[62]

Paternalistic and Competitive Models

Van den Berghe's book is the most sophisticated of the last-mentioned examples. In it the author reviews dominant trends in the study of race relations, many of which have already been touched on in previous discussion, and then explicates several key concepts, particularly race and racism. Offering an operational definition similar to that suggested by Marvin Harris, van den Berghe writes: "We consistently use the term race . . . to refer to a group that is socially defined but on the basis of physical criteria."[63] To avoid confusion with the layman's usage, he would call groups sharing certain cultural characteristics, such as a language or religion, ethnic groups or ethnicities. The important difference is that, like races, ethnic groups are socially defined; but their definition is based primarily on cultural rather than physical criteria.[64]

In this view racism is defined as "any set of beliefs that organic, genetically transmitted differences (whether real or imagined) between human groups are intrinsically associated with the presence or the absence of certain socially relevant abilities or characteristics, hence that such differences are a legitimate basis of invidious distinctions between groups socially defined as races."[65] Although such racism is to be found in all eras of human history and in various parts of the world, van den Berghe focuses on Western racism and racial stratification. The latter is said to result from one or more of the following conditions: military conquest (in which the victor establishes his political and economic domination over an indigenous group, such as the European powers in tropical Africa); gradual frontier expansion (in which one group pushes back, overruns, or exterminates the native population, such as European expansion in North America and Australia); involuntary migration (such as the capture and transportation of African slaves into the United States, Brazil, and the West Indies); and voluntary migration (in which alien groups move into new lands seeking political protection or economic opportunities, such as the old European and recent Puerto Rican, Mexican, and Cuban migrations to the U.S. mainland).[66]

Western racism is a fairly widespread phenomenon with definite historic and cultural roots. Of special importance is (or was) its congruence with certain prevailing forms of economic exploitation (including slavery in the New World and colonial expansion there and elsewhere).[67] (Debate still continues over the question of pre–eighteenth-century racism. I would contend that racism, even as defined by van den Berghe, is a much older phenomenon.)

In any case, van den Berghe is correct when he points to the fact that Darwinism gave legitimacy to the ideology of racial superiority, particularly for those who had taken up the White man's burden. He has an interesting addendum to this point:

> The egalitarian and libertarian ideas of the enlightenment spread by the American and French Revolutions . . . paradoxically contributed to [racism's] development. Faced with the blatant contradiction between the treatment of slaves and colonial peoples and the official rhetoric of freedom of equality, Europeans and white North Americans began to dichotomize humanity between men and submen (or the "civilized" and the "savages").[68]

> The scope of applicability of the egalitarian ideals was restricted to "the people," that is, the whites, and there resulted what I have called *"Herrenvolk* democracies,"—regimes such as those of the United States or South Africa that are democratic for the master race but tyrannical for the subordinate groups.[69]

According to van den Berghe, *Herrenvolk* democracies are apt to be more highly developed economically and socially more complex. In Karl Mannheim's terms, they would be more democratic than aristocratic in spite of obvious disparities (often explained in social Darwinist terms).[70]

Attempting to go beyond the traditional theories that rarely seem able to relate race relations to the total society, van den Berghe offers his own paradigm. To avoid the pitfalls of the past, he seeks to provide a system of classification which meets the criteria of comparative applicability, historical usability, specification of variables, and integration (meaning the integration of the specific syndrome of race relations within the rest of the social structure). Pointing out that one frequently finds similarities in *social structural relations* which transcend cultural differences (such as the plantation systems in North and Latin America), van den Berghe states:

> If two societies with widely different cultural traditions can more or less independently develop similar racial situations and institutions, if, conversely, the history of a given country can be marked by profound changes and discontinuities, and, furthermore, if abrupt qualitative changes in race relations can be shown to coincide with structural changes in the society at large, it is reasonable to accept that basic aspects of the social structure exert a considerable degree of determination on the prevailing type of race relations.[71]

He then presents two ideal types: the traditional master/servant pattern of paternalism and the modern competitive one. A series of schematic outlines illustrate the independent, dependent, and social-control variables associated with such polarity.[72]

Van den Berghe also introduces (or reintroduces) the concept of pluralism. His usage differs from the Tocquevillian—and Riesman-esque—view of a variety of competing interest groups each with some sort of veto power (political pluralism) and from the widely used sociological notion of cultural pluralism.[73] To him, as to J.S. Furnivall, J.H. Boeke, and M.G. Smith,[74] the defining criteria of a plural society are institutional duplication *and* cleavage between corporate groups. In theory, "social pluralism . . . is present in pure form to the extent that a society is structurally compartmentalized into analogous and duplicatory but culturally alike sets of institutions, and into corporate groups which are differentiated on a basis other than culture." In practice, social pluralism sometimes goes hand in hand with cultural pluralism because racial groups as previously defined often learn to share certain common values and beliefs and form subcultures of their own. Van den Berghe calls this "secondary cultural pluralism," arising from structural pluralism.[75] Again, one thinks of the situation of enslaved Black Africans who became Negro Americans and are now developing a new Afro-American or Black American ethnicity.[76] Still, recognizing the persistence in this country of social separation and cultural assimilation for many American minorities (like the Irish, Poles, and Jews), theoretical distinction remains relevant for empirical purposes. This is further evident in *Race and Racism*.

Van den Berghe uses case studies of four segmented or plural societies—Mexico, Brazil, the United States, and the Union of South

Africa—each of which is the product of a historically unique set of factors resulting from the colonial expansion of Europe after the late fifteenth century.[77] He examines similarities and differences between them on such dimensions as the respective degree of acculturation, the role of religion, the character of indigenous social organizations, the fate of the local population, the extensiveness of miscegenation, the presence of slaves, demographic and economic features, the major cleavages and dimensions of intergroup conflict, and the attitudes of those in dominant positions. The body of his book is concerned with these comparisons but, since this is only tangential to our immediate theoretical interests, I will only summarize his general findings:

> The system of race relations developed in the pre-modern phase of the four societies examined showed great similarities despite great differences in the cultures of both dominant and subordinate groups. In all instances a typically paternalistic system united in symbiotic interdependence a servile or quasi-servile labor force . . . the stereotypes of subordinate groups were similar . . . the dominant group rationalized its position by virtue of cultural and racial superiority. . . .

> The paternalistic regimes were all characterized by two social processes . . . physical intermixture or miscegenation . . . [and] the extensive and relatively rapid assimilation of the subject groups to the culture of the dominant group. . . .

> [Differences are apparent in] the contrasting role of Catholicism and Protestantism. . . .

> Another "generalizable difference" between the four cases concerns the nature of the indigenous cultures which the conquerors encountered. . . .

> In all four cases the paternalistic systemof race and ethnic relations was undermined by a series of changes in the social infra-structure. In the political sphere aristocratic, colonial, or white settler regimes became transformed into "representative" governments with wider participation in the polity, though in South Africa and until recently in the United States the democratic process was still restricted to the dominant racial caste.[78]

One last summarizing point must be added, the one that links van den Berghe's findings to his overall theory and relates back to the paternalism-competition axis. It is his statement that

> even these *Herrenvolk* democracies are clearly different from the colonial government or the planter slave-owning oligarchy which preceded them, if only because they were legitimized in terms of an ideology that could be effectively used to challenge the racial status quo. Thus these *Herrenvolk* democracies contained the ideological seeds of their own destruction, providing the educated elite within the oppressed groups

and the progressive minority of the dominant group with a set of values to deny legitimacy to the established order.[79]

As noted, "race" and "racism" are perceived in different ways by the members of various disciplines.

> To the physical anthropologist "race" in the genetic sense is a case of subspeciation in *homo sapiens*; to a social psychologist racism is a special instance of prejudice; for the philosopher racism is a particular body of ideas; the political scientist may regard racism as a special kind of political ideology; to an economist race is one of the "nonrational" factors, influencing, to be sure, economic behavior but falling outside the scope of his discipline; a historican may look at race and racism as by-products of, and rationalizations for, Western slavery and colonial expansion; a cultural anthropologist may regard race and racism as traits in the cultural inventory of a people.[80]

Sociologists, according to van den Berghe, should limit themselves to seeing these phenomena as special instances of *structural* or *social* pluralism. Whether one agrees with so narrow a view or not, it is significant to note that van den Berghe, perhaps better than anyone else, indicates that "cultural and social pluralism are not simply two facets of the same reality." He continues: "Since race is a more rigid basis of cleavage than ethnicity, social pluralism can subsist longer and, indeed, even in the nearly total absence of cultural pluralism, whereras the converse is not true."[81] This is why several sociologists have attempted to draw clear distinctions between racial and ethnic groups even in the study of American society.[82]

When one uses the concept of social pluralism, four levels of society must be examined: groups, institutions, individuals, and values. Boundaries are significant in the first instance; duplication in the second. (It is said that "institutional pluralism is the opposite of functional differentiation." Thus a segregated school system is pluralistic; an alternative one is not.) At the individual level, mobility through both structural and cultural space is most relevant. Finally, at the value level, consensus or its absence is crucial (for instance, "freedom does not mean the same to most whites and to most Negroes in the United States").[83]

Value consensus is often considered the critical level and key to social stability, at least by those concerned with the study of whole societies. A problem arises when societies are not homogeneous but socially pluralistic. What, then, is the basis of social integration? Some would claim that pluralistic societies are in constant turmoil and always lacking in integration, although the evidence belies such a claim. Van den Berghe and others believe that many pluralistic societies are held together by a combination of political coercion and economic interdependence (he suggests that neither alone is sufficient to maintain stability).[84]

Here van den Berghe has touched on a critical theoretical debate of particular relevance for those wishing to apply sociological perspectives to the study of intergroup relations. I refer to the controversy over functionalism versus conflict theory. Despite an impressive amount of research in race relations (particularly within the United States), there has been a dearth of theory. Race relations was not particularly important to the founding fathers of sociology; few wrote much on it as a subject per se, and few modern theoreticians have shown much interest in it either.[85]

I have already indicated the biases of most American sociologists who have worked in the area of racial and ethnic relations and have stressed the ideological character of their concern, the pragmatic approach to data gathering, and the melioristic orientation by which they hope to save society or its victims. One fact alluded to previously (in a passing reference to a swing of the sociological pendulum from Chicago to the East), is the bias of many theorists, at least since the mid-1930s. Imbued with a structural-functional orientation that emphasizes stasis and system maintenance through the acceptance of certain values by society's members, it was difficult to cope with race relations, which are contentious almost by definition (at least the definitions most popularly used). Michael Banton pursues this point in a brief review of race relations theory (or its lack). He suggests that "by its very nature this [structural-functional] approach is not well suited to the study of circumstances in which two societies interact or in which social patterns are maintained by force rather than agreement."[86]

Some alternatives have been offered. One is Ralf Dahrendorf's thesis as presented in *Class and Class Conflict in Industrial Society* (1959), which begins with a very different basic assumption from that of Talcott Parsons and other functionalists. To them, "integration" means largely what A.R. Radcliffe-Brown (and Emile Durkheim before him) had contended. Social behavior and the institutions of society are seen in terms of the functioning of the social system (the individual being "adjusted" if he accepts his place, "deviant" if he does not). To Dahrendorf this is only one view. Another is the "coercion thesis," the argument that society is held together by various constraints.

Banton illustrates the dual perspectives of consensus and coercion rather cleverly in the following example:

> It may be useful to view the attitudes of miners towards work underground in terms of coercion theory: they work because they have to, not

because they want to. At the same time, it may be more profitable to view their leisure behavior in the welfare centre from the standpoint of the consensus theory, highlighting their common outlook and values concerning matters outside the employment situation.[87]

Though it may seem obvious that, in the case of the study of race relations, there is no alternative but to use the coercion approach, Banton says that "no sociologist has linked up race relations studies to the intellectual tradition behind the coercion theory, permitting the lessons learned in this long controversy to be applied to the racial field."[88] No one, that is, except Pierre van den Berghe and Richard Schermerhorn (two men of whose most recent work Banton seems unaware).

Conflict and Consensus: The Critical Dialectic

For many years Schermerhorn, the author of *These Our People* (1949) and *Society and Power* (1961), has been concerned with the strains in plural societies and the relative position of members. An early inclination to favor what has been called "the conflict approach" gave way to a less dogmatic view. In a paper entitled "Polarity in the Approach to Comparative Research in Ethnic Relations," published in 1967, Schermerhorn asserted that "the task of intergroup research is to account for modes of integration-conflict (as dependent variables) in the relationships between dominant groups and subordinate ethnic groups in different societies."[89] As for independent variables, he suggests two that are "most promising": (1) the degree of enclosure in the subordinate ethnic group[90] as measured by such indices as endogamy, ecological concentration, institutional duplication, associational clustering, and the like; and (2) the control of scarce values by dominant groups.[91] In addition, the direction of "movement" toward or away from one another by those who hold and those who lack power is "the contextual feature" and, as an intervening variable, must also be taken into account.

His idea may be graphically presented as in Diagram 9.1.[92] *A, B, C,* and *D* are various patterns of intergroup relations. The first two represent situations where there is agreement regarding the maintenance of stability (though in one case it is through togetherness and in the other through institutionalized separation), and the latter two indicate situations where there is a collision between the desires of the separate parties toward their respective positions and lifestyles.

The important point is Schermerhorn's graphic portrayal of the necessity to consider both systemic and relational matters (the whole-

Diagram 9.1   Congruent and Incongruent Orientations toward Centripetal and Centrifugal Directional Movement by Superordinate and Subordinate Groups

	A		B	
Superordinates	Cp		Cf	Tending toward
Subordinates	Cp		Cf	Integration
	Assimilation		Cultural Pluralism	
	Amalgamation		Federalism	
	C		D	
Superordinates	Cf		Cp	Tending toward
Subordinates	Cp		Cf	Conflict
	Forced segregation		Forced assimilation	
	with resistance		with resistance	

Cp - centripetal
Cf - centrifugal

to-part "functionalist" orientation and the part-to-whole "conflict" orientation) at least when considering intergroup relations at a macro-sociological level. This concern with a "dual perspective" is one of the main issues discussed by Schermerhorn in his latest work, *Comparative Ethnic Relations*.[93]

A central question of comparative research in ethnic relations is: What are the conditions that foster or prevent the integration of ethnic groups into their environing societies? Here integration is not seen as an end state (as would be the "integration" of Blacks in the United States), but as "a process whereby units or elements of a society are brought into an active and coordinated compliance with the ongoing activities and objectives of the dominant group in that society." Again, integration and conflict are viewed as dependent variables subject to a variety of social and historical factors.

To the question—How are societies as wholes maintained by their constituent elements?—those following the Durkheimian tradition would tend to say:

> Societies as wholes can survive as "going concerns" only if fundamental needs are met. These needs, usually called functional imperatives or functional requisites . . . include such items as provisions for physiological functioning and survival, reproduction and replacement, shared goals and perspectives, socialization, communication, organization of roles, control and regulation of deviance, and general regularization of activities in patterned forms . . . if these needs are to be met reliably and predictably, they must be supported by structures, i.e. by uniformities of action that recur when called for by the situation. Here generic princi-

ples must become specified into determinant patterns and organizations and institutions.

Whatever character societies assume, they must be, according to functional theory, mutually supportive to maintain stability.

Two other principles of functional analysis are relevant here as well. One is that of hierarchy, or what some would call "the functional basis for stratification."[94] The other is the principle of symmetry. The latter is best illustrated by such Parsonian terms as complementarity, boundary maintenance, mutuality of role expectations, pattern consistency, and the like.

Robin M. Williams, a functional theorist in his own right, sums up the approach in the following statement, also quoted by Schermerhorn: "Even with all its careful disclaimers and qualifications, the [structural-functional] scheme does have the net effect, for many readers, of emphasizing stability, and, by omission, understating the problem of radical discontinuities and rapid, massive, and violent conflicts and changes in social systems with sub-systems."[95]

Schermerhorn asks whether it is possible that some functional requirements may contradict others. Although the answer is affirmative, he does not conclude that one should dispense with the concept of system altogether. Rather, it "means that any use of system analysis must be more flexible, relativisitic, and circumspect, alert at the same time to inductive and categorical difficulties." One factor that Schermerhorn feels has inhibited greater flexibility is "the excessive dependence on cultural factors to carry the explanatory load." Here he is referring to the tendency of Parsonians to be "ends-oriented," stressing norms and values rather than means, especially scarce means. "If we are to take systems analysis seriously," Schermerhorn claims, "it must encompass the structures of both ends and means."[96]

Continuing along this line of reasoning, he asserts that those who study social systems must bear in mind the admonition of Georg Simmel that "contradiction and conflict not only precede unity but are operative in it at every moment of its existence."[97] They must do, in part, what the conflict theorists do—look at the other side and, in Lenski's words, see social systems "as stages on which struggles for power and privilege take place."[98]

What Schermerhorn calls "power-conflict theory" would seem, in the face of it, far better suited to the study of racial and ethnic relations. In a way it is:

> Beginning with the immediate experience of limited social encounters, the power-conflict theory stresses the obvious fact of inequality in most

interactions, i.e. that what one has, the other wants, what one wants, the other has. . . . What divides the two contenders is the inherent scarcity of means. The attempt to control these means leads directly to open or concealed conflict in which the exertion of power is needed to attain the goal. Such encounters occur at all levels of society and between all sorts of concrete groupings like nations, political parties, regional associations, ethnic groups, labor vs. management, rural vs. urban sectors, and the like.[99]

But this angle of vision is also seen as limiting. A better approach is to view system analysis and power-conflict theory as dialectically related perspectives, at least with regard to ethnic relations. Keeping in mind the typology referred to earlier, in which there is a graphic if limited portrayal of this dialectic, Schermerhorn's thesis may be summarized as follows:

1. Comparative study requires a view of ethnic groups in a macrosociologial perspective, i.e. in their relation to total societies [a point made forcefully by van den Berghe and discussed above]. . . .

2. In observing these relations one should be aware of the two main theoretical interpretations of total societies given by the system analysts and the power-conflict theorists (Talcott Parsons and Marion Levy representing the former; Gerhard Lenski and, to a lesser extent, Ralf Dahrendorf representing the latter).

   a. Applying system analysis to comparative ethnic relations actually centers attention on the function the ethnic group performs for the entire system, viewing the ethnic group itself as a sub-system gradually fitted into the wider society by a series of adaptive adjustments regulated by the norms and values of its institutions that eventually become internalized by members of the ethnic groups involved.

   b. From the standpoint of power-conflict theory, one can view each ethnic group as being in an embattled position, fighting for its life, its identity, or its prestige, subject to perpetual constraints that threaten its survival, its freedom, or its life chances in a precarious world.

3. Actually, neither perspective can exclude the other without unwarranted dogmatism. As Robin Williams has stated, "all interacting human populations show both coerced and voluntary conformity."

4. The problem is, at bottom, an empirical one. It is important, therefore, to search out, by inductive inquiry, observation, and analysis the meaning of williams' proposition (as well as A.R. Radcliffe-Brown's statement that "opposition, i.e. organized and regulated antagonism, is . . . an essential feature of every social system"). No field of inquiry is better fitted to exemplifying the dual relevance of such ostensibly clashing theoretical perspectives than the sphere of ethnic relations.[100]

Evident throughout the remainder of Schermerhorn's study is inter-play between the two dominant perspectives. For example, in a chapter on "Some Unexplored Types of Integration," he considers the problems of legitimation, cultural congruence, and goal definitions from the point of view of those holding power and attempting to maintain a particular system and of those who are subordinates (minor-ities as well as mass subjects). I will dwell only on the last problem.

Here the question is, in part—how do minority group members see themselves in relation to others and what are they prepared to do about this conception? Louis Wirth had outlined policies adopted by minority group members. His famous paradigm suggested these alternatives: assimilation, pluralism, secessionism, and militance.[101] I have also addressed attention to this problem and to certain choices offered to indicate various responses to discrimination in the United States. My own typology (Diagram 9.2, originally published in 1964) was based on responses to two theoretical questions: Does the subordinate accept or reject the dominant group's image of his group's inferiority? Regard-less of the answer to the first question—is he willing to play (or even desirous of playing) a segregated role?[102]

Diagram 9.2   Dominant Image of Subordinates' "Inferior Status"

	Dominant Image of Subordinates' "Inferior Status"	
	Accepted	Rejected
Segregated role?		
Yes	Submission	Separation
No	Withdrawal	Integration

Although this typology goes somewhat farther than Wirth's, it has, in Schermerhorn's terms, the same inherent problem. It emphasizes only the attitudes and behavior of the subordinates and *assumes* discrimination on the part of the dominant group. Its utility is limited to the specific cultural context for which it was designed, namely the United States.

Schermerhorn points out that such typologies tend to examine only one side of the transaction. It is essential to consider what dominant groups want the subordinates to attain. Here he reintroduces the idea of centripetal and centrifugal tendencies and offers a slightly revised version of the typology presented in his earlier paper and referred to above.[103]

Schermerhorn goes on to discuss many other matters tangential to the problem of "the *development* of race studies." Included here are other "typologies of problem relevance," classification schemes that divide societies into "multinational sectors" or along a continuum according to the dominance of either the polity of the economy (as "Pol-Ec Societies" or "Ec-Pol Societies"), discussions of cross-sectional research on plural societies in which he illustrates attempts at rapprochement between diachronic and synchronic approaches,[104] and more. These latter chapters are richly illustrated with data drawn from a wide variety of empirical reports on ethnic relations in various parts of the world.

Propositions and Possibilities

Often during the early days of research in this field, American sociologists (and others) followed the lead of physical anthropologists. They deduced that if dark-skinned people were backward in technological and "moral" matters while white-skinned people were more advanced and civilized, there must be some connection between the color of their skin and their ability to perform complicated tasks (including that of governing themselves). Somewhat later, with the advent of cultural anthropology and particularly with the "Boasian challenge," there came a growing concern with the impact of society on its members and vice versa. (Many sociologists first became involved because of their worries about the effects newcomers were having on American society).

In time more and more sociologists became concerned with the victims of discrimination and the causes of prejudice. Research on minority communities and on the attitudes of members of dominant groups began in earnest. The findings tended to corroborate the view that racism was pervasive and that discrimination was damaging to those marked by oppression. Some propositional inventories began to appear and, though limited to a single society, there was some discussion of "a theory of intergroup relations." Robin M. Williams's SSRC Bulletin, *The Reduction of Intergroup* (1947), is the best example of this approach. Such inventories were useful indicators of endemic problems and were guidelines for action. They were also helpful sources for those who wish to compare American racial attitudes and, to a lesser extent, behavior with that in other societies.

More typical of sociologists who ventured, literally and figuratively, beyond America's borders to make comparative studies of racial and ethnic relations are those who have set forth inductive typologies for measuring their findings. Using the conceptual and methodological tools of their discipline, they have begun to fashion models of inter-group relations offering what Richard Schermerhorn calls "scaffolding for subsequent theory." Perhaps the most significant point is that sociologists like Shibutani and Kwan, van den Berghe, and Schermerhorn are beginning to fight against the main currents of a discipline where practitioners often seem better and better equipped to learn more and more about less and less. This is a significant movement away from microanalysis and a return, in many ways, to macrosociology.

Before leaving this matter of "direction" one last caveat must be stated. Macrosociology (at least in the realm of ethnic studies) is becoming fashionable among rather different groups of sociologists. First, there are those who eschewing what is seen as nothing more than quantophrenia, they want to get at the "broader issues," the subjective aspects of human relations, to make their contributions more effective.

Then there are those who advocate a New Sociology (sometimes called "underdog sociology"). They are quite explicit in their answer to the question—"Which side are you on?" Such sociologists feel that many of their colleagues (especially the sort just cited) are agents, or at the least, naive collaborators of the "welfare-warfare establishment" and contributors to the continued exploitation of those with whom they wish to align themselves: the poor, the sick, the downtrodden in every part of the globe. Finally, there are those who are less concerned with debates over quantitative versus qualitative study, over involvement versus detachment. Their goal is expanding the horizons of knowledge.

Such sociologists are primarily interested in describing and explaining the reasons for differential patterns of race relations. They are only secondarily concerned with the policy implications of such patterns. This is as it must be if honest appraisal is to mean anything. Their work should be an important complement rather than a substitute for policy studies and for the cross-national research of political scientists, social psychologists, and anthropologists such as Almond and Verba, Buchanan and Cantril, Stein Rokkan and his colleagues, Beatrice Whiting, Campbell and LeVine.

At bottom, comparative sociologists are addressing themselves to a basic question about research in race relations: whether one can eventually come up with a grand theory replete with postulates of relevance to all (or most) contingencies. This is a large order, but a goal worth pursuing. We need such theorizing. Of course, this is not all that is needed. There are many other problems—and challenges—facing sociologists and other social scientists concerned with both theoretical and applied race studies. I would suggest that particular attention be paid to the following:

1. Further examination of the functions and dysfunctions of racial categorization in particular societies and cultural areas, with attention to *all* parties. Such studies, closely akin to some of the best recent work conducted in the United States (e.g. Milton M. Gordon's *Assimilation in American Life,* 1964) or in the Caribbean (e.g. H. Hoetink's *The Two Variants on Caribbean Race Relations,* 1967) would be a boon to comparative research. They would be particularly useful for:
2. Comparing societies along the same critical dimensions (or variables) of power and size, ideology and institutional structure, attitudes toward subordinates, types of participation, "minority reactions," and the like. This would further the development of:
3. Propositional inventories (like Robin M. Williams's) but with implications for both social theory and social policy at a *regional* and *international* level. This would help to bridge concerns with:
4. National and international systems, particularly with regard to assessments of race (and ethnicity) in relation to other critical factors in the growth of new political movements and the matter of pannational racial identity, or what has here been called "direct and indirect linkages."

Notes

1. See William Stanton, *The Leopards' Spots: Scientific Attitudes toward Race in America, 1815-59* (Chicago: University of Chicago Press, 1960).
2. Jacques Barzun, *Race: A Study in Modern Superstition* (London: Metheun, 1938): 159.
3. Ibid., p. 162.
4. See Ruth Benedict, *Race, Science & Politics,* rev. ed. (New York: Viking, 1943, ch. 3; Gustav Retizus, "The Development of Race Measurements and Classifications," in *Source Book in Anthropology,* ed. Alfred L. Kroeber and Thomas T. Waterman, rev. ed. (New York: Harcourt, Brace, 1931): 94-102.
5. See Juan Comas, "Scientific Racism Again?" *Current Anthropology* 2 (October 1961): 303–40; Benedict, esp. ch. 7; Pierre L. van den Berghe, *Race and Racism* (New York: Wiley, 1967):esp. 1-18.
6. See UNESCO, *The Race Question in Modern Science* (New York: Whiteside & Morrow, 1956).
7. See George E. Simpson and J. Milton Yinger, *Racial and Cultural Minorities* (New York: Harper & Row, 1965): 41-48.
8. Franz Boas, *Aryans and Non-Aryans* (New York: Information and Service Associates, 1934): 11.
9. Theodosius Dobzhansky, "Comment," *Current Anthropology* 2 (October 1961): 31.

10. Ibid., p. 317.
11. Manning Nash, "Race and the Ideology of Race," *Current Anthropology* 3 (June 1962): 285.
12. Marvin Harris, "Race," in *International Encyclopedia of the Social Sciences* (New York: Macmillan, 1968): 285.
13. Ibid. See also Bruce K. Eckland, "Genetics and Sociology: A Reconsideration," *American Sociological Review* 32 (April 1967): 173–94.
14. Harris, p. 264.
15. H. Hoetink, *The Two Variants of Caribbean Race Relations* (New York: Oxford University Press, 1967): 120; Michael Banton, *Race Relations* (New York: Basic Books, 1968): 54-62.
16. See C. Wright Mills, "The Professional Ideology of Social Pathologists," *American Journal of Sociology* 49 (September 1943): 165–80.
17. William Graham Sumner, *Folkways* (Boston: Ginn, 1906): 13.
18. Ibid., p. 238.
19. See E.B. Reuter, "Racial Theory," *American Journal of Sociology* 50 (May 1945): 452–61.
20. William I. Thomas, "The Psychology of Race Prejudice," *American Journal of Sociology* 9 (March 1904): 593-611.
21. Thomas, *Source Book of Social Origins*, p. 156.
22. Sigmund Freud, *Group Psychology and the Analysis of the Ego* (New York: Boni & Liveright, 1950): 55.
23. See E. Digby Baltzell, *The Protestant Establishment* (New York: Random House, 1964): 104.
24. See Robert E. Park and Ernest W. Burgess, *Introduction to the Science of Sociology* (Chicago: University of Chicago Press, 1924): 578. Italics added.
25. See Robert E. Park, "The Nature of Race Relations," in *Race Relations and the Race Problem*, ed. Edgar T. Thompson (Durham: North Carolina University Press, 1939): 3-45. Italics added.
26. See Reuter, "Racial Theory," pp. 452–61. See also Herbert Blumer, "Reflections on a Theory of Race Relations," in *Race Relations in World Perspective*, ed. Andrew W. Lind (Honolulu: University of Hawaii Press, 1955); 3-21.
27. See Brewton Berry, "The Concept of Race in Sociology Textbooks," *Social Forces* 19 (1940): 11; Chester L. Hunt, "The Treatment of 'Race' in Beginning Sociology Textbooks," *Sociology and Social Research* 35 (March-April 1951): 1277-1284.
28. Donald Young, *American Minority Peoples* (New York: Harper, 1932): xiii.
29. Louis Wirth, "The Problem of Minority Groups," in *The Science of Man in the World Crisis,* ed. Ralph Linton (New York: Columbia University Press, 1945): 347.
30. Ibid., p. 348.
31. Ibid.
32. See E.K. Francis, "The Nature of Ethnic Groups," *American Journal of Sociology* 52 (March 1947): 393-400.
33. See Louis Wirth, *The Ghetto* (Chicago: University of Chicago Press, 1928).
34. Reuter, p. 455.

35. Ibid.
36. Robert E. Park, "Our Racial Frontier on the Pacific," *Survey Graphic* 9 (May 1926): 196.
37. For synopses and critiques of "race relations cycles" see Brewton Berry, *Race and Ethnic Relations* (Boston: Houghton Mifflin, 1965), ch. 6; van den Berghe, *Race and Racism,* pp. 25-34; Banton, *Race Relations,* ch. 4.
38. See Robert E. Park, "Racial Assimilation in Secondary Groups with Particular Reference to the Negro," *Publications of the American Sociological Society* 8 (1913): 66-83; Robert E. Park, "Human Migration and the Marginal Man," *American Journal of Sociology* 33 (May 1928): 881–93; Everett V. Stonequist, *The Marginal Man* (New York: Scribners, 1937). See also Robert E. Park, "The Concept of Social Distance," *Journal of Applied Sociology* 8 (1924): 339–44; the following by Emory S. Bogardus: "Measuring Social Distance," *Journal of Applied Sociology* 9 (1925): 299-308; "Social Distance: A Measuring Stock," *Survey* 56 (May 1926): 169–70; *Immigration and Race Attitudes* (New York: Heath, 1928).
39. See John Dollard, *Caste and Class in a Southern Town* (New Haven: Yale University Press, 1937); Gunnar Myrdal, *An American Dilemma* (New York: Harper, 1944); Bruno Bettelheim and Morris Janowitz, *The Dynamics of Prejudice* (New York: Harper, 1950), and their restudy, *Social Change and Prejudice* (New York: Free Press of glencoe, 1964); Melvin M. Tumin, *Desegregation* (Princeton: Princeton University Press, 1961); Robin M. Williams, Jr., *Strangers Next Door* (Englewood Cliffs: Prentice-Hall, 1964); Kenneth B. Clark, *Dark Ghetto* (New York: Harper & Row, 1965); Gary T. Marx, *Protest and Prejudice* (New York: Harper & Row, 1967); Elliot Liebow, *Tally's Corner: A Study of Negro Streetcorner Men* (Boston: Little, Brown, 1967). See the brief discussion of such work by Hoetink, *The Two Variants in Caribbean Race Relations,* pp 62-67.
40. Personal correspondence with Everett C. Hughes, 9 December 1965.
41. Louis Wirth, "Problems and Orientations of Research in Race Relations in the United States," *British Journal of Sociology* 1 (1930); 118–19.
42. Everett C. Hughes and Helen MacGill Hughes, *Where Peoples Meet* (Glencoe: Free Press, 1952): 8-9. See also Hoetink's discussion of "sociologistic visions" and prevalent optimism in his *Two Variants on Caribbean Race Relations,* pp 86-90.
43. See Richard Christie and Marie Jahoda (eds.), *Studies in the Scope and Method of "The Authoritarian Personality" (Glencoe: Free Press, 1954); John P. Davis* (ed.), *The American Negro Reference Book* (Englewood Cliffs: Prentice-Hall, 1966); Milton M. Gordon, "Recent Trends in the Study of Minority and Race Relations," *The Annals* 350 (November 1963): 148–56; John Harding, Bernard Kutner, Harold Proshansky, and Isidor Chien, "Prejudice and Ethnic Relations," in *Handbook of Social Psychology,* ed. Gardner Lindsey (Cambridge: Addison-Wesley, 1954); 1021–61; Otto Klineberg, *Tensions Affecting International Understanding: A Survey of Research* (New York: Social Science Research Council, Bulletin 62, 1950); Raymond W. Mack, "Race Relations," *Social Problems: A Modern Approach,* ed. Howard S. Becker (New York: Wiley, 1966): 317–58; Elizabeth W. Miller, *The Negro in America: A Research Guide* (Bloomington: Indiana University Press, 1965); Theodore M. Newcomb, "Social Psychology and Group Processes," in *Annual Review of Psychol-*

ogy, ed. Calvin P. Stone and Donald W. Taylor (Stanford: Annual Reviews, 1953): 183-214; Arnold M. Rose, *Studies in the Reduction of Prejudice* (Chicago: American Council on Race Relations, 1947); Peter I. Rose, *Joint Newsletter on Desegregation* (1961), *Joint Newsletter on Intergroup Relations* (1962), *Research Bulletin on Intergroup Relations* (1963 and 1964)(all published in New York: Anti-Defamation League for the Society for the Study of Social Problems and the Society for the Psychological Study of Social Issues); Melford E. Spiro, "The Acculturation of American Ethnic Groups," *American Anthropologist* 57 (December 1955): 1240–52; Edward A. Suchman, John P. Dean, and Robin M. Williams, Jr., *Desegregation: Some Propositions and Research Suggestions* (New York: Anti-Defamation League, 1958); Melvin M. Tumin, *Segregation and Desegregation: A Digest of Research* (New York: Anti-Defamation League, 1957), and *Supplement: Segregation and Desegregation* (same publisher, 1960); Melvin M. Tumin, *An Inventory and Appraisal of Research on American Anti-Semitism* (New York: Freedom, 1961); Melvin M. Tumin, *Research Annual on Intergroup Relations, 1965* (New York: Praeger, 1966); Erwin K. Welsch, *The Negro in the United States* (Bloomington: Indiana University Press, 1915); Robin M. Williams, Jr., *The Reduction of Intergroup Tensions: A Survey of Research on Problems of Ethnic, Racial, and Religious Group Relations* (New York: Social Science Research Council, Bulletin 57, 1947); Robin M. Williams, Jr., "Racial and Cultural Relations," in *Review of Sociology: Analysis of a Decade,* ed. Joseph B. Gittler (New York: Wiley, 1957): 433–64.

44. Gordon W. Allport, *The Nature of Prejudice* (Cambridge: Addison-Wesley, 1954); Brewton Berry, *Race and Ethnic Relations,* 3rd ed. (Boston: Houghton Mifflin, 1965); Ina C. Brown, *Race Relations in a Democracy* (New York: Harper, 1949); E. Franklin Frazier, *Race and Culture Contacts in the Modern World* (New York: Knopf, 1957); Eugene L. Hartley, *Problems in Prejudice* (New York: King's Crown, 1946); Charles F. Marden and Gladys Meyer, *Minorities in American Society,* 2nd ed. (New York: American Book, 1962); Edward C. McDonagh and Eugene S. Richards, *Ethnic Relations in the United States* (New York: Appleton-Century-Crofts, 1953); Arnold Rose and Caroline Rose, *America Divided* (New York: Knopf, 1953); Peter I. Rose, *They and We: Racial and Ethnic Relations in the United States* (New York: Random House, 1964); R.A. Schermerhorn, *These Our People* (Boston: Heath, 1949); Tamotsu Shibutani and Kian M. Kwan, *Ethnic Stratification: A Comparative Approach* (New York: Macmillan, 1965); George E. Simpson and J. Milton Yinger, *Racial and Cultural Minorities,* 3rd ed. (New York: Harper & Row, 1965); Pierre L. van den Berghe, *Race and Racism* (New York: Wiley, 1967); James W. Vander Zanden, *American Minority Relations,* 2nd ed. (New York: Ronald, 1966); Charles Wagley and Marvin Harris, *Minorities in the New World* (New York: Columbia University Press, 1958); Paul A.F. Walter, Jr., *Race and Culture Relations* (New York: McGraw-Hill, 1952). See also the following "readers": Milton Barron, *Minorities in a Changing World* (New York: Knopf, 1967); Francis J. Brown and Joseph C. Roucek, *One America,* 2nd ed. (Englewood Cliffs: Prentice-Hall, 1945); Raymond W. Mack, *Race, Class, and Power* (New York: American Book, 1963); Talcott Parsons and Kenneth Clark, *The Negro American* (Boston:

Houghton Mifflin, 1966); Earl Raab, *American Race Relations* (Garden City: Doubleday, 1962); Arnold Rose and Caroline Rose, *Minority Problems* (New York: Harper & Row, 1965); Bernard E. Segal, *Racial and Ethnic Relations* (New York: Crowell, 1966); Marshall Sklare, *The Jews: Social Patterns of an American Group* (Glencoe: Free Press, 1958); Edgar T. Thompson and Everett C. Hughes, *Race: Individual and Collective Behavior* (Glencoe: Free Press, 1958).

45. See Peter I. Rose, *The Subject Is Race: Traditional Ideologies and the Teaching of Race Relations* (New York: Oxford University Press, 1968), esp. chs. 7, 8, 9.

46. A very important exception to this trend is found in Hubert Blalock's *Toward a Theory of Minority-Group Relations* (New York: Wiley, 1967).

47. Shibutani and Kwan, p. 15. See also Melvin M. Tumin, "The Functionalist Approach to Social Problems," *Social Problems* 12 (Spring 1965): 379–88.

48. Shibutani and Kwan.

49. Ibid., ch. 4.

50. See Donald L. Noel, "A Theory of the Origin of Ethnic Stratification," *Social Problems* 16 (Fall 1968): 157–72.

51. Shibutani and Kwan, p. 572.

52. Ibid., p. 573.

53. Donald Noel says that "Ethnic stratification is a system of stratification wherein some relatively fixed group membership (e.g. race, religion, or nationality) is utilized as a major criterion for acquiring social positions with their attendant differential rewards" (p. 157).

54. Shibutani and Kwan.

55. See Edward T. Hall, *The Silent Language* (Garden City: Doubleday, 1959).

56. Shibutani and Kwan, p. 574.

57. Ibid., p. 575.

58. Ibid.

59. Park, "Our Racial Frontier on the Pacific," p. 196.

60. The comment appears in Schermerhorn's newest work, *Comparative Ethnic Relations* (New York: Random House, 1970).

61. See Gabriel A. Almond, "A Functional Approach to Comparative Politics," in *The Politics of Developing Areas,* ed. Gabriel A. Almond and James J. Coleman (Princeton: Princeton University Press, 1960), ch. 1.

62. One other book Schermerhorn might have mentioned is Michael Banton's *Race Relations* (New York: Macmillan, 1967). He may have decided not to do so because it is far more difficult to pigeonhole than, say, van den Berghe's. Banton's book is a potpourri: part text, part treatise, part description, part analysis. It is built in large measure on an earlier work, *White and Coloured* (1959), some of his previously published journal papers, and the excellent Munro Lectures he delivered at Edinburgh in 1966. Though not divided as such, the result is the presentation of several "books" in one, each of which fits rather fortuitously into one or another of Schermerhorn's categories.

63. *Race and Racism,* p. 9.

64. Ibid., pp. 9-10.

65. Ibid., p. 11.

66. Ibid., p. 14.

67. Ibid., pp. 14-15.
68. Ibid., pp. 17-18.
69. Ibid., p. 18.
70. See Karl Mannheim, "The Democratization of Culture," in *Essays on the Sociology of Culture* (London: Routledge & Kegan Paul, 1962):171-246. This essay and the dichotomy discussed in it was brought to my attention by Professor H. Hoetink.
71. Ibid., p. 26.
72. Ibid., pp. 31-33.
73. See Milton M. Gordon, *Assimilation in American Life* (New York: Oxford University Press, 1964). And see discussion of the uses of the term *pluralism* by Schermerhorn below.
74. See J. S. Furnivall, *Colonial Policy and Practice* (Cambridge: Cambridge University Press, 1948); J. H. Boeke, *Economics and Economic Policy of Dual Societies* (New York: 1953); M. G. Smith, "Social and Cultural Pluralism in the Caribbean," *Annals* 83 (1960): 763-77; *The Plural Society in the British West Indies* (Berkeley: University of California Press, 1965).
75. Van den Berghe, pp. 34-35.
76. Robert Bierstedt has described this phenomenon in terms of the development of societal groups. See Robert Bierstedt, "The Sociology of Majorities," *American Sociological Review* 13 (December 1948):700-10.
77. See M. G. Smith, *The Plural Society in the British West Indies* (Berkeley: University of California Press, 1965).
78. Van den Berghe, pp. 122-26.
79. Ibid., p. 126.
80. Ibid., p. 132.
81. Ibid., p. 135.
82. See Rose, *They and We*.
83. Van den Berghe, pp. 136-38.
84. Ibid., p. 139. See also his article "Dialectic and Functionalism: Toward a Theoretical Synthesis," *American Sociological Review* 28 (1963): 695-705.
85. Three notable exceptions to this generalization are Milton M. Gordon, Robert K. Merton, and especially Robin M. Williams, Jr., although even their theoretical work on the subject has been confined to the American scene.
86. Banton, *Race Reltions,* p. 63.
87. Ibid., p. 64.
88. See Richard A. Schermerhorn, "Toward a General Theory of Minority Groups," *Phylon* 25 (1964): 238-46.
89. Richard A. Schermerhorn, "Polarity in the Approach to Comparative Research in Ethnic Relations," *Sociology and Social Research* 51 (January 1967): 235-40.
90. Elsewhere Schermerhorn defines an ethnic group as follows: "A collectivity within a larger society having real or putative common ancestry, memories of a shared historical past, and a cultural focus on one or more symbolic elements defined as the epitome of their peoplehood."
91. A dominant group is defined by Schermerhorn as "that collectivity within a society which has prominent authority to function both as guardians and sustainers of the controlling value-system, and as prime allocators of rewards in the society." Such dominant groups might be restricted elites, majorities, or an ethnic group, according to his description.

92. Schermerhorn, "Polarity in the Approach to Comparative Research in Ethnic Relations," p. 238.

93. Schermerhorn, *Comparative Ethnic Relations,* p. 192.

94. See Kingsley Davis, "A Conceptual Analysis of Stratification," *American Sociological Review* 7 (1942): 309-21; Kingsley Davis and Wilbert E. Moore, "Some Principles of Stratification," *American Sociological Review* 10 (1945): 242-49; Melvin M. Tumin, "Some Principles of Stratification: A Critical Analysis," *American Sociological Review* 18 (1953): 387-94.

95. See Robin M. Williams, Jr., "Some Further Comments on Chronic Controversies," *American Journal of Sociology* 71 (1966): 717-21.

96. Schermerhorn, *Comparative Ethnic Relations,* pp. 20-39.

97. Ibid., p. 38. See full statement in Georg Simmel, *Conflict,* trans. Kurt Wolff (New York: Free Press, Macmillan, 1955): 13. Also Lewis A. Coser, *The Functions of Social Conflict* (Glencoe: Free Press, 1956).

98. Gerhard Lenski, *Power and Privilege: A Theory of Social Stratification* (New York: McGraw-Hill, 1966): 17.

99. Schermerhorn, p. 40.

100. Ibid., pp. 48-59 passim.

101. Wirth, "The Problem of Minority Groups," pp. 354-63.

102. See Rose, *They and We,* pp. 131-46. In the early printings Type 3 was called "Avoidance," not "Separatism"; now the latter term is being used (see 7th printing).

103. Two modifications include substituting the word *Incorporation* for *Amalgamation* in Type A and *Autonomy* for *Federalism* in Type B.

104. Again, see Hoetink, *The Two Variants on Caribbean Race Relations;* Sidney Greenfield, *English Rustics in a Black Skin.* In the latter volume, a study of family life in Barbados, Greenfield stresses the dual perspectives he used, structural-functional and cultural-historical. See also Gabriel Almond and Sidney Verba, *The Civic Culture* (Princeton: Princeton University Press, 1963); William Buchanan and Hadley Cantril, *How Nations See Each Other* (Urbana: University of Illinois Press, 1953); Stein Rokkan, "International Action to Advance Comparative Research: The Role of UNESCO," in *Comparing Nations,* ed. R.L. Merritt and Stein Rokkan (New Haven: Yale University Press, 1966); Beatrice Whiting (ed.), *Six Cultures* (New York: Wiley, 1963); Donald T. Campbell and Robert A. LeVine, "A Proposal for Comparative Cross-Cultural Research on Ethnocentrism," *Journal of Conflict Resolution* 5 (March 1961): 82-108.

10
Problems in Conveying the Meaning of Ethnicity:
The Insider/Outsider Debate

(1978)

Several years ago, with a lightbulb flash of recognition, I realized that I was witnessing one of those events secretly dreaded by ethnographers. The natives were challenging the outsider's description of themselves. The challenge was not very dramatic nor even very vocal. It consisted of whispers and the ultimate put-down, shrugs of dismissal. To those who belonged to the group in question, it was just one more piece of evidence to confirm the fact that acquaintance with something is very different from true understanding, that there is a wide chasm between *Kennen* and *Verstehen*. Outsiders might know a bit of another person's history and some cold facts; but it is much more difficult for them to feel the undertones.

It was not the Australian Aborigines, the Bushmen of the Kalihari, or Thai peasants being discussed, but some fellow Americans who, it turned out, were middle-class Jews. Those who described them were students who had spent several weeks culling through the literature to present summary papers on the American Jewish community. What I experienced did not really surprise me. Yet somehow I found myself troubled and rather uncomfortable.

The setting of my discomfort was a small seminar of fifteen junior and senior students who had come together to study four ethnic groups—Jews, Italians, Blacks, and Puerto Ricans—as they related to their own "brothers and sisters" and to each other in one American city, New York. Together the students and I were embarking on an examination of the backgrounds and experience of the four critical groups in an attempt to better understand such specific issues as the debate over community control of schools and other crises then extant.

The seminar roster included nine students from Smith, five from

Amherst, and one from the University of Massachusetts. There were four Jews, four Blacks, and one Irish Catholic. The rest were White Protestants, two of them from the South. Ordinarily their ethnic, religious, racial, and regional connections would have had little relevance to my concerns or their own. The mix was not uncommon. But it turned out that in this particular setting it made a world of difference.

During the first part of the semester the students were asked to decide on which of the four groups they wanted to concentrate and then to give me a preference listing indicating their choices. They were to develop whatever expertise they could in a short period of time. To ensure adequate breadth of coverage, not more than four were to be permitted to deal with a single one of the chosen minorities. For whatever reason, none of those whose first choice was New York's Jews was Jewish. It was the report of one of them that triggered the shrugs and sighs and the unsaid message to me and several others in the class that "they just don't get it."

At the time I let the looks pass. I was not even sure that everybody saw them or, if they did, understood what was happening. But I did, and so did the speaker. He shuddered a bit and pushed on with it, further confounding his credibility by innocuous but telling evidence of seeming insensitivity. For example, to make an important point about the Reconstructionist movement in contemporary Jewish life, he began by saying that, "To most people, the Jewish church in America has but three divisions—Orthodox, Conservative, and Reform." Apparently he did not realize that despite its functional similarity to other religious bodies, no Jew would ever use the word *church* in such manner.

To help out a bit, I pointed out this fact of Jewish life to the smiles of my all-knowing fellow Jews in the room and to the blank stares of some of my classmates. Eventually we got back to the more general subject of Jewish settlement and mobility presented in the student reports. Discussion followed that day and on into subsequent meetings. To my undeniable relief, several times the somewhat embarrassed presenters bested the too smug insiders in arguments over points of fact. Feelings, they found, they could hardly touch.

Several weeks later we spent three hours on New York's Italians and debated the differing viewpoints of sociologists and historians who had written about them. We discussed migration patterns, religious beliefs, and the nature of life for those often referred to as "birds of passage." We discussed the character of Little Italy and the role of family, church, and workplace. We discussed stereotypes and reactions to them. It was a lively session. As I left the seminar, I asked myself why it was so different from the previous ones. Then it hit me. No shrugs this time. No sighs. No Italians either.

I was reminded of several classes on The Negro in America I had taught not long before when no black faces had been in evidence and everyone had enthusiastically discussed interpretations of what we now call "The Black Experience." Commenting on this to a colleague, he said, in utter seriousness, that it was easier to be objective in those days. Perhaps. Maybe our debates about the writings and researches of Campisi, Nelli, Lopreato, Panunzio, Tomasi, and the others were better than they might have been had one or more of the students been named Carbona or Marselli. Maybe there were advantages in being unchallenged assessors, playing the role of dispassionate observers. From discussions during the preceding weeks, we had all become sensitive to the fact that there are obvious risks to including the subject of one's research in the discussion of it. About ten years ago, a Jules Feiffer cartoon character made the point with righteous simplicity. His button-down, gray-flanneled liberal character stated: "Civil rights used to be so much more tolerable until the Negroes got into it."

And what about those Negroes? In the third set of sessions we came to New York's Blacks. This time two of the reporters were Black, two were White. Though they had read the same material, general studies of urban Blacks including parts of St. Clair Drake and Horace Cayton's *Black Metropolis,* Karl and Alma Taeuber's *Negroes in Cities,* and Kenneth Clark's *Dark Ghetto,* and specific studies of New York City including James Weldon Johnson's *Black Manhattan* and Gilbert Osofsky's *Harlem: The Making of a Ghetto,* it was clearly apparent that the latter two (the White students) constantly deferred to the former two (the Black students). Whenever the Black students presented their ideas, the White students tended to take them down with little or no challenge. Neither they nor the remaining Blacks did the same when the White students gave their part of the report. On those few occasions when questions were asked about behavior, attitudes, or social conditions, the tension was palpable. If a straightforward answer was given, everyone seemed relieved. If the speaker, almost invariably one of the Black students, seemed annoyed, tensions mounted again. Part of the problem was that everyone was playing out their appropriate roles circa 1970—the Black students playing the insider's game and saying, in the words of the old Negro spiritual, " 'Nobody knows the trouble *I've* seen'—and nobody can."

Lastly came the Puerto Ricans. Again, with no representatives present and little general knowledge save for the "I-want-to-be-in-Amer-i-ca" imagery portrayed in *West Side Story,* we reverted to academic one-upmanship. We reviewed and debated what some of the experts, including Oscar Lewis, Elena Padilla, Eduardo Seda-Bonilla, Clarence Senior, and Melvin Tumin had described. For example, considering the role of race in Puerto Rican society, one reporter began with the contention that "there is a difference between people raised in a racially continuous society, one where there are people in all walks of life of varying shades, and those who grow up in a racially dichotomous one, where there are Whites and non-Whites, like ours."

"True," said another, "Clarence Senior makes the same point. But do you really think race is the main basis of difference?" "I do," said the first speaker, "though I note that it is not such an important factor in the writing of Oscar Lewis. His use of the idea of the culture of poverty would suggest that things are not very different on the island or here, at least for those who are poor. And *he* knows!"

I end my description of the events that led up to this essay with that last almost verbatim comment of the White Southern Amherst student who wrote and spoke about Puerto Ricans, people he had admittedly never met, and about the late Oscar Lewis. It seems fitting because it was Lewis himself who, perhaps more than anyone, tried to get outsiders inside the experience of others, who tried to convey the true meaning of culture "in their own words," who provided nonmembers with a vision of what it was like to be poor and Puerto Rican, and Mexican, and East Indian. As is well known, even Lewis had difficulty convincing some that he was telling it like it really was, and even more difficulty convincing others that he had the right to attempt it.

Personal Reflections

In all, that seminar set me to thinking again about a problem that has long plagued all of us who study and teach about ethnic experiences. I say "again" for the seminar I described was not the first time I had encountered these issues or tried to wrestle with them. The first large-scale study I ever conducted was on the meaning of isolation to minority group members who were strangers in the midst of alien territory. In 1957, I began to explore the character of Jewish life in rural towns and to test certain thoughts I had about the nature of a process sociologists have come to call "the exemption mechanism" and laymen know as the "some-of-my-best-friends are . . . syndrome."

As I got the small-town Jews to help me tell their stories, I became increasingly intrigued by two phenomena: the first was their incredible allegiance to a group they could "feel" though they could not "touch." They were Jews and they reported, almost to a person, that they constantly felt obligated to play the role of ambassador to the Gentiles. Moving from village to village and gathering life histories and attitudes and opinions about how they were faring and how successful they were in their ambassadorial roles, I had a growing sense that they might have distorted notions about how they were being received. That concern led to a parallel study of some twenty rural communities with less than 5,000 inhabitants, half of which had Jewish families in residence (about whom I already had information) and half of which had no Jews. I learned that stereotypes persisted in both sets of communities, the only difference being that, in the communities with Jews, exemptions took place: "Oh, the Cohens are not like other Jews. They're different." And what of those other Jews? They fulfilled the then–commonly held images to a "T"—or to a "P," for prejudice.[1]

Several years later, still concerned with the problem, I tried to piece together the various ideas American sociologists had about racial and ethnic relations in a little book whose title highlighted the dichotomy between outsiders and insiders. It was called *They and We*. Shortly after the book was published, a group of Smith College students and I sought to learn what others were doing about conveying the meaning of ethnicity through a nationwide survey of university-level courses on racial and ethnic relations. From the study, conducted in the mid-1960s, it was learned that most courses on the subject, despite their different titles, were quite similar. Most teachers concentrated on prejudice but rarely dealt with the issue of power (White or Black). Most described in detail the attitudes of dominant group members and the patterns of discrimination they imposed, but too often skimmed over the nature of minority reactions and even more rarely attempted to deal with ethnic experiences themselves. Focusing on Black/White tensions, most instructors firmly pronounced that color-blind integration was the answer when, it seemed, they really meant white-washed assimilation.[2] Using a single standard for judging others, they appeared to reflect exactly what James Farmer had said so eloquently in his book *Freedom—When?* published around the time of our study. There he wrote:

> We have found the cult of color-blindness not only quaintly irrelevant but seriously flawed. For we learned that America simply couldn't *be* color-blind. It would have to *become* color-blind and it would only *become* color-blind when we gave up our color. The white man, who presumably has no color, would have to give up only his prejudices. We would have to give up our identities. Thus we would usher in the Great Day with an act of complete self-denial and self-abasement. We would achieve equality by conceding racism's charge: that our skins were afflicted; that our history is one long humiliation; that we are empty of distinctive traditions and any legitimate source of pride.[3]

Looking at the data on over 800 different courses I felt that Farmer's charge, leveled at many of his friends and colleagues and comrades in arms, including a number of sociologists, rang true. Many seemed to interpret most things from the perspective Richard Schermerhorn once labeled as "victimology."[4] That they were victims was not to be disputed; that they were *only* victims without culture or character was quite another matter. But few had bothered to listen to what *they* were trying to say.

I addressed myself to some of these matters in several lectures and in a lengthy essay in the *Social Science Quarterly* [a version of which appears in this volume as "The Black Experience].[5] The essay was a sort of gamble, for I was trying personally to cross the barrier mentioned previously, attempting to deal in some detail with someone else's experiences. That I was partially successful was poignantly conveyed at a conference where I was presenting a paper. A Black conferee came up and said that he felt betrayed. He had read and liked my essay, but was disappointed to find that I was not a "brother." Somebody, he said, must have helped me. The assumption was, once again, that nonmembers can never really cross the threshold. Another conferee was disturbed because he claimed that I said some things that, he felt, were best left unsaid or should be discussed only within "the family." These views, while troubling, were not unfamiliar. Just about that time, I wrote about these very issues in a Foreword to Marshall Sklare's excellent book, *America's Jews:*

> Most of what is written about American Jews comes from the pens of Jewish specialists—novelists and playwrights, journalists and Yiddishists, many outside the formal academic community (some within) whose primary concern is to contribute to continuing deliberations with fellow Jews about themselves and their problems. Too frequently it appears that the *sine qua non* for understanding interpretations of Jewish history, the nuances of religious practice, or even contemporary problems is that the reader already be *au courant.* ("If you don't know what I'm talking about, you will never be able to understand.")[6]

The last line sounds quite similar to that of Louis Armstrong who said: "If they don't know, you can't tell them." Still, despite the argument recently expressed by Jules Chametsky that "it isn't the job of the oppressed to educate the oppressor, but simply get him off their backs,"[7] there is a price to pay for insulation and chauvinism. Playing "We've Got a Secret" is no way to help others alter erroneous views. But then there is that other side, as the non-Jewish sociologist Ernest van den Haag discovered after he published *The Jewish Mystique.*

"Show and Tell" is not appreciated either—at least not by those written about. In recent years various "minority" writers, politicians, and professors have decried what they claim are the unwitting and intentional distortions by so-called experts on race relations. Whether the criticisms are justified or not, there is no question but that a major part of the effort of those promoting a new ethnic consciousness has been to question the right of *any* outsider to attempt to explain what it means to be something they are not.

Some Political Aspects of an Epistemological Debate

The problems I have been discussing fall within the general realm of the sociology of knowledge and in that part of it popularly referred to as the "insider/outsider debate." As Robert K. Merton has recently stated: "The sociology of knowledge has long been regarded as a complex and esoteric subject, remote from urgent problems of contemporary life."[8] But, as he indicates, that is certainly not true in the present instance. The insider/outsider debate is complex but far from esoteric. Everyone, it seems, has gotten into it. It reaches far beyond the groves of academe, although it is on the campuses where some of the fiercest arguments and confrontations about "who speaks for whom—and who can?" have taken place.

That question has obvious ramifications in all current attempts to understand the nature of dominant-minority relations, the structure and character of plural societies, and ethnic identity itself. But in the present temper, it is not surprising that scholarly and dispassionate discourse about sources of knowledge, means of discovering truth, methods of inquiry, and questions of freedom of expression and the control of ideas get embroiled in and often overwhelmed by ideological considerations, by the *political* aspects of the old epistemological controversy.

Since the beginning of modern sociology, there have been two contending views about which is the better way to assess social phenomena, through observation or participation. Any history of sociology or textbook on social research will describe the two ideal types: the spectator position which claims the advantages of distance and detachment, and the participant position which claims that only through intimacy and involvement—but not necessarily actual membership—can one ever get to know the subtleties of rules, roles, and social relationships.[9]

While these approaches have been discussed and debated by Emile Durkheim, Max Weber, and countless others, and have been variously labeled, for our purposes I will only say that we might refer to the former as the "Walter Cronkite Approach" and the latter as the "Walter Mitty Approach." In the first case the idea is that the researcher looks at society or some segment of it as if through a one-way screen (like watching a battle or a sports event from the sidelines, being able to see how all combatants act, interact, and react from afar). The second type, in its ideal form, is one in which the participant takes on all the characteristics of the object of his concern, blending into the scene in order to partake of the activities at first hand. Sometimes he has the added advantage of membership, but this is rarely discussed and when it is, it is passed over lightly, since the assumption is that Walter Mitty can learn to play anybody's role.

Many empirically oriented sociologists have long found themselves hedging their bets. Recognizing the difficulties of both total detachment and full involvement has led to various compromises. One of the most popular techniques taught to American graduate students is that of "participant observation," where investigators are trained to go into the field to record the doings of one group or another not as one of them (a most difficult task in most instances), but by playing roles that give apparent legitimacy to their presence, such as claiming to be historians trying to learn about the background of communal life or journalists trying to get a fix on a particular issue. Key informants become critical sources of information in order "to get a point of view of the natives." But there are inevitable limits to what gets reported and what is withheld by the real insiders. Many social scientists have become increasingly concerned about such limitations. Others have abandoned any efforts to do so, retreating into quantophrenia and claiming that "if you can't count it, it doesn't count." Still there are those who continue to pursue their traditional goals, probing and prodding their human subjects in the hope of finding out not only the nature of life among the Ceylonese, the Cheyenne, or the Chicano (to the best of their limited ability), but to better grasp the broader implications of what they find to the understanding of social interactions, social stratification, and social change. This, they will argue, is, after all, what it is really all about.

If the sociologists in this last group were to accept the damnation of those who claim no outsider can know another's character, then they, along with historians and ethnographers, would have to resign themselves to seeking new careers! Like much of sociology, history and ethnography are also based on the assumption that the outsider *can* know and *can* understand. In the essay referred to earlier, Merton spoke to this issue:

> If direct engagement in the life of a group is essential to understand it, then the only authentic history is contemporary history, written in fragments by those most fully involved in making inevitably limited portions of it. Rather than constituting only the raw materials of history, the documents prepared by engaged Insiders become all there is to history. But once the historian elects to write the history of a time other than his own, even the most dedicated Insider, of the national, sex, age, racial, ethnic, or religious variety, becomes the Outsider, condemned to error and misunderstanding.[10]

The ethnographer, as Merton reminds us, is very like the historian. Both may be concerned with societies other than those in which they live. Merton quotes Lévi-Strauss to illustrate the point:

> Whether the *otherness* [or "outsiderism," in our terms] is due to remoteness in time (however slight) or to remoteness in space, or even to cultural heterogeneity, is of secondary importance compared to the basic similarity of perspective. All that the historian or ethnographer can do, and all that we can expect of either of them, is to enlarge a specific experience to the dimensions of a more general one, which thereby becomes accessible as *experience* to men of another country or another epoch. And in order to succeed, both historian and ethnographer must have the same qualities: skill, precision, a sympathetic approach, and objectivity.[11]

We must take note of four key words: *skill, precision, sympathy,* and *objectivity.* The assumption remains that one can be properly trained to use the latest in data-gathering techniques—ranging these days from one-way mirrors, to interviewing, to camouflaged entry; that one can learn to separate the important from the trivial and know the difference; that one can be sympathetic and understanding; that one can hold one's own values in abeyance being the true cultural relativist. The question is not whether these directives are reasonable goals for a social scientist to strive for but whether they are possible to attain. That is the rub.

I once facetiously defined an ethnographer as "a social scientist who faithfully records his biased views of somebody else." Kidding aside, I believe that some bias is endemic and inevitable in the sort of work we do. What is important is to seek ways to minimize its intrusion. But bias is not the only problem that confronts the reflective investigator. His presence is often enough to alter the social system itself and to cause various changes, some immediate, some longer-ranging.

When I was a graduate student in anthropology we used to describe the Navaho nuclear family as "mother, father, children, and anthropologist." It was not really so funny. Numerous commentators on social change in the Southwest have attested to the impact of the field worker. And others have mentioned their own disruptive effects on those they sought to study with sensitivity and compassion. Oscar Lewis, for example, was greatly concerned when the real "children of Sánchez" gained worldwide recognition and celebrity and were, in his words, "never able to be themselves again."

So intrusion *is* an issue and it cannot be dismissed (I will have more to say about it further along). Before going on, however, I should like to remind us all that Walter Cronkite and Walter Mitty, the nonpartici-pant and the full participant, are both *outsiders*. Though they may claim expertise, they are not (or rarely are) part of that which they are studying.

Insiders are different. In general, they are not methodologists but members; they share not a set of professional tools but what many claim is a sort of "privileged access" to that which only they say they can know and feel.[12] Their concern about themselves is not abstract but immediate; it is not intellectual but visceral; it is not objective but highly subjective. In the broadest sense, whether corporate execu-tives, college professors, guest workers, Pakistani villagers, Blacks in Bedford-Stuyvesant, or small-town Jews, they are united by an inter-dependence of fate and a fellowship that, most argue, cannot be penetrated. Monopolists of culture, *they* are the "We," as Kipling said, and "everyone else is They."[13] They belong, in the words of William Graham Sumner, to "in-groups," and few would deny their own ethnocentrism.

Sumner claimed that "each group nourishes its own pride and vanity, boasts itself superior, exalts its own divinities, and looks with contempt on outsiders . . . the most important fact is that ethnocen-trism leads a people to exaggerate and intensify everything in their own folkways which is peculiar and which differentiates them from oth-ers."[14]

Insiders, the subject of much of our research, dubious about the premise that outsiders are value-free or ethically neutral, rarely make such claims for themselves. Most, if asked—and until recently, rarely have they been asked—to explain their lives would stress that it is in the very values, biases, and nuances of personal existence, in the folkways and mores, that the true warp and weft of the social fabric is to be comprehended. Further, their spokesmen would argue that only they and a few enlightened souls who share their outlooks, if not always their statuses or appearances, have access to their *sanctum sanctorum*, whether village or neighborhood, barrio, ghetto, or psy-chological turf.

Sociology in Black and White

In recent years, this point of view has been most explicitly articulated by certain Black intellectuals, including those who contend "that only black historians can truly understand black history, only black ethnologists can understand black culture, only black sociologists can understand the social life of blacks, and so on."[15] Typical of the views reflecting this stance are Joyce Ladner's remarks in the introduction to her edited volume, *The Death of White Sociology.*

> Why a book on "Black sociology"? Is there such a discipline? Many readers, indeed, will argue that sociology, like physics, is without color and can validly apply the same methodology and theoretical framework, regardless of the ethnic, racial, and other backgrounds of the group under investigation.
>
> But sociology, like history, economics, and psychology, exists in a domain where color, ethnicity, and social class are of primary importance. And, as long as this holds true, it is impossible for sociology to claim that it maintains value neutrality in its approach.[16]

This bold statement is supported by a selective review of the writings of some of the most prominent sociologists whom generations of students and scholars came to believe had some objective understanding of Black life. Ladner suggests that many of them misrepresented what they were purportedly trying to describe. Robert E. Park, for example, former newspaperman, advisor to Booker T. Washington, and founder of the famed Chicago School of Sociology, and his collaborator Ernest W. Burgess, described Negro character as follows:

> The temperament of the Negro as [we] conceive of it consists in a few elementary but distinctive characteristics, determined by physical organizations and transmitted biologically. These characteristics manifest themselves in a genial, sunny, and social disposition, in an interest in and attachment to external, physical things rather than to subjective states and objects of introspection, in a disposition for expression rather than enterprise and action.[17]

And Edward B. Reuter, author of *The American Race Problem,* one of the first textbooks in the sociology of race relations, boldly asserted:

> [The Negroes] were without ancestral pride or family tradition. They had no distinctive language or religion. These, like their folkways and moral customs, were but recently acquired from the whites and furnished no nucleus for a racial unity. The group was without even a tradition of historical unity or racial achievements. There were not historic names,

no great achievements, no body of literature, no artistic productions. The whole record of the race was one of servile or barbarian status apparently without a point about which a sentimental complex could be formed.[18]

Ladner says that "one could argue that the doctrines of racial inferiority which these men sought to document scientifically have been disposed of."[19] In fairness, she might have pointed out that Park and many of his colleagues repudiated some of their earlier contentions in view of what they learned. And what they learned often came from the research and writings of a number of Black commentators, such as W.E.B. DuBois, James Weldon Johnson, Bertram W. Doyle, Charles S. Johnson—to name but a few of the better-known figures.

Despite the backing-off of some of the harsher judgments about the lack of a meaningful past or of a significant culture, certain themes have persisted. Not surprisingly, many prominent historians and sociologists continue to be cited as reflecting an incredible lack of sensitivity about the ambiguous meaning of being Black in White America. Consider the following statement by Nathan Glazer and Daniel Patrick Moynihan, made in the first edition of *Beyond the Melting Pot:* "It is not possible for Negroes to view themselves as other ethnic groups viewed themselves because—and this is the key to much in the Negro world—the Negro is only an American and nothing else. He has no values and culture to guard and protect."[20]

Not only Black critics have charged the mainstream sociologists with bias, ignorance, or naiveté. In 1972 Stanford Lyman presented a devastating critique of the way in which many prominent experts failed in their efforts to deal with Black ethnicity. His argument is interesting. He contends that neither Park, John Dollard, Gunnar Myrdal, Gordon Allport, T.W. Adorno, nor Talcott Parsons (who edited a large *Daedalus* volume on *The Negro American)* ever really understood "the American dilemma."

Condemning the proclivity of these and other social scientists to follow the Aristotelian view "that science could only study that which behaved in accordance with slow, orderly, continuous, and teleological movement," Lyman argues that they were led "to make racial separation of events from processes."[21] As legatees of evolutionary anthropology and nineteenth-century functionalism, many sociologists seemed to have been wedded to notions of unilinear development, set stages, fixed trends. In chapter after chapter, Lyman attempts to explain what is wrong with such assumptions and then offers a backhanded compliment to those he criticized saying: "Despite the contradicting arguments of these studies, they have supplied valuable insights on the race issue, sensitized many readers to hitherto unnoticed features of American life, and, with widely varying degrees of optimism, suggested that a resolution to the black problem might be found."[22] The sociologists of race relations reflected, in many ways, one of the most significant leitmotifs of the discipline itself, a kind of liberal conservatism, a faith in the system which many believed was capable of righting historic wrongs inflicted on the victims of past injustices, of dealing with but never solving the dilemma.

To Lyman and an increasing number of other commentators, the proper sociology of Black people (and others in similar straits) has to address existential matters and deal with the disjunctive, marginal, and often absurd position of those caught between two worlds. For too long, Lyman claims, the mainstream sociologist's view of the Black has, in Camus's terms, "divorced him from his [real] life, removed the actor from his setting, denied that he has any existence at all—no past, no future."[23] Although Camus might not have used such words, I would add, "no soul."

Ladner in her way and Lyman in his—and a host of others—argue that Blacks have always been measured against an alien set of norms. As Ladner puts it:

> Mainstream sociology . . . reflects the ideology of the larger society, which has always excluded Black lifestyles, values, behavior, attitudes, and so forth from the body of data that is used to define, describe, conceptualize, and theorize about the structure and functions of American society. Sociology has in a similar manner excluded the totality of Black existence from its major theories, except insofar as it has deviated from the so-called norms.[24]

The generalization is sweeping but bears more than a kernel of truth. Blacks have too frequently been seen as a residual category or deviant group, not as part of the general cross-section. One simple example is the tendency of statisticians and survey analysts to use the White/non-White dichotomy as a critical one, often dropping the latter from analysis because they are *assumed to be so different,* even when close examination would indicate that other variables, as gender, level of education, and social class are more critical in distinguishing people on many issues than race or ethnic group membership.

There is a strange paradox in all this. These days school administrators, government officials, and social scientists find themselves damned when they fail to draw distinctions based on race or ethnicity after having been berated for making such "discriminating distinctions." The charge is, once again, that outsiders fail to recognize the uniqueness of those who are different.

A growing number of "minority" social scientists and even more lay people have begun to echo the sentiment. The argument is that old and unfamiliar cry of insiders: not only can no outsider comprehend what others experience, they have no adequate frame of reference with which to assess it. Lerone Bennett speaks for many Blacks when he writes:

> It is necessary for us to develop a new frame of reference which transcends the limits of white concepts. It is necessary for us to develop and maintain a total intellectual offensive against the false universality of white concepts, whether they are expressed by William Styron or Daniel Patrick Moynihan. By and large, reality has been conceptualized in terms of the small minority of white men who live in Europe and in North America. We must abandon the partial frame of reference of our oppressors and create new concepts which will release our reality, which is also the reality of the overwhelming majority of men and women on this globe. We must say to the white world that there are things in the world that are not dreamt of in your history and your sociology and your philosophy.[25]

Bennett carries the argument to the extreme by advocating not a universalistic model but one which looks at the world from *his* rather than someone else's perspective. A Black view to replace a White one!

The political scientist Martin Kilson, among others, has recently warned against this sort of exchange. Referring to early debates over Afro-American Studies, he writes:

> "We must be frank about this, what this amounts to is racism in reverse—black racism. I am certainly convinced that it is important for the Negro to know of his past—of his ancestors, of their strengths and weaknesses—and they should respect this knowledge, when it warrants respect, and they should question it and criticize it when it deserves criticism. But it is of no advantage to a mature and critical understanding or appreciation of one's heritage if you approach that heritage with the assumption that it is intrinsically good and noble, and intrinsically superior to the heritage of other peoples. That is, after all, what the white racists have done; and none of my militant friends in the black studies movement have convinced me that racist thought is any less vulgar and degenerate because it is used by black men.[26]

Kilson does two things in his essay. He challenges the assumption that only the insider has access to truth (and beauty) and he does so as a member of the very group in question. As a Black political scientist he is a sort of "insider without," the equivalent, in this particular context, to the "outsider within," the person who has successfully penetrated the veil of suspicion.

Insiders without are called by many names. "Tom" is one. But it is not the only one, as many who labeled Kilson "courageous" will attest. Outsiders within are also called different things, the two most common are "friend" and "foe." Friends are those acceptable strangers who are exempted from the rule that claims that membership is the key to understanding. The bona fides of friends depend in large measure on their ability to reflect the current ideological stance regarding the position of those they study. This is not to denigrate their efforts, but one cannot help but point out that even the fortune of friends is fickle.

If, for example, William Styron had published his version of *The Confessions of Nat Turner* ten years earlier, it is conceivable that he would have been praised rather than damned for making the protagonist a religious-type leader rather than a revolutionary. And even Senator Moynihan, that *bête blanche* of so many critics, might have been applauded instead of excoriated for saying what a number of Black scholars, including Kenneth Clark, had already said, had he presented *The Negro Family: A Case for National Action* a decade earlier. By contrast, a decade before, Robert Blauner might have been attacked for turning the race problem into a class problem, which many feel it is.

But Styron and Moynihan, as Joyce Ladner stated in the essay quoted earlier, were not to be viewed as friends in the 1960s. They were foes or "ofays." Foes are seen as members of the enemy camp who pretend to be your friend but are really engaging in exploitation. They are not there to learn from you, the argument goes, but to take from you. And they often engage in surreptitious entry. It may well be that there is great suspicion of outsiders not because they cannot ever learn the insider's problems (à la Louis Armstrong's contention), but because in fact they have got his number. This underlies much of what is objected to by those who see the outsider—whether social scientist or politician or simply as an agent of The Man—as able to expose their innermost thoughts and exploit their weaknesses.

This view, the last I shall discuss, is expressed with brutal clarity not only in the writings of some Black (and other minority) sociologists, but by many essayists, novelists, poets, and playwrights like Ishmael Reed, Claude Brown, Don L. Lee, and Leroi Jones. Take Jones for a moment and his bitter play *The Dutchman*. The setting is a subway in New York. Two characters, Lula, a White woman (the symbolic outsider), and Clay, a Black man, are engaged in a heated conversation. Lula taunts Clay: "You're afraid of white people. And your father was. Uncle Tom Big Lip!"

Clay slaps her as he can across the mouth and Lula's head bangs against the back of the seat. When she raises it again, Clay slaps her again. "Now shut up and let me talk," he says. And then, with rising anger he begins to berate her. As the argument continues, Clay pushes Lula back into her seat. "I'm not telling you again, Tallulah Bankhead! Luxury. In your face and fingers. You telling me what I ought to do. Well don't! Don't you tell me anything! If I'm a middle-class fake white man . . . let me be. And let me be in the way I want."[27]

He lets loose a tirade of vituperation and venom mocking Lula and all she stands for. But beneath the surface one feels a tension, a tension between being found out and of losing control because somehow Lula/outsider seems to know Clay's vulnerability. Clay is an insider whose psychic space has been invaded by Lula, the embodiment of White power and White intrusion. But when she realizes that Clay knows she knows, she must destroy him and she does. She stabs him and he dies. The circle is closed and the oppressor remains in control.

Dialectics and Dialogues

So, where are we? It is apparent that the suspicions of insiders are as inhibiting to any attempts to understand the meaning of ethnicity and to reduce intergroup tensions as are the biases of outsiders. Is there any way out of the dilemma? How does one answer the following sets of questions? First, can outsiders ever become expert enough to know the right questions to ask, to obtain meaningful information about others, and be able to interpret them? Even if this is possible—is it right? Who is to define the boundaries between acceptable inquiry on the one hand and unacceptable intrusion on the other? The investigator? The subjects of research? If the latter—how does one seek and obtain permission to enter their physical domain or cultural space?

Second, insiders may know themselves—but do they fully understand why they are the way they are? Does it matter? If it does, who is to help them? An outsider? If insiders accept that there is some merit in having others enter, especially as friends, will they be willing to lower their guards enough to let those outsiders have access to personal information and innermost thoughts? Or will the acceptable strangers invariably have to be on guard against the pontification of "inside dopesters" who tell only what they think the others want to hear or what they think others should hear rather than what they truly believe and feel?

Finally, recognizing the limits of both distance and intimacy, of detachment and involvement, accepting that there are and will always be competing claims to truth and insight, and being mindful of the very real political aspects of the whole debate, can we ever get our students and others to comprehend the full meaning of ethnicity and get inside someone else's world? It would take far more time than we have here to even begin to answer many of the questions. Still, given my personal concerns and the circumstances that led to my interest in the whole subject, I would like to end by addressing the last set.

There are things I still believe a well-trained social scientist brings to any situation—not least a framework of inquiry, a comparative focus, and an interest in the particular, mainly (though I can hardly say exclusively) to better understand the more general. There are things that must remain at more than arm's length, things that can never be directly experienced. As a white person, I will never be Black; as a man, I will never be a woman. But in addition to the obvious fact that there are Black social scientists and female ones (who may have my problems in reverse), it is also possible to experience things vicariously, through careful study of the acts, art, and artifacts of others, through what they do, say, and produce for themselves *and* for others. I am referring not only to the materials based on formal interviews, field studies, or responses to questionnaires, but also to the commentaries and polemics of "members" and to portraits painted in the lofty and lowly literature of a given group. I am referring not only to what my colleagues and I can gather as we stand on the outside peering in, but to what people say to and for each other.

Too many sociologists have been so concerned about gaining and maintaining respectability as hard-headed scientists that they have often overlooked or avoided dealing with one if the richest lodes of empirical data there is for understanding cultural phenomena in modern societies—the novels, poems, plays, essays, and letters home that, long ago, such masters as Florian Znaniecki warned us not to ignore.[28]

If there is any way to close the gap, to turn the debate into a dialogue, it is to recognize that what many outsiders seek and many insiders produce for themselves may be governed by an implicit norm of receprocity. "As your words and works help me to know you better, I will be better able to help you." By "help" I do not mean direct aid but assistance in having others begin to comprehend the meaning of being something they are not, and perhaps learn what makes *them* think the things they do and why *they* are the way they are.

To recognize this is to begin to abandon the either/or dichotomy and to look for ways of integrating what professional observers are seeking and insiders are saying. To do it is to find that the gap may be considerably narrower than the champions of Abstract Empiricism (to use C. Wright Mills's famous phrase) or Extreme Insiderism (to use Merton's) would have everyone believe. The approach I am suggesting is closer to the tradition of the symbolic interactionists and some of the ethnomethodologists than to other schools of sociological thought, for it is essential to be as concerned with posturing and posing, with fronts and masks, as with what underlies them. It is as important to be as concerned with perceptions of reality as reality itself.

The scholarly, political, literary, and personal works of insiders offer special insights into the character of societies and communities and the minds of those within them. The writers and their subjects—and their characters—are, in a very real sense, key informants, better ones in many cases than the sycophants we have often had to rely on in our scientific surveys. Lerone Bennett is thus a key informant; so is Leroi Jones or Imira Baraka. So, too, are Lula and Clay. Richard Wright is such a key informant as are Bigger Thomas and "The Man Who Lived Underground." Maya Angelou is one; so is her "Momma." The same can be said for Jewish commentators real and fictitious from Abraham Cahan and David Levinsky to Philip Roth and David Kepesh; it can be said for James T. Farrell, Studs Lonigan, and Danny O'Neill; for Mario Puzo and his fortunate pilgrims; for Oscar Lewis and for Cruz; for Harry Patrakis and the descendants of Pericles. It can be said of hundreds of writers whose descriptions and characterizations allow readers to be temporarily transported into another world, to feel what it is like to have another *Weltanschauung,* to sense the tension of marginality so simply but poignantly portrayed fifty years ago in Countee Cullen's brief poem, "Incident":

> *Once riding in old Baltimore,*
> *Heart-filled, head-filled with glee,*
> *I saw a Baltimorean*
> *Keep looking straight at me.*
>
> *Now I was eight and very small,*
> *And he was no whit bigger,*
> *And so I smiled, but he poked out*
> *His tongue and called me, "Nigger."*
>
> *I saw the whole of Baltimore*
> *From May until December:*
> *Of all the things that happened there*
> *That's all that I remember.*[29]

Cullen helps us to feel what it means to be a Black child in White America. His words are a part of what I see as an expanded data bank, to be included in our analyses alongside the facts and figures and technical assessments. They add substantive gristle to the theoretical bones and cold statistics.

Reading real literature along with what we are wont to call *the* literature, looking at cultural material not conventionally considered as "data," may have the latent function for social scientists of reconnecting us with our humanistic brothers and sisters. It does not mean abandoning the sociological perspective. That orientation still provides the framework within which to understand what is being read, the larger picture of the systems in which people live, work, play, and suffer, the context in which to indicate and test the variables that relate to human affairs everywhere.

After all, Blacks like Whites, Jews like Gentiles, Chicanos like Anglos, Irishmen Protestant and Catholic, institutionalize their behavior patterns, set criteria for the conferring or denying of status, indicate the tolerance of limits of accepted and expected behavior, and maintain social systems of great intricacy even when they have difficulty articulating their character. To explain these things is and should remain the primary role of the sociologist.

Beyond this thought there is no real conclusion to this series of ruminations, save for the fact that I now feel very strongly that much of our work is like that of the Japanese judge in *Rashomon,* the one who asks various witnesses and participants to describe a particular event as seen through their own eyes. Like the judge, neither teachers of sociology nor our students can be allowed to get off the hook. We must analyze the disparate pieces of evidence and then try to figure out how they fit together. If we use the suggested approach of broadening what in the trade we call our data base, perhaps we will be better able to know the troubles others have seen and be better able to understand them.

Notes

1. See Peter I. Rose, *Strangers in Their Midst: Small Town Jews and Their Neighbors* (Merrick, N.Y.: Richwood, 1977).
2. See Peter I. Rose, *The Subject Is Race: Traditional Ideologies and the Teaching of Race Relations* (New York: Oxford University Press, 1968).
3. James Farmer, *Freedom—When?* (New York: Random House, 1965): 87.
4. Richard A. Schermerhorn, *Comparative Ethnic Relations* (New York: Random House, 1970): 8–9.
5. See Peter I. Rose, "The Black Experience: Issues and Images," *Social*

Science Quarterly 15 (September 1969): 286-97: idem (ed.), *Slavery and Its Aftermath,* vol. 1, and *Old Memories, New Moods,* vol. 2 of *Americans from Africa* (New York: Atherton, 1970).

6. Peter I. Rose, "Foreword," in *America's Jews,* by Marshall Sklare (New York: Random House, 1971): ix.
7. Jules Chametsky, "Race in American Life: A Personal View," *Fresh Ink* (20 October 1977): 3.
8. Robert K. Merton, "Insiders and Outsiders: A Chapter in the Sociology of Knowledge," *American Journal of Sociology* 24 (July 1972): 9.
9. See Norbert Elias, "Problems of Involvement and Detachment," *British Journal of Sociology* (1956): 226–52; John Goudsblom, *Sociology in the Balance* (Oxford: Basil Blackwell, 1977): esp. 180-86.
10. Merton, p. 32.
11. Claude Lévi-Strauss, *Structural Anthropology* (New York: Basic Books, 1963): 16 (originally published in 1949).
12. Merton, pp.11–12.
13. Rudyard Kipling, "We and They," in *Debits and Credits* (London: Macmillan, 1926): 327–28.
14. William Graham Sumner, *Folkways* (Boston: Ginn & Company, 1906): 13.
15. Merton, p. 13.
16. Joyce A. Ladner, "Introduction," in *The Death of White Sociology* (New York: Random House, 1973): xix.
17. Robert E. Park and Ernest W. Burgess, *Introduction to the Science of Sociology* (Chicago: University of Chicago Press, 1924): 138–39.
18. Edward B. Reuter, *The American Race Problem* (New York: Crowell, 1970): 365 (originally published in 1927).
19. Ladner, p. xxii.
20. Nathan Glazer and Daniel P. Moynihan, *Beyond the Melting Pot* (Cambridge, Mass.: MIT Press, 1965): 53.
21. Stanford M. Lyman, *The Black American in Sociological Thought* (New York: Capricorn, 1972): 24. See also pp. 28–31, 166–68.
22. Ibid, p. 175.
23. Ibid, p. 183.
24. Ladner, p. xxiii.
25. Lerone Bennett, "The Challenge of Blackness" (as quoted in Ladner, p. xiii).
26. Martin Kilson, "Black Studies Movement: A Plea for Perspective," *Crisis* 76 (October 1969): 329–30 (as quoted in Merton, p. 26).
27. Leroi Jones, *The Dutchman* (Sterling Lord Agency, 1964).
28. Florian Znaniecki, *The Method of Sociology* (New York: Farrar & Rinehard, 1934).
29. Countee Cullen, "Incident," in *On These I Stand* (New York: Harper, 1925).

11
It's Almost 1984: Sociological Perspectives on American Society*

(1982)

In 1976 Americans celebrated the bicentennial of the founding of their nation. Many traveled to Boston, Philadelphia, Washington, D.C., and Williamsburg. Special charter flights brought tourists to visit the historic sites. Over the next five years there seemed to be continuing interest in the character and quality of American life. Much of this interest was a sort of living remnant of bicentennial fervor, but some was prompted by internal social and economic problems and by perceived external threats to the society.

Teachers spent extra time discussing the meaning of "the American dream"; preachers gave sermons about the freedoms granted under the Bill of Rights and the religious bases of many of our ideals; politicians declaimed about the uniqueness of the American way; merchants and travel agents cashed in on the business of patriotism; and social scientists continued to debate the character of the American system.

The American system is indeed fascinating to social scientists. The United States is a land of complexities and contradictions, a nation of many nations—a melting pot to some and a seething caldron to others. It is a "house that we call freedom" and "the home of liberty"; it is also both racist and sexist. Ours is a culture in which success is often seen as the ultimate value, in which achievement and drive are most highly rewarded; yet it has a tradition of rooting for the underdog, and a number of its young people today are dropouts from the materialist, competitive world.

These contradictions are known to most Americans. We grow up learning about them—and living them. It is this point that intrigues both supporters and critics of the United States: those who see it as a model democracy and those who view it as a stage for conflict between

---

*With Myron and Penina Glazer.

the masses and certain power elites who manipulate the press, public opinion, and major institutions for their own benefit.

In recent years much has been written and said about the American system by social scientists. Books with a variety of intriguing titles discuss the dilemmas of democracy: S.M. Lipset's *The First New Nation*, Max Lerner's *America as a Civilization*, Jean-François Revel's *Without Marx or Jesus*, Raymond Mack's *Transforming America*, Maurice Zeitlin's *American Society, Incorporated*, Michael Lewis's *The Culture of Inequality*, Henry Etzkowitz's *Is America Possible?*, Vance Packard's *A Nation of Strangers*, William Manchester's *The Glory and the Dream*, and Andrew Hacker's *The End of the American Era*.

The issues are debated during the day in classrooms and seminars and at night on radio and television. The following hypothetical talk show is fairly typical. The setting is a studio in Washington, D.C. Three sociologists have been invited to join moderator Tom Kelly to discuss the subject, "It's Almost 1984: Sociological Perspectives on American Society."

Moderator: *Good evening. I'm Tom Kelly, and this is the National Public Broadcasting Corporation's "Weekly Forum." This is the second program in our series "American at the Crossroads." Last week three noted historians looked at the history of the United States. The discussion was lively, to say the least, and you may have wondered at times whether our three guests were talking about the same country. While one kept insisting that ours was the first new nation to have had a truly democratic revolution, another said the nation was new but the revolution far from democratic. And the third, in case you missed her, said that the founding fathers purposely gave power to the privileged and left the majority—including women and racial minority groups— powerless. All conceded that social changes had occurred, but differed on how to interpret them.*

Tonight I am pleased to have with me three sociologists noted for their work on American society and culture. Professor Cyrus Wyckham teaches at Warren University here in Washington. His speciality is political sociology, and he has recently published a two-volume work entitled Freedom and Control: The American Contradiction. *Our second guest is Janice Fisher, professor of sociology at Blaine College. Professor Fisher has written extensively on American social structure. Her well-known books include* Meritocracy *and* Democracy: A Functionalist Analysis. *Finally, we have Professor Terry Jordan, a sociologist on the staff of St. George University. Professor Jordan also teaches courses on American social structure, with an emphasis on the American people themselves. She is the author of* Peasants to Parvenus *and* The Plural Society, *and her latest book is an edited volume called* Consensus and Dissension: The American People at Bicentennial.

As you may have guessed from the titles of their published works, all three of our guests deal with the broad issues of social structure and belief systems. They are all what some of their colleagues call "macrosociologists," for they see societies and their institutions as the basic units of analysis. As we agreed when today's three guests were invited to participate, each is to make a brief statement summarizing his or her position regarding the nature of the American system today. Professor Fisher, would you begin?

Fisher: *I see American society as a functioning system whose mechanisms are constantly at work trying to solve major social issues. I should stress that all sociologists know how problematical it is to maintain the social order. There are constantly new members to be socialized, deviant behavior to be controlled, tensions to be managed, needs to be met, decisions to be made, resources to be allocated, physical and social environments to be adapted to. This is such a complicated undertaking that it is impressive that any modern industrial society can continue functioning at all while providing the freedom to its members that ours does. It can only do so if there is substantial agreement on basic values and structural arrangements to support them. The United States is effectively held together by such cultural and social factors.*

The founding fathers created a unique set of social institutions whose norms underscored the values they felt were pertinent in achieving what sociologist Seymour Martin Lipset has called "the first new nation." Freed from the legacy of feudalism that restricted most European nations, the United States emphasized individual achievement, not birthright; equality before the law; an open marketplace relatively free from restraints; and an enlightened public who could participate in the processes of government.

What was created was a system, or series of systems, designed to carry out both lofty and mundane goals. While few of the founding fathers anticipated the changes that would affect the course of national development—the influx of millions of immigrants, the challenge to the practice of involuntary servitude, the problems of urbanization and industrialization—they did provide the cement in the mosaic that was to become the modern United States. That cement—the core values of the society—has been amazingly resilient.

A society must be judged by the extent to which it establishes and maintains a meaningful equilibrium among its various parts. This equilibrium depends in large measure on a general agreement about what the priorities should be and how to achieve them. In judging American society, I would say the structures have served their functions well and that we have an extraordinarily stable society. A concrete example should help make my perspective clearer.

Within the last two decades this nation has suffered the removal of two presidents: Kennedy by assassination, Nixon by forced resignation. Events like these are sufficiently grave to undermine almost any nation's stability. But our people held firm. Our values and laws supported the peaceful transfer of power. Widespread consensus and commitment to the system were clearly evident. In other countries, takeovers by the military would have been the order of the day. And many were certain that the United States was also going to succumb to the rule of the generals. What they failed to understand was the ability of American political institutions to adapt to crisis.

I am not suggesting that a society of more than two hundred million people does not have serious problems. Nowhere in human history is there evidence of a true utopia free from conflict. What I do look at in my analysis of this country is the ability of its various components to work together smoothly and to correct the society's course where necessary without destroying its basic structure.

In contrast to some of my colleagues, I would argue that the persistence of the "American way" is based far more on the will of the people, the masses of people, than on pressures by some powerful elite of bankers, politicians, and military leaders. We can test that assumption by asking the people their views. The majority will agree with my own that, by and large, we are doing very well.

Moderator: *Thank you. Professor Fisher has argued that this country is basically sound, that the American system, for all its problems, works. What do you say, Professor Wyckham?*

Wyckham: *Professor Fisher is what we sociologists call a functionalist. To me, functionalism avoids asking certain very serious questions. I see society—any society—from a rather different point of view. Take the bicentennial we celebrated a few years ago. Every sociologist knows that such events are patriotic rituals. Traditional societies reaffirm their values and their group solidarity at annual group rites and festivals. Lately, worried about our future, Americans have been subjected to a bombardment of rhetoric about our glorious past and our allegedly stable society. Tonight I'd like to introduce another function to this ritual—one that is perhaps more appropriate. I'd like to propose a little more introspection, to probe the overwhelming prob-*

lems that surround us. Frankly, I think the issue is one of survival, and I want to point to the critical problems that may spell our decline.

The first is racial violence. Despite the Supreme Court decision in 1954 ordering desegregation of public schools and despite the vast civil rights movement of the 1960s, I see little evidence that our racial problems can be solved—or even that the system is working toward solving them. We are faced with the widespread belief that busing children from Black ghettos to decent White schools leads to violence, riots, and hatred, and further encourages the White exodus to the suburbs. Many Blacks are still confined to the decaying centers of cities and are increasingly alienated. They hold little hope of improving their lot. The same is true of millions of Puerto Ricans, Chicanos, and Native Americans. This despair has brought us the highest rate of violent crime in the history of the nation—from terror in city subways to gun battles on Indian reservations. Perhaps even worse is the hopelessness and apathy that pervade broken neighborhoods and families.

I think we have neither the will nor the way to solve the problems of race, urban decay, and national violence. As a sociologist I would say that the social structure inhibits meaningful change. The socialization process transmits the beliefs and values of the past to the social participants of the future. This is true in any society. It means that the social structure perpetuates itself. Unfortunately, the values that most members of our society hold do not encourage them to make sacrifices to achieve equality or justice—or even to support the Bill of Rights. The results of some studies show that many people rejected the contents of the Bill of Rights when they appeared, reworded, on a questionnaire.

Our society is dominated by the profit motive. Great power is concentrated in the hands of corporations and their military and political allies. It may be in their interest to overthrow unfriendly governments in foreign countries, but it isn't in their interest to increase the power and opportunities available to poor people here or abroad.

Most of the rest of us are trapped by our commitment to the system's values and rules. We don't want to give up a promotion in order to let someone from a deprived group get ahead. We don't want our kids going to integrated schools for fear that they won't get as good an education—even though it would improve the educational opportunities for minority kids. We don't want our "property values" to go down because other, less privileged people have moved into the neighborhood.

These are the social values we live by, and they seem so reasonable. Yet the difficulty is that they're based on an incorrect assessment of the situation. Many of us are taught to blame the poor for their poverty, their lack of skills, their violent outrage. But even among those of us who see poverty as a manifestation of the stratification of our society, rather than as the fault of the poor, few blame those in power for this structural inequality. We accept the system, so we go on defending the interests of the powerful against the weak.

I realize my time is running short, but I want to give one more example of our inability to make the basic changes we so desperately need. This is the richest country in the world. We comprise only 6 percent of the world's population, but consume 50 percent of the world's annual output of natural resources. These resources are limited. So what happens in the face of an energy crisis? First of all, you've got to remember that our entire economy is geared toward the ever-increasing production of consumer goods—from toasters to automobiles. Any immediate cutback would result in a deepened recession, more unemployment, and falling profits. This structural problem could be averted only by massive reorganization of the economy. It would amount to a virtual revolution, which simply does not appear in the offing.

The government is so big and so influenced by vested interests that it cannot come up with decent policies to deal with the energy crisis, pollution, or the production of dangerous products. We used to worry about destroying ourselves through a nuclear holocaust. That's still a possibility; but I think we are more in danger of choking ourselves to death from smog, poisoning ourselves from cancer-producing materials in the water supply, or spraying ourselves to death with aerosol cans. Cigarette companies don't care about lung cancer. They care about profits. Oil companies have used the oil shortage to raise prices and profit margins and to lobby for tax benefits and unrestrained offshore drilling. They don't care about the rest of society. Profit is the name of their game. I'll close by saying the problems are getting worse—and bigger. Unfortunately, the solutions are not keeping pace.
Moderator: *You sociologists differ as much in your interpretations of modern American society as the historians did in their views of its history. Professor Wyckham's society is very different from Professor Fisher's. Wouldn't you say so, Professor Jordan?*
Jordan: *Frankly, no. Their differences represent two basic perspectives of society that sociologists have debated for years. To my way of thinking, my two colleagues would look at any society from either a "consensus" or a "conflict" view. But our concern here is with the*

United States. *No, they are not looking at different societies, but they're looking at this country from different angles and theoretical positions.*

To me the United States is not so easily praised or damned. It is a tension-ridden social system, and in those tensions lie both its promises and its problems. This has been true for a long time. The United States is a vast land. It is many peoples with many voices. It is a nation of contradictions. It is held together by powerful interests that often appear more concerned with the private good than with the public welfare. But it is also a place where the dream of mobility has proved to be more than a slogan, more than a catch phrase. It is also a society that can and has changed.

Changes in American society have rarely come about through the good will of those in power. But they have occurred. The pressure of the people has been the primary motivating force. What was not accomplished by the ballot box was often accomplished in the streets. Voices in the wilderness—labor agitators, civil rights demonstrators, feminists, student radicals—who first met with hostility and violence, were not easily stilled. In time—often a long time—others joined them. Little movements grew into great campaigns, and time and again employers, government officials, and representatives of other powerful sectors of society began to make concessions. Most interesting to me is the willingness of opponents of change to change themselves, once they recognize that the force of public opinion is running against them.

There are areas where progress has been slow. And there are areas where we have not yet found the way or the will to make broader changes that will affect all who suffer from some of our greatest problems. Our cities are decaying and unmanageable; our environment is becoming polluted; economic recessions have caused thousands of publicly and privately employed citizens to be laid off. Perhaps these problems, which are not unique to the United States, are unavoidable in postindustrial societies. Perhaps they are so enormous that we cannot deal with them all. But so far such a view is not widespread in our society. There is still a fundamental optimism about our ability to deal with adversity.

Moderator: *You feel, then, Professor Jordan, that the American people think they are capable of solving their problems?*

Jordan: *I do. While many Americans are frightened of what they see around them, they still seem to have a fundamental belief in the soundness of the system. This may be naive on their part. As I tried to point out, the problems that confront us today are far greater and more ominous than those we have faced in the past.*

Fisher: *I disagree. The problems of today are not greater, they are different. There were very great problems in the earlier days of this country, and most were solved quite successfully. They were solved because of a common spirit that almost everyone—rich and poor—felt. It was a spirit or belief that no problem was too big to handle.*
Jordan: *You really think Americans can do just about anything?*
Fisher: *Perhaps I was overdramatizing, but I do think that too much is said about how we've failed and not enough is said about the strengths and successes of this country. Those successes are not based on some abstract notion of patriotism but on a combination of institutional forms and values that bind us together in an integrated society. Even those who are most removed from the mainstream have a sense of their Americanness.*

I am concerned by those who continually promote the idea that there are no common interests, that there is no strength in the social fabric. I think they give people false expectations that complex problems are the fault of a wicked conspiracy. I think it is irresponsible to undermine the emotional bonds that give us a sense of interdependence. The "hyphenated Americans"—Irish-Americans, Polish-Americans, Jewish-Americans, even Black-Americans—feel it. At the core of whatever they are is something that binds them. After all—why do Blacks prove to be among the most patriotic citizens in public opinion polls?
Jordan: *I'll tell you why. It's not because they're Black but because they're Southern. Southern Protestants, to be more accurate. And they're poor. Take those three variables, and you've got a winning combination for political conservatism. Of course, they're not conservative when it comes to racial or bread-and-butter issues. But on anything else they're conservative. Although it's hard for many critics to accept, members of the working class—whether White, Black, or something else—are more conservative on many issues than any other sector of society. Let me cite just a few examples. Studies of sexual attitudes and behavior reveal greater permissiveness among members of the middle class than among the working class. Opinion polls about desegregation and the rights of minorities reveal more support for these values among members of the middle class. Studies of attitudes toward the war in Vietnam also showed greater opposition to the war from the middle class than from those lower down the ladder.*
Wyckham: *But that doesn't mean that working-class people are enamored with the system. Their conservatism may simply reflect a fear of the changes that other, more powerful people are always advocating at their expense. They stick to the straight and narrow because they are not really able to strike out at the source. They are taught to believe*

their problems are personal rather than political, they are encouraged to blame Blacks or Puerto Ricans for slums, filth, and crime. No one suggests to them that the big banks may have something to do with urban decay. Sociologists call that "blaming the victim."

Jordan: *It isn't entirely true that working-class people aren't able to fight the system. When members of the working class really want to mobilize around issues that are important to them, they can and have. I wouldn't say working-class people were being manipulated.*

Fisher: *I believe they have accepted the values of the dominant culture and feel they can achieve something. They are not outsiders; rather, they are integrated into the wider society.*

Moderator: *Professor Fisher—why do you persist in saying this is an integrated society? It seems to me we have substantial evidence that the United States is still segregated.*

Fisher: *I mean integrated in the Parsonian sense. As the late sociologist Talcott Parsons argued, the whole system functions fairly smoothly because of the harmonious intermeshing of its various parts. In this sense I believe that our society is integrated. If it were not, it wouldn't work—and ours works amazingly well. Our institutions mesh, our stratification hierarchy allows for considerable social mobility, our people find that, by and large, they are far better off than nine-tenths of the world's population.*

We do have our problems. But everything is relative in two ways: relative to other societies and to what existed before. Take the first. Can you think of any place that is as complex as our society, that has so many different groups of people from so many places, that has done better than we? The assimilation of millions of immigrants and their considerable mobility is but one example of the ability of this system to function and adapt to change as needs arise. On the second point of comparison, think what life was like for the early settlers. They didn't land in a bed of roses; they landed in a wilderness. They slaved and suffered, and many of them died trying to open up this country. The birth rate was high, but the death rate was too. Most people lived only forty to fifty years—if they were lucky. Today we have problems too: polution, heart disease, the threat of nuclear accident. But in the "good old days," the manure that piled up in city streets was a far worse menace than the auto fumes of today; the scourge of epidemics like dysentery, malaria, and tuberculosis hung over people like the Sword of Damocles.

Jordan: *But isn't it true that many of the problems of those days still exist, Janice? You haven't even touched on some of the major ones Cy mentioned: poverty, racism, military power. These are the real issues*

*that threaten to pull our society apart. The saving grace is that we are
aware of them and have begun to deal with them. It isn't easy, but at
least every American today is aware of the fact that so many are poor
in this land of riches, that so many are discriminated against, that . . .*
Wyckham: *So they know. They still turn their backs, except when they
are personally affected. When people get laid off themselves,* then *they
begin to understand what it is not to work. When their own kids have to
register for the draft, then they wake up to what we have been doing.
When . . .*
Fisher: *Now just a minute. You know better than any of us, Cy, that
things can change. You were in the forefront of the civil rights
movement. We've seen more changes on the racial front in the last
twenty years than in the previous hundred.*
Wyckham: *Right. And they came about when people were willing to
stand up and be counted. When they really challenged the old system.
But even that wasn't enough. What happened was that the people in
power did what they always do in this country when there is real
pressure: they engaged in tokenism. They gave little to save a lot.*
Fisher: *I agree with you, in part; only I see that as the genius of the
system. It says, in essence: "I think you're wrong, but I hear what
you're saying. Let's compromise." It says: "You cool it, and we'll
work something out." And often something is worked out. More jobs,
perhaps. More access to the universities. More recognition. Maybe
some new facilities.*
Wyckham: *That's cooptation. That's simply a slick way of conning
some of the protesters into thinking they have made real gains and
then using them to defuse the protest. What's really happening is an
attempt to integrate a select few into the system.*
Fisher: *Precisely. And it works.*
Wyckham: *Come on, Janice. It works for how long? People can be part
of what you call an "integrated system" and still be on the short end of
the stick. A functionalist like you should know that. What is important
is that the system works, right? Equality has nothing to do with it—
you've said that before. Face facts. This country is not so tolerant. It is
an oppressive society where only the rich and powerful have any real
clout. They are the gatekeepers. They decide who to let in—and how
far. And they're not about to let anyone tear down the gates.*
Jordan: *But there are times when the people can have clout too. If we
have time I'd like to illustrate how changes have come about in this
society by using three examples: the assimilation of immigrants,
women's roles, and our sexual mores.*
Moderator: *Go ahead, Professor Jordan.*

Jordan: *In colonial times, this country was an Anglo-Saxon nation to which newcomers were "invited." They were welcome as long as they shed their foreign ways. Later on, when it was apparent that not all who came wished to assimilate so completely that they lost their former identities—when ethnic enclaves dotted the expanding maps and when ethnic neighborhoods began to abound in the cities—we began speaking of the United States as a "melting pot," a place where the ingredients of varied civilizations would be blended into a new social stew. This did happen to some extent through social mixing and intermarriage. At least, many people paid lip service to the idea of the melting pot and prided themselves on their contribution to the overall heritage.*

But again reality intruded. Many ethnic groups coexisted within society but were not assimilated into it. This fact of persisting cultural pluralism led us to recognize that the nation was not so much a melting pot as, in Horace Kallen's words, an orchestra. Each group is like a section—strings, brass, percussion, woodwinds—with its own timbre and tonality. Together the various ethnic and religious groups provide the harmonies and dissonances of a vibrant society. Cultural pluralism was a fact in American society before it became a theory. Today pluralism is recognized as a characteristic of American life.

I recognize that our racial problems have not been resolved in this way. Until very recently, non-Whites had to try to adopt the characteristics of Whites to be accepted. Pluralism for them was considered unacceptable separatism. Nevertheless, the civil rights and Black Power movements made great strides in getting political, business, and labor leaders to begin redressing the grievances of those discriminated against. Although in the past few years there has been a retreat on the commitment to civil rights, so that not all the goals have been met, Blacks have made headway against strong resistance. And it's undeniable that Black people feel differently about themselves from the way they did two decades ago. In the years ahead we will see a return to the commitment to justice for all. It may well take another wave of unrest and civil disobedience, but it is inevitable.

My second example concerns American women. The colonists had rather traditional views of the role of women in the political life of societies. With some rare exceptions, women were considered beyond the pale of political activity. Although they toiled at home and in the fields side by side with the menfolk, they were, on the one hand, put up on a pedestal, and on the other, put down by those who said they didn't have heads for making the tough decisions of life. They had no vote and few privileges of their own. Even the Bill of Rights expressed the view that all men *were created equal—and were to be treated as equals. Not women. In the 1840s and 1850s, spurred by their involvement in the antislavery campaign then going on, a number of women began to challenge the character of their own "servitude." Their women's rights movement won several skirmishes, but it was cut off by the Civil War. When women resumed their battle for equality at the end of the nineteenth century, they concentrated their efforts on the struggle for suffrage. Finally, in 1919, this culminated in passage of the Nineteenth Amendment to the Constitution.*

The suffragist fight was the second wave of the struggle for "women's liberation." The third was and is the most far-reaching. While women achieved many rights in law, they still faced discrimination in almost every sphere of life. In fifteen years their persistent pressure on institutions, organizations, and political parties, on men in general and on husbands, fathers, brothers, and lovers in particular, has brought about significant changes. Consciousness-raising has stretched the old norms beyond their limits, and new norms—and new ideas about women—have begun to replace the old.

Moderator: *Are you saying that women are really different as a result of these pressures?*

Jordan: *Yes, I think we are. And I think men are too. I think society is different.*

Wyckham: *There is still ample evidence of sexism in our society. Just look at our training of future mechanics and future presidents.*

Fisher: *That's not the point. Women's liberation is great. Even I benefit from it. I've had more attractive job offers in the last five years than in the previous twenty. But as a professional, I think that those who are impatient and want to change things too quickly are disrupting more than they realize. Plenty of men are unfairly discriminated against because quota systems are replacing qualifications. A backlash is setting in. If women start competing in earnest for scarce jobs, something's got to give. For men to be out of work is more devastating than for women. After all, our society is still oriented to having men be breadwinners and women take care of the home. Those are still generally followed norms. And the data indicate that unlike middle-class women, many working-class women like it that way. They aren't too eager to work at some of the deadly dull jobs open to them.*

Wyckham: *But if we had a different system, we wouldn't have to worry constantly about who was going to be laid off. If our system were designed to give priority to full employment instead of to profiteering, women and men wouldn't be pitted against each other in a scramble for scarce jobs. We don't really know what working-class women* *would like if they weren't subjected to so much economic insecurity. No wonder they want their men to be breadwinners. Look at the alternatives open to these women—low-paid factory and service jobs. You yourself said they were "deadly dull."*

Moderator: *Let's go back to Professor Jordan. I'm going to ask her for her third example, and then I want to pose one final question to you all.*

Jordan: *I mentioned changes with regard to ethnic groups and women's rights and roles. Let me take an even more loaded subject: sex. For centuries a double standard has existed: males could sow their wild oats—so long as they did so on the other side of the tracks—and prove their masculinity by words and deeds. "Nice" women were expected to be virginal, saving themselves for their husbands. Women's liberation has altered this view considerably, and premarital sex between men and women has become normative if not formally sanctioned.*

But these changed mores are nothing compared with the changes in attitudes that have occurred relating to homosexual behavior. Until very recently, homosexuality was considered sinful, degenerate, and sick. No self-respecting person could openly display sexual attraction to members of the same sex. In the wake of civil rights activities relating to racial minorities and to women, homosexuals began, in their own words, "to come out of the closet." Gay liberation, a movement that began in the late 1960s, has brought about profound changes not only in sexual behavior but also in attitudes toward it. As a result of pressure and publicity from people who no longer accept social views of what are proper and improper sexual relationships, homosexuals and their supporters have gained recognition for their cause.

Fisher: *I'd like to comment on something that Terry suggests but does not say. It is an important sociological point that relates her examples to something about which I feel quite strongly. While it is true that changes of all kinds have occurred in recent years—the three she mentioned are but a sampling—many people seem to feel that these changes demonstrate the willingness of our society to stretch its tolerance limits to satisfy the needs of individuals who feel left out or discriminated against. That society is willing to do so is true. But it is also true that the reason authorities are willing to do so—whether they be employers, college administrators, or government officials—is that they see acquiescence as a means of preserving the system.*

Wyckham: *Exactly.*

Fisher: *Wait, Cy, I'm not finished. You see, you think it's a bad thing to try to absorb the dissidents. I don't. I think it's essential to the well-*

*being of a society that reform be orderly and at a pace that the society
can absorb. If not, the entire equilibrium of society can be upset, and
chaos cannot benefit any group.*
Wyckham: *That's my basic disagreement. I think there is a real
question about whether you can gradually patch up a failing welfare
system, an alienated labor force, or a swollen military establishment,
given the highly uneven distribution of power we have. Sure, the
country will stay afloat a while longer, but it's destined to sink. That's
the United States as we head for 1984—not George Orwell's totalitar-
ian regime but a ship stuck together with bandaids.*

*Making your sort of concession to protesters simply cools them
down. It's clever. Any attempt at genuine revolutionary change is
dampened by expanding what's acceptable. The outsiders—Blacks,
women, homosexuals, and others—are taken into the fold and, feeling
grateful for admittance, lose their zeal to overturn the system. What I
think is less visible is the seething anger that most Blacks still feel in
their slums, the potential violence that may explode in a way we can't
control—not because changes will have occurred too rapidly, but
because unemployment, poverty, and racism will have continued at
their present levels. And. . .*
Moderator: *I must get to that last question, since time is fleeting.
Where are we going from here? I gather from Professor Wyckham's
remarks that he thinks we're going nowhere, that the period some have
called "the American era" is coming to a sad ending.*
Wyckham: *Not sad. Just an ending. As you know, I have little faith in
this society. It uses warfare to build itself up and welfare to keep
people thinking everything is just fine. It is built on a mystique of
individualism that is belied by the fact that the little guy can never run
an even race. The United States was founded on lofty values and ideals
that no one can fault: life, liberty, the pursuit of happiness. But it never
seems able to realize its own proclaimed destiny. It is a society crying
for a real revolution—not one like the war of 1776. That was really just
a civil war between British monarchists and British republicans. I'm
talking about a true revolution. And yet I fear it will never occur. There
will be protest, violence, rebellion, but it won't come to anything,
because the people are controlled by the powerful. The people are
forever told that they really have the best of all possible worlds. You'd
no doubt say the fabric is too strong.*
Fisher: *I think you've just admitted something that many of us have
tried to say. Like it or not, the American system is an integrated
society, and it's going to last a very long time. It will last, because it
will continue to be what it has been in the past—a dynamic society that*

values its heritage. It recognizes that one of the most significant aspects of that heritage is a future orientation, a belief that the past was good, the present is better, and the future will be better still.

Jordan: *I think we're in for some rough sledding and our famous future orientation will be undergoing some rude reorientations in the years ahead. In recent years the raw wounds of this society have been exposed. Our tensions and fears have been expressed. We have suffered—through misadventure, mismanagement, or sheer bullheadedness—in foreign policy and domestically. But we've also proved that we can deal with defeat, disillusionment, even corruption in the highest places. As many people said in the wave of relief after the Nixon impeachment hearings: "The system works."*

Moderator: *Our time is up. Once again, we're left with a variety of views and no clear answers to our questions. What the three sociologists have done is provoke our thinking about the nature of our society. That, I suppose they would all agree, is really the function of such discussions. I leave you with some questions I posed to them: Is the United States an integrated society? How does it deal with its many problems, and how should it deal with them? What are the responsibilities of those in its mainstream? And what is the future of those on its margins?*

Index